The Man Wit...

The Unlikely Rise of ....

LONGLISTED FOR THE 2012 SAMUEL JOHNSON PRIZE

'This book is full of surprises . . . Gessen has sounded an alarm, and it is high time the West stopped blocking its ears' *Mail on Sunday*

'[A] courageous, enlightening account' *Independent on Sunday*

'A luminous study . . . Gessen has written a brave book, demolishing the numerous myths and legends that have accumulated around her subject' *Guardian*

'The Putin who emerges from this brave and important book appears to be a grudge-driven mass murderer and extortionist . . . Gessen's engaging prose combines a native's passion with a mordant wit and caustic understatement that are characteristically Russian' AD Miller, *Telegraph*

'To sound clued-up about current affairs, read Masha Gessen's biography of Vladimir Putin . . . she charts the rise of the Russian prime minister from anonymous bureaucrat to scary potentate' *Observer*

'Provides a compelling and exhaustive portrait of a man who rose without trace from being a minor KGB and St Petersburg bureaucrat to become what Gessen describes as "the godfather of a mafia clan"' *Sunday Telegraph*

'[A] clear, brave book . . . Gessen offers intriguing details of the scratching, biting, hair-tearing, undersized, brawling boy Putin, refusing to be bullied in the grubby back yards of Leningrad' James Meek, *Observer*

'Gessen conveys the atmosphere – whether of the last months of the Soviet Union, the chaotic years of Yeltsin, the strange transfer of the presidency to Putin or the disappointments of his period – more accurately than any recent chronicler of the period' *Independent*

'[A] brilliant new book by Russian-born author Masha Gessen' *Daily Mail*

'An essential source for anyone interested in the rise of Mr Putin' *Economist*

'A non-fiction book that I can't imagine anyone being brave enough to write in the first place' *Scotsman*

'Gessen's account of the fortunes of those who have suffered at Putin's hands is persuasive and even moving' *Irish Times*

'Gessen's portrait of the obscure young Putin is of a cold, contained youth in whom sentiment and feeling were reserved for institutions rather than people' *Herald*

'A coruscating exposé' *Word*

'A thorough analysis of one of the world's shadiest democratic leaders' *Traveller*

'Gessen has clearly put in the hours and the miles finding people to tell her about Putin's days in the KGB, in the St Petersburg City Administration, and in the Kremlin. She paints a portrait of a man who dislikes democratic movements, who is committed to the ideals of the KGB, who is happy siphoning money from the state for his friends, and who would rather fight than negotiate' Oliver Bullough, *Sunday Telegraph*

Words Will Break Cement

The Passion of Pussy Riot

Masha Gessen

GRANTA

Granta Publications, 12 Addison Avenue, London W11 4QR

First published in Great Britain by Granta Books 2014
First published in the United States by Riverhead Books,
a member of the Penguin Group (USA) LLC, New York

A CIP catalogue record for this book is available from the British
Library.

1 3 5 7 9 10 8 6 4 2

ISBN 978 1 84708 934 2
eISBN 978 1 84708 935 9

Book design by Tiffany Estreicher

Offset by Avon DataSet Ltd, Bidford on Avon, Warwickshire

Printed and bound by CPI Group (UK) Ltd, Croydon, CR0 4YY

MIX
Paper from
responsible sources
FSC® C020471
FSC
www.fsc.org

CONTENTS

PART 3
Punishment

Words Will
Break
Cement

IK-14

GERA WANTED TO PEE. Again. In the eleven hours we had spent in the car the day before, she had alternated every five minutes between asking if we were there yet and demanding to be allowed to pee. She did not sleep a wink, even though we arrived at one in the morning. Now, barely eight hours later, we were back in my car, on our way to the penal colony, and Gera wanted to pee.

"Gera, you cannot pee every five minutes!" said Petya to his four-year-old daughter. "You cannot appraise a work of art from the point of view of effectiveness." Now he was speaking into a lapel mic that belonged to the German television crew following us in another car. Before we left the hotel in Zubova Polyana where we had spent the night, I had to pull the car away from the back porch so the Germans could film the lanky Petya running to the car with huge plaid Chinese-made rectangular bags we were taking to the colony for Nadya, Petya's wife and Gera's mother. "This is the sixth time I've been filmed loading bags into a car for Nadya." He laughed as he got into the passenger seat. He always seemed to enjoy the publicity connected with his wife's imprisonment, and only now, more than a year after I first met him, was I starting to appreciate how hard, tedious, and unceasing was the work he did on her behalf.

While one of the Germans was miking Petya up, another tried to interview Gera, but she went suddenly tight-lipped and petulant. When the reporter walked away, I tried, in a sudden fit of competitiveness, to ask Gera some questions too. We had, after all, become familiar to each other after spending a day in the car together.

"When was the last time you saw your mom?"

"I don't remember anymore." She shrugged.

"Why is your mom in jail?"

"I don't even know." She shrugged.

"Who put her there?"

She shrugged again. "Putin."

Then her father and grandfather were finally in the car, and we started driving. And she wanted to pee. Again.

"If you keep peeing in the cold, you will freeze your bottom and won't be able to have any children," said Andrei, the grandfather.

"I don't need any children," Gera shot back.

"I don't either," said Andrei. "But you see, they just happen to you."

Andrei was not the kind of man you would want talking to your daughter. At fifty-six, he was well-worn, but you could tell he used to be movie-star handsome. He was impatient. He was occasionally inappropriate, as when he started berating Petya in front of Gera. He was immature. When a tired Gera threw a tantrum, demanding that she be taken to her mother, her grandmother, and back to the hotel—immediately, and all at the same time—he threw a tantrum too, demanding that Petya give him his cup of coffee, then giving it back, then taking it again. The rest of the time he talked and played with Gera, to her evident delight, but when I heard him teaching her to say the word *entropiya* (entropy), I found myself stifling the impulse to explain to him that children are not circus acts. I assumed such remonstrations had been attempted many times before by other women, to no evident effect.

"Mama does not want to see you," Gera told Andrei now, kicking her foot against the floor. She had taken to calling her grandmother, Petya's mother, "Mama." It drove Andrei crazy, and he made no effort hide it.

"I don't want to see her either," he declared.

"You scared of her?" asked Gera.

"Well, she is a woman," Andrei responded, with what I thought was uncharacteristic candor.

———————

WE HAD SPENT THE NIGHT at a hotel on the third floor of the House of Homekeeping—a peculiar name given, back in Soviet times, to buildings that contained services ranging from hair salons to shoe repair shops. In 2013, the House of Homekeeping in Zubova Polyana, Mordovia—population just over ten thousand—contained a half-dozen clean hotel rooms with simple pine furniture, a pool hall, a café, and a reception desk for the hotel that also sold a mind-boggling assortment of hair dyes in the narrow color range from pink to copper, and two kinds of flags: a flag of the Russian Federation for the equivalent of ten dollars and one of Mordovia for about twelve. The café in the House of Homekeeping was named "13," after the number featured on Mordovian license plates—as distinct from the numbers associated with each of the other eighty-two regions that make up the Russian Federation. As in the Western tradition, thirteen is an unlucky number in Russia, "the devil's dozen," and it seemed an appropriate designation for the region with not only Russia's but the world's highest concentration of prison inmates among its residents.

We had about twenty-five miles to go to get to Nadya's penal colony, Correctional Colony Number 14, or IK-14. Petya pointed out local landmarks. Here was a rusting metal board with the words RESTRICTED TERRITORY. NO PASSING WITHOUT STOPPING, but there was no checkpoint at which to stop—it had apparently been eliminated some years ago, when another high-profile female inmate was serving time here and someone high up decided the checkpoint looked bad on film. A men's maximum-security colony straddled both sides of the road; a covered bridge concealed by tin sheeting connected the structures, allowing inmates to be taken across the road out of sight of drivers. Another men's colony, a women's one, then a bland stretch of road with an identical flat forest on either side, then, finally, the village of Partsa, which consisted of IK-14, a small variety store, and a smattering of houses where IK-14 employees lived.

The penal colony hid behind a tall gray fence, with only a couple of structures reaching above it: a sizable church—Orthodox churches were erected in all the surrounding colonies in the 1990s—and one of the colony's standard gray concrete buildings with a wall-size poster of a girl child on it. Petya told me the caption, obscured by the fence, said YOUR FAMILY IS WAITING FOR YOU. We entered a two-room structure for visitors. It had been freshly built, most likely because Nadya was expected to draw media attention here, and it even included a carpeted playroom with a crib, a set of toddler-appropriate Legos, and a rocking donkey. Gera and Andrei took off their shoes and started building a Lego prison from which a rubber duck was going to help her friend the princess escape by means of a plastic fire truck with a telescoping ladder.

Petya planted himself and the bags in the larger room. One of its walls was entirely taken up with bulletin boards. A small one labeled THE SOCIAL MOBILITY SYSTEM featured charts and flyers geared to show that "malicious repeat offenders" would come to no good in prison while "positively character- ized convicts have hope for the future." A large board labeled INFORMATION was completely covered with sample applica- tions: an application to be granted a visit with an inmate; an application to have a package delivered to an inmate; excerpts from laws relevant to the business of visiting inmates; and de- scriptions of attempted violations colony authorities had suc- cessfully intercepted. In both of the cases described, visitors had tried to smuggle cell phones to inmates during a visit and had paid a high price, forfeiting not only the phones but visi- tation rights.

A lonely LED display hung on the back wall. On it, a cor- pulent middle-aged woman in a federal prison–authority uni- form was reading out rules and regulations and excerpts from the Penal Correctional Code. It was a twenty-minute recording playing on a loop, and by the time our wait was over, we had absorbed the rules in all their monotonous detail. Petya took off his parka and, wearing one of his apparently endless supply of checkered fitted Ralph Lauren shirts, sat down at a desk facing the window, with his back to the woman on the screen, and started making a complete list of the contents of the large plaid bags.

Assorted fruit
Bedding

Inmates are allowed only plain white bedding; last time, a pillowcase was turned away because it exhibited piping, which is apparently not allowed, despite also being white. The opposite rule applies to underwear: it must be plain black. Petya dropped an empty Uniqlo thermal-underwear package to the floor.

Books:
My Testimony *by Anatoly Marchenko*

Marchenko was a Soviet dissident who spent years writing this exhaustive accounting of the lives of political inmates in Soviet camps; he died behind bars in 1986, following a hunger strike to demand the release of political prisoners. Nadya had asked for this book specifically; Petya had been unable to find a copy for sale, so we brought the one from my personal library. Two human rights activists who had been helping Petya had added another eight books by and about dissidents. A Russian translation of a book by the philosopher Slavoj Žižek rounded out the list of ten—the maximum number of books allowed at one time. Nadya had been corresponding with Žižek, and she had said she liked the idea of carrying on a conversation with the man and his books at the same time. Months later, only the Žižek volume will have gotten past the prison censors.

The uniformed woman on the screen was reading out a list of items prohibited from being passed to prisoners. *Markers, colored pencils, copying paper*—all potential tools of escape. Early that morning, when Petya printed out a map of the surroundings, a House of Homemaking staffer had quipped, "Is this an escape plan?" Meanwhile, in the adjacent playroom, Gera grew bored with playing out the rubber-ducky prison-escape scenario and started throwing a large red gym ball at the prison she and Andrei had constructed. She was barely bigger than the ball, so throwing it proved both difficult and ineffectual, but she kept at it with furious determination. Petya continued making the list:

Yellow plastic basin
Blue plastic basin
Green plastic ladle

All of this was intended for washing clothes, though there was also hope that Nadya might be allowed to use the multi-colored plastic equipment to wash her long hair. Petya was entering the colony in possession of a precious document: a letter from the federal prison authority stating that the Penal Correctional Code placed no limitations on the frequency of hair washing. In theory, this might be interpreted to mean Nadya and the other thirty-nine women in her barracks could be allowed to wash their hair in between their weekly bath-house visits. The theory would eventually prove wrong. The on-screen officer continued her litany of banned objects: *maps, compasses, books on topography or dog training.*

In all, the preliminaries lasted nearly three hours—with the making up of the lists and the visitor applications and the waiting for a young woman officer to come and get the docu-ments and then waiting for her to come and get the visitors, it was nearly one in the afternoon by the time Petya, Andrei, and Gera entered the facility. They were shown out at four. With a short wait inside, they were cheated out of one and a half of the four hours allotted once every two months.

They spent the two and a half hours of the visit in the guest cafeteria, the facility's pride and joy, featured on the Mordovia prison authority's YouTube channel. Gera sat in her mother's lap the entire time. The four of them played a board game called To Catch the Koschei (Koschei the Deathless be-ing an evil character in a number of Russian folktales); the grown-ups kept getting distracted, giving Gera the opportu-nity to cheat. She, meanwhile, let no one get away with the slightest deviation from the rules. In a phone conversation a couple of weeks later, Nadya would, with a mixture of pride and regret, cite this behavior as evidence that Gera was far better grounded at the age of four than Nadya herself would ever be: "I think she will be an excellent leader of middle-class protest." All along, a junior visiting-room inspector sat in the corner of the cafeteria looking absent. She did not even stop Petya and Nadya from hugging each other, which made this visit, overall, a lot better than the one two months earlier, when they had not even been allowed to hold hands.

While Petya, Gera, and Andrei were inside, I drove around taking pictures of penal colony landmarks. The Zubovo-Polyanski District, of which the town of Zubova Polyana was the administrative center, was in essence a company town formed around the prison authority. A penal colony was the economic and architectural center of each village, with small, impermanent-looking wooden residential houses clinging to the mass of the colonies' concrete buildings and tall churches. I found one ongoing construction project: an apartment building for prison authority staff across the street from the district prison authority itself. Judging from the tall fence around the construction site and watchtowers in its every corner, the building was being put up by inmates.

Down the street from the district penal authority sat the district administration, housed in a neoclassical building that used to be a secondary school. The building's once-proud, columned and porticoed facade was peeling, but someone had lovingly retouched the red kerchiefs on the pockmarked sculptures of two Young Pioneers on either side of the porch. It was a striking sight in a region that, for many Russians, had once been synonymous with political prisoners; Marchenko and several of the other Soviet-era dissidents whose books we had brought for Nadya had served their prison sentences here.

But the region's ideology seemed less neo-Soviet than, simply, penal. Another colony featured over its entrance a large banner that said THOSE WHO WANT TO WORK FIND THE RE-SOURCES. THOSE WHO DO NOT WANT TO WORK FIND EXCUSES. When I stopped to take a picture of this banner in all its Nazi-concentration-camp glory, I saw a policeman spot me and drive away. In a few minutes I was detained and taken to the Zubova Polyana precinct, just down the street from the House of Homemaking, to make an explanatory statement about the purpose of my work here. I had just left the police station when Petya called to say they were done.

That was that: eleven hours in the car, a brief night in the House of Homemaking, two and a half hours with Nadya—and here we were again, strapped in for the three-hundred-mile drive back to Moscow. Gera, who had been stoic throughout the previous day's long drive and today's tedious waiting, was now acting up, shouting, demanding that she be taken back to the hotel, to her mother, and to her grandmother. Andrei was shouting too, calling Gera a spoiled brat. Petya was trying to tell me about the visit but constantly getting distracted by calls coming in on one of his two cell phones, then absently scrolling through Twitter posts, apparently forgetting that he had been in the middle of a story. He did not feel like finishing it because there was not much to tell. Nadya's life now consisted of fighting for a working sewing machine in the colony factory, where her job was putting pockets on the trousers of police uniforms, and of trying to find tiny islands of common ground with other inmates. When you lose your freedom, you lose, first and foremost, the opportunity to choose the company you keep. The women who now surrounded Nadya might as well have come from a different planet. The only person who had even walked the same streets and read some of the same newspapers was the colony's other high-profile prisoner: an ultranationalist sentenced to eighteen years behind bars for the murders of a human rights lawyer and a journalist.

Occasionally, Nadya and Petya succeeded in fashioning her surroundings into tellable stories, like the one about an inmate who everyone said had eaten her lover; or the one about an inmate who had waited four years for her lover to get out of prison, then two weeks later came home to find him in bed with another woman and stabbed them both to death; or the one about an inmate who gets regular visits from her dead husband's parents, who think that when she killed him he got what he deserved. But just now Petya did not feel like telling stories. Everyone in the car was tired, no one had gotten what he or she wanted out of this trip, and no one but me had freely chosen to be stuck in the car for hours in the company of the other three. While we were driving back to Moscow, Petya got a letter from Nadya's friend and fellow Pussy Riot prisoner Maria Alyokhina; it seemed she was upset with him for talking about her solitary confinement in a different penal colony as though it were some sort of blessing—just because she did not have to interact with other inmates.

We got into Moscow at three in the morning on a dirty-snow early March Friday. The following Monday would mark one year since the Pussy Riot women were arrested; that meant Nadya and Maria had exactly one more year left behind bars. The same day, Gera turned five.

PART 1

Becoming
Pussy Riot

ONE

Nadya

HERE IS WHAT I was trying to figure out: how a miracle happens. A great work of art—something that makes people pay attention, return to the work again and again, and reexamine their assumptions, something that infuriates, hurts, and confronts—a great work of art is always a miracle.

The temporal borders of this miracle were fuzzy. Certainly it had begun earlier than the morning of February 21, 2012, when five young women entered the Cathedral of Christ the Savior in central Moscow to stage what they called a "punk prayer" against the backdrop of its over-the-top gaudy, gilded interiors. It had begun earlier even, I thought, than the fall of 2011, when a larger, ragged-edged group of women started to call themselves Pussy Riot and engage in punk rock performances. It had begun, in fact, years or even many years earlier.

To create, and to confront, one has to be an outcast. A constant state of discomfort is a necessary but insufficient condition for protest art, however. One also has to possess a sense that one can do something about it, the sense of being entitled to speak and to be heard. I asked Nadya where she got that.

Our communication was awkward: we had no more than a passing acquaintance before she was arrested (soon afterward I realized with a jolt of regret that she had "poked" me on Facebook—an attempt at communicating I had cavalierly ignored in part because I was unsure how one responds to being "poked"), and now I wrote to her in the penal colony, knowing that my letters as well as Nadya's responses would be seen by the censors. "I am trying to understand the origins of the independence of your thinking and your ability to shape your own education . . ." It was not just the expectation of the censors' eyes that made my writing feel stilted; it was also the fact that I was using a pseudonym, one suggested by Nadya in a rare note smuggled out past the censors. In it, she laid out the terms of our correspondence: never mention writing a book or any intention of publishing our correspondence; bear in mind that the letters will be read by censors; consider using a pseudonym—say, Martha Rosler. So I came to sign my letters with the name of a contemporary American feminist artist who I am sure had no awareness I was using her name as a cover-up.

Hello, Martha,

On the subject of independent education and the origins of a rebellious personality type. A significant role in my story was played by my father, Andrei Tolokonnikov. He

*managed, amazingly, to focus my vision in such a way
that now I am able to find things that are interesting,
challenging, and curious anywhere at all. That includes
the experience of being incarcerated. My father gave me
the ability to receive all kinds of cultural production, from
Rachmaninoff to the [ska punk] band Leningrad, from
European art-house film to* Shrek. *At the age of 4 I could
distinguish a Baroque building from a Rococo one, and by
the age of 13, I loved [Venedikt Yerofeyev's profanity-filled
novella of alcoholic rumination]* Moskva-Petushki *and
[nationalist opposition activist, former émigré writer and
poet known for sexually explicit writing]* Limonov. *The
lack of censorship in my education and, in fact, the
concentration on that which could not pass the censorship
of official Russian education pushed me to be passionate
about possessing knowledge that privileged the culture of
rebellion.*

Nadya's writing, I assumed, was stilted for some of the
same reasons as mine: she was writing for me, for the censors,
and for eventual publication in a foreign language. She was
also writing about things rarely discussed in Russian, at least
rarely discussed with the earnestness that her work—and my
enterprise—seemed to demand. In addition, there was something profoundly wrong with the power dynamics of our epis-
tolary relationship. I wrote to her by e-mail, using a service
called Native Connection (no hint of irony here either). When
I sent a letter, I had the option of requesting a response and
putting a page value on it. I asked for three pages the first
time and it proved insufficient, so from that point on I always

asked for five. Each page cost fifty rubles (roughly $1.70) and the amount for the requested number of pages was immediately deducted from my Native Connection account. In essence, I was giving Nadya writing assignments—and paying for them.

A few days after I sent my letter by e-mail, Nadya would receive a printout of it along with blank pages in the quantity I had requested. She would write her responses in longhand—her script got smaller and harder to decipher if she was running out of space or more sprawling if she was running out of things to say with a page or so still to go—and I would eventually receive scans through the Native Connection website. If Nadya chose not to fill a page at all, she would have to write "Opportunity to respond rejected" on the blank page—and I would receive a scan of that as well.

Andrei shared Nadya's idea that he had been the architect of her independence, her personality, and even her art. "I am an expert in the upbringing of girls," he informed me. "I approach it as a total performance." He added that he had "authored the words 'holy shit,'" the refrain that had been the ostensible source of some of his daughter's problems.

Andrei came out of the woods to talk to me. For more than a decade he had been living in a friend's house about an hour outside of Moscow. He called it his lair, and he said he cleaned it once a year. Our interview fell between these annual cleanings, so he said a visit was out of the question. Instead, I picked him up by the side of the highway and we drove around looking for an eatery that had both heat and electricity: less than fifty miles from Moscow, we were on the disintegrating fringes of civilization.

Andrei was born at civilization's true fringe, in the world's northernmost large city (where *large* is defined as having a population over a hundred thousand). "Half the population is behind bars and the other half is guarding them," Russians have said of their country since the times of Stalin. In Norilsk, this was literally true. Founded in the mid-1930s, the city served as the center of Norlag, the mining-and-metallurgy arm of the gulag. Though the number of prisoners decreased in the 1950s following Stalin's death and the Norlag was officially dissolved, forced prisoner labor was used in the mines through the 1970s.

Andrei's father had been on the guards' side of the prison fence. He had landed in Norilsk after World War II as a Party worker. He was, according to Andrei, a well-known and roundly hated Norilsk character. The young Andrei hated everyone back. "When I was five, I remember seeing elderly intellectuals in the streets—former Norlag inmates. Then they all died off, of course, and all that was left was *bydlo*." Dictionaries suggest translating that Russian slang word as "cattle," but that word does not come close to conveying the concentration of disdain and disgust educated Russians pack into the epithet for their compatriots: it is "white trash" but more derogatory, "redneck" but more frightful.

Andrei was educated as a doctor (this did not require nearly as many years or as much effort as an American medical education—and in his case, very little effort indeed was expended), but he did not feel like working as a doctor or, really, working at all. He thought of himself as an artist, though he was not sure what kind of art he should be making. He finagled his way into the Arts Institute in Krasnoyarsk, the nearest truly large city, as a correspondence student in music; he pretended to play the piano. During one of his visits to the institute, he met Katya. She was, unlike him, "an actual musician," he told me; she played piano. She would even go on to study at a conservatory, and then to teach music to schoolchildren. She was generally more serious and better grounded than Andrei, and this pronounced difference between them might have ended their marriage sooner or prevented it altogether had it not been for one thing: they were oblivious, because they drank. Everyone in the Soviet Union did, more drunks and more drinks with every passing year. In the early 1980s, Soviet rulers came and died in quick succession—Brezhnev died, then Chernenko, then Andropov—but not before promising to do something about the epidemic of alcoholism. Mikhail Gorbachev appeared in 1985 and launched an all-out war on the drink. Andrei and Katya, then newly in love, drank. And drank. And drank. And had Nadya.

She came as a surprise, conceived on a night of heavy drinking and arriving on Revolution Day, November 7, 1989, one of the most vodka-soaked days of the year. By then, Gorbachev's war on alcoholism was at its peak, with the vineyards in the south razed and vodka rationed across the land. So for many Soviet citizens it was a day soaked in industrial alcohol, cologne, or, as was the case with Andrei, medical spirits. No one had been expecting Nadya. She was given the name Nadezhda, which means "hope," and parked, for the next few years of her life, with Andrei's mother, Vera, which means "faith."

Vera lived in Krasnoyarsk. Katya lived in Norilsk. Andrei lived in various places; when Nadya was conceived and born, for example, he was living in a village outside of Arkhangelsk, in the very north of the European part of Russia. He had a gig as chief doctor at a rural hospital, unfettered access to medical spirits, and rare access to his wife. "That's part of the reason we parted ways. I think that distance is important and a relationship works better when people take breaks from each other." The distance in this case exceeded a thousand miles. "I guess Katya had a different opinion. She said I killed the woman in her. It's a strange accusation, though I'm not a woman, so I wouldn't know. And anyway, it's not like she was wasting time herself." All the more reason to be surprised by Nadya's arrival.

Shipping the baby off to Krasnoyarsk was not an unusual arrangement: young Russian couples often placed their children with grandparents, who themselves had likely been raised by their parents' parents. Katya showed up at regular intervals, while Andrei was always anything but regular: "I am a holiday. I was always highly prized—both because girls always privilege men and because I provide a contrast to the women's strict ways."

In the early 1990s, Andrei moved to Krasnoyarsk and Katya followed him. They had plans, a friend who had secured funding for a medical center, a view to making a home for their family. But the Soviet Union collapsed, and soon so did the friend's funding scheme, and Andrei and Katya's marriage. Andrei left for Moscow. Katya took the child and returned to Norilsk.

NORILSK WAS A DARK PLACE. Forty-five days out of the year the city fumbled in the pitch-blackness of polar night; for another six months the blackness took turns with a gray haze that was neither day nor night. And when polar day arrived in May, it exposed snowbanks hardened by the winter and blackened by the fine particles with which the metals plants showered the city year-round. As the snow melted, more blackness emerged— all the way to the banks of the Norilskaya River, where some natives swam despite temperatures that rarely exceeded fifty-five degrees, even in July. The banks were coarse sand and rocks filled with the metals that made Norilsk the mining mecca it is. And one of the ten most polluted places on the planet.

In the summers, Andrei yanked Nadya out of the darkness and transported her to hectic Moscow or the green leafy outskirts of Krasnoyarsk, where his mother still lived. Some summers, Katya finagled a ticket to a seaside summer camp in the Russian south and informed Andrei of its location so he could find a rental cot nearby and take Nadya out of camp for a few weeks. The colorful, warm, light-soaked environments in which Nadya spent time with Andrei no doubt enhanced the magical effect of father "the holiday."

"She would come and see ducks [in a Moscow canal] and she wouldn't just say, 'Ducks!' She would ask, 'Are these real ducks?' She lived at the end of the earth, her only image of *duck* was virtual, like a computer-generated sign," Andrei told me. And then he would commence his performance. How did he do it? Andrei took the question very seriously: self-effacement does not run in the Tolokonnikov family. "A hypnosis teacher of mine used to say you have to aim your arrow low: all this talk of superego or social phenomena makes no sense; what makes a difference is the biological, reptilian, sleeping life of the brain. The trick is to awaken that sleeping volcano—that is where true creativity begins. That's what I worked on. Of course, I might have gone overboard. She might have taken my instruction too literally. But we will see what happens when she is released from prison." When Nadya returned from a visit with Andrei at the age of seven, Katya's new husband, Misha, demanded to know what Andrei had done to the child: a wallflower had been transformed into a rebel.

For most of the dark majority of her year, Nadya studied. "She was a straight-A student," Andrei told me without a hint of pride or admiration. "She would spend five or six hours a day studying at home. There is a picture of her sleeping at her computer. I don't know where she got it: certainly not from me or her mother. And it's not like her mother made her study. It may have been a way to escape from reality, by running not into the street or to bad company, but to textbooks."

By her penultimate year of secondary school, Nadya had worked out an autodidact program she followed rigorously. "My education began the moment I came home from school," she wrote to me. "I would sit down with alternative textbooks I had ordered from the library, books on literary criticism and books for the soul." For the soul she read turn-of-the-century Russian existentialist philosophers Nikolai Berdyaev and Lev Shestov, as well as Sartre, Schopenhauer, and Kierkegaard. Whatever gave Nadya the idea she should be reading these books—I was never able to pin her down on this matter in our correspondence—the books gave her ideas. "During regular classes I was either dying from the emptiness of what was going on or actively fighting to impress upon the school administration the primacy of the critical impulse in education."

Whatever ammunition Nadya used in this fight—this too she would not describe in detail, possibly for fear of arming her jailers with the means to assail her character in her endless court and disciplinary hearings—it led to conflict. One time she was directed to write an explanatory note to the school principal. Instead of the standard acknowledgment of wrongdoing and assurances of reform, Nadya wrote a paragraph on the importance of "crisis, watershed moments" in the development of young people. "I have devoted myself to creating such critical moments," she wrote. "And I do this solely out of concern for the school, so it may develop faster and better."

That particular incident centered on a jar of glue. The way Andrei remembered Nadya telling him about it, she had borrowed the glue from a classroom windowsill to use on a school project. The way a former teacher recalled it, still outraged, Nadya had taken a jar of linoleum glue being used by repair workers and moved it to a girls' bathroom—"she was just testing the teachers, but technically it was theft and the policeman told us if we had filed a report she would have gotten two years." I do not know what Nadya remembers of the glue taking because we could not correspond about something that could, however absurdly, be considered a crime.

The principal summoned Nadya to his office over the PA system. She took the opportunity to lecture him on her crisis-fosters-growth theory. "He didn't understand a word of it but asked me angrily why I had signed my statement the way I did." Rather than the customary juvenile "Nadya Tolokonnikova, grade 11A," fifteen-year-old Nadya had signed "Tolokonnikova, Nadezhda Andreevna," as an adult would have. The principal demanded she rewrite her statement and append a proper signature. "This is exactly the way my relationships with representatives of the state have developed ever since," she wrote to me in a letter from her penal colony.

The books or Andrei or both—and something else too—gave Nadya the idea, rarely expressed in Russia, especially in Norilsk, that things could be different—and she demanded that they be so. When she was fifteen, she submitted an article to *Zapolyarnaya Pravda* ("The Truth Beyond the Arctic Circle"), the local daily, and the paper published it under the headline WHAT IS THIS WORLD COMING TO? It was a poorly organized, cliché-ridden rant that condemned Nadya's contemporaries for being shallow and unmotivated, blamed this on all sorts of factors including the popularity of a transvestite singer on television, attributed Marx's maxim that "social being determines consciousness" to the wisdom of Nadya's mother, but concluded, incongruously, with a call to dare effect change because, after all, "It's a wonderful life." When I found the article, I was reassured to learn that Nadya had not come out of the womb quoting Theory, as I had at times suspected, but had been a haphazardly informed and typically judgmental adolescent—just an unusually active one.

The triumphant publication of the article—no Tolokonnikov had ever been in print before—gave either Nadya or Andrei or both the idea that she could be a journalist. Moscow State University's journalism department preferred its applicants with a few publications to their name. Andrei and Nadya collaborated on several pieces they submitted to a Krasnoyarsk paper as Nadya's. There might, however, have been more Andrei than Nadya in them, for the editor rejected them, saying that journalism dealt in fact, not fantasy—an assertion that still appeared to offend Andrei's sensibilities when he recounted the story to me seven years later. Nadya would not be applying to the journalism department.

In THE MID-1990s, the mining giant Norilsk Nickel, by far the city's largest employer, was privatized by a pair of emerging oligarchs. In a few years, the junior partner, Mikhail Prokhorov, decided to become the hands-on manager of the plant and the man who would modernize not only production but the very lives of workers. He inserted himself into Norilsk housing construction, the planning of Norilsk leisure, and the city's cultural life.

As it happened, Prokhorov was unusually close to his older sister, Irina, whose publishing enterprise he had started funding with some of the first money he made years earlier. Irina Prokhorova started and ran the country's best and biggest intellectual publishing house, putting out books, a scholarly journal, and a more-popular intellectual magazine. In 2004, when Mikhail (who generally left the reading of books and other lofty pursuits to his sister) launched a culture foundation, he asked Irina to run it—and to bring the intellectual wealth of her publishing house to Norilsk. For years, when light started dawning in Norilsk, Irina would put together a large group of Moscow writers, artists, and photographers and airlift them to Norilsk for weeks of performances, lectures, and seminars. This was how Nadya saw Prigov. Dmitry Alexandrovich Prigov was a visual artist, a performance artist, and a Conceptualist poet, and he sounded, looked, and moved like no one Nadya had ever seen before. He once explained, "I don't produce text, I produce artistic behavior." He wrote poems like:

I've spent my whole life doing the dishes
And writing highfalutin poetry
From this, my wisdom and judiciousness
Therefore my character, so mild and steady

I understand the water flowing from my faucet
Outside my window, it's the people and the state
If I don't like something, I just forget about it
I keep my mind on things that I can tolerate.*

He took turgid Soviet language, which Nadya had been unsuccessfully trying to use, and made it his own: he bent it, molded it, made it funny, and even more incredibly, made it poignant. This made Prigov and the Moscow Conceptualist school different from any writers Nadya had read or seen before: they did not turn up their noses or turn their faces away from official Soviet culture but, acknowledging its thoroughly false nature, made hay—that is, art—out of it. They reappropriated Soviet expressions like *collective action*—the Moscow Conceptualists staged a series of performances under that title

---

*Translation by Bela Shayevich.

in the 1980s—and other staples of Soviet officialdom, as Prigov had done with the bureaucratic habit of addressing people by their name and patronymic; he made it his artistic name.

Nadya added the Moscow Conceptualists to her extracurricular list of "reading for the soul." And she decided to apply to the philosophy department of Moscow State University. "The philosophy department appeared to me as paradise," she wrote to me from prison, "a place where everyone (or so I thought) was a researcher and an experimenter and everyone had his own little pocket Chernyshevsky, his own little critical thinker." (Nikolay Chernyshevsky was a Russian materialist philosopher.) Nadya's mother said the philosophy department would be hell. She started smoking in the apartment and having constant extremely loud telephone conversations to give Nadya a taste of life in a dormitory. In fact, after sixteen-year-old Nadya miraculously gained admission to the philosophy department despite having no connections in high places, she was assigned to a dorm room with two pious Russian Orthodox fourth-year students who made dorm life feel infinitely better than home. Otherwise, though, the philosophy department was hell.

It took a few letters back and forth to get Nadya to describe precisely what was wrong with the philosophy department— other than everything. It seemed a topic she found almost too distasteful to discuss. "I was flummoxed," she finally wrote, "by the students' immaturity, the irresponsibility of their worldview, their mediocrity, their constant readiness to act true to type, to stick to the norm, their lack of passion—of something that would be authentic, eccentric, outside the norm." Nadya herself stuck to the philosophy department student norm for one semester. "I hate that time and I hate who I was during that time. And I cannot understand how people can spend five years out of their finite lives in such a talent-less, slavish, bureaucratic manner."

At the start of her second semester, Nadya met Petya. He was older—twenty—and in his fourth year in the philosophy department, and he was worldly in a real and almost unfath-omable way. When he was a teenager, his parents had accepted an extraordinarily generous offer from friends in Toronto, who had suggested sending their troubled adolescent to stay with them and go to high school there. After two years, Petya spoke near-native English; then he spent a year in Japan, where his father was working at the time. He had actually seen the poststructuralist feminist philosopher Judith Butler give a talk on the University of Toronto campus. He used the phrase *contemporary art*—words that Nadya had held sacred ever since she first saw Prigov—as though they belonged to him. Or he to them.

Like anyone who ever met Nadya, Petya was struck first by her looks: she looked perfect—like a circle drawn with a compass looks perfectly round or a cut diamond placed on velvet looks perfect with the light falling directly on it. She was tall and taut and curvy in all the places that are theoret-ically appropriate for the qualities of tautness and curviness, and in practice she inhabited this perfection with perfect ease. She had long straight brown hair that shone as hair should shine, and she had a perfectly symmetrical face with large brown eyes and a striking, mesmerizing mouth with full, fleshy, exaggerated lips. Which she used to speak.

"What struck me—aside from the way she looked," said

Petya, acknowledging the obvious, "was that she was this girl from Norilsk, a first-year student, and she had an idea of who the Moscow Conceptualists were. You have to understand that as far as the aesthetics chair of the philosophy department was concerned, Andy Warhol was edgy." Whereas Petya and Nadya knew that Andy Warhol was ancient history, Moscow Conceptualism was the past, and they were the future.

TWO

War

"THEORY WRAPPED ME in an entire climate of description. Theory was simply, shoulder-shruggingly, the only thing that helped me to see what I was and where," writes the American memoirist Marco Roth. "Part of what Theory promised was an idea that another world was still possible, not in some mythical afterlife, but on this earth, now, that the life around me did not have to be the only one. There was no fixed human nature except to take in and shape what was around us. And almost everything around us was now the result of some sort of human endeavor, like the soy formula I'd been nursed on. We were culture and artificiality and engineering all the way down. What was made could thus be unmade."

I recognized that description. And this too: "Semiotics is the first thing that smacked of revolution. It drew a line; it created an elect; it was sophisticated and Continental; it dealt with provocative subjects, with torture, sadism, hermaphroditism—with sex and power." This from Jeffrey Eugenides's novel *The Marriage Plot*.

Nadya described it as "getting shivers." This happened to her when she read the French philosopher Gilles Deleuze. Even in 2007, long after the generation of students who felt they had discovered Theory had grown old enough to write about it wistfully, and long after the humanities had been declared dead in the West, repeatedly, it made her feel like the world was becoming clearer and infinitely more complicated at the same time. It was exhilarating.

The world outside Moscow State University at the start of 2007 was just as stultifying as the world inside it. Vladimir Putin, once a low-level KGB staffer, was in his eighth year of running the country. His luck showed no sign of running out. The price of oil, which had grown nearly fourfold since 2000, had begun its steepest climb yet: it would nearly double in a year. Russia was flooded with money. Luxury boutiques could not keep goods in stock. Nor could the Bentley dealership that had opened up a block from the Kremlin: the country's yearly quota of the latest model would be bought up in a matter of days—for cash. Russia's most popular writers were a man and a woman who authored what barely passed for fiction about the lifestyles of the Russian rich. Each commanded a million dollars a book and they could not keep up with reader demand.

The liberal right wing—the economic reformers of the 1990s—had started out on and by Putin's side, then a number of them broke ranks, tried to establish opposition parties, and failed. In the years it had taken them to change their minds,

Putin had systematically disassembled the country's electoral system and taken over all federal and most local television channels, so that there was little left for opposition politicians to work with, or for. The left-wing establishment—the Communist Party and its satellites—was firmly and comfortably in the Kremlin's pocket. In 2005, chess champion Garry Kasparov, one of Russia's most respected and beloved men, announced he was giving up chess to take up the cause of toppling the Putin regime. He found himself unable to rent a hall anywhere in the country. He did, however, succeed in hammering together a ragtag coalition that staged a series of street protests called the Marches of the Disagreeable. These dissipated in 2008 after the police started detaining known activists in the days leading up to scheduled protests.

In December 2006, at the end of Nadya's first semester in Moscow, more than five thousand people showed up for a March of the Disagreeable, for which a permit had been denied by the authorities. They tried to force their way through a police cordon; more than a hundred people were detained. Four months later, as many as a thousand activists were detained as they left their homes to go to another banned march. Still, about five thousand people showed up and several hundred managed to break through a police cordon and march for about half a mile before the protest was broken up by police. To Petya and Nadya, who took part in some of these protests, it did not exactly feel like change was in the air but it was at least clear that they were not the only people in Russia who would speak out against the suffocating political uniformity, the overwhelming mediocrity, and the obsessive consumption of Putin's Russia.

PETYA'S BEST FRIEND, Oleg Vorotnikov, a philosophy department graduate, had been trying on the role of contemporary artist. Oleg's wife, Natalia Sokol, was a physicist turned photographer, and in 2005 they had formed what they called an art collective, though it appears to have comprised only the two of them and it is not entirely clear what kind of art they did—or, really, whether they did any. Now the two couples, Oleg and Natalia plus Petya and Nadya, would form a new art group. By February 2007, they settled on a name: Voina, or "War."

There remained the question of what this art group was going to do. It was definitely not going to rebroadcast the message of the opposition, which was as stilted as any set of political clichés anywhere—it was a miracle this language had inspired anyone to come out into the streets. The small art scene hardly offered an alternative. The scene was dominated by commercial giants like AES+F, a four-person art group that represented Russia that year at the Venice Biennale with a video called "Last Riot," in which planes collided without bursting into flames and gangs of staggeringly beautiful teens clashed without shedding blood. The art world's emerging star was Victor Alimpiev, who created ethereal works that looked like traces of snow against a pleasantly gray sky and who emphasized that his work was in no way tied to current events or, more generally, to the place and time in which it was created. A group called the Blue Noses provided an alternative to the high gloss of the mainstream art scene; its work was all irony all the time, which basically meant it was a collection of caricatures.

It was not the artists' or the politicians' fault, this desolate state of affairs. To a large extent, it was the Soviet Union's fault. In all societies, public rhetoric involves some measure of lying, and history—political history and art history—is made when someone effectively confronts the lie. But in really scary societies *all* public conversation is an exercise in using words to mean their opposites—in describing the brave as *traitorous*, the weak as *frightening*, and the good as *bad*—and confronting these lies is the most scary and lonely thing a person can do. These are the societies of Aldous Huxley's *Brave New World* or Yevgeny Zamyatin's *We*, which preceded it. In Zamyatin's utopia, the guillotine was known as the Machine of the Benefactor, people were known as Numbers, and the power of words was well understood: "Whoever feels capable must consider it his duty to write treatises, poems, manifestos, odes, and other compositions on the greatness and beauty of the United State." Zamyatin had based his dystopia on the Soviet state he witnessed being constructed. Half a century after his death, real words that corresponded to actual facts and feelings broke through in a sudden, catastrophic flood and brought down the Soviet Union. But that heady period of Russian history was winding down by the time Petya and Nadya were learning to talk. Voina faced a challenge that perhaps exceeded challenges faced by any other artist in history: they wanted to confront a language of lies that had once been effectively confronted but had since been reconstructed and reinforced, discrediting the language of confrontation itself. There were no words left.

A few other artists were struggling with the same issues. Petya had spent some months helping the performance artist

Oleg Kulik mount a large collaborative show called *I Believe*.
The show was preceded by a series of collective soul-searching
sessions during which each participant strove to identify what
he believed in. Petya found this approach unnervingly and
embarrassingly modernist. Here was another complication:
these philosophy students (and one physicist) wanted to use
their intellectual tools to deconstruct what they were confronting, but the shifty and shifting language resisted decon-
struction. In the summer of 2007, they went to see Prigov.

PRIGOV LIKED THEM—of course he did—and happily agreed to
perform with them. This was to be Voina's first real action,
after six months of talking all the time, and once throwing
cats (actual live stray cats) over the counter at McDonald's in
a joint action with the art group Bombily ("Gypsy Cabs"),
which was really just Kulik's stepson Anton Nikolaev, a former
student who emailed me links to footage of Voina's actions.
Voina called him the Crazy One.

Prigov was going to get inside a fireproof metal safe and
Voina members were to carry the safe with the poet up twenty-
two floors in the main building in Moscow State University.
The entire time, Prigov was to be in conversation with himself, presumably in his usual melodic, prayerlike manner. He
wrote a piece to launch his monologue:

> The image of him who sits in the closet, in a shell, in a case,
> is long familiar. He has gone into hiding, he has gone un-
> derground, he is doing his work in secret; the work of his

soul and of his spirit is concealed from outside view. He is like Saint Jerome in his cave when the ray of Providence enters to take him up to the heavens. So has the man in the closet waited long enough for the moment of his ascension, when he shall be taken up to the twenty-second floor and this shall be his reward for the pain and suffering inflicted by the world and for the feats of his spirit, as yet undisclosed. No plain worker of the ordinary physical world—no one whose job it is to transfer regular physical or fleshly burdens from one place to another—could be entrusted with the labors of this ascension. It would be a day's work for them, whether their remuneration was miserly or generous. No, the higher power demanded the untrained hands of those for whom this labor would be a heroic feat, the work not of muscle but of soul and spirit.

The piece was called *Ascension* and reflected the spirit of excessive symbolism with which Voina would imbue its first action. Moscow State University's main building, one of seven Moscow skyscrapers modeled on the Manhattan Municipal Building in a blatant act of architectural plagiarism, is one of the city's tallest buildings, sitting atop its highest hill. So the top of that building is truly as high as one could rise in the Russian capital. Several thousand gulag inmates were used in the construction of the building, and the twenty-second floor actually housed a temporary *lagpunkt* (labor camp unit) when work inside the building was under way. Although the philosophy department was located in a different building, the main building still symbolized all of the university—and all of Russian education, and all of Russian knowledge, and much of Russia's ambition. And it would be by the tender, untrained hands of former and current Moscow State University students (not unlike the untrained hands of inmates who had built the university) that Dmitry Aleksandrovich Prigov would finally be installed at the pinnacle of Russian culture, albeit in a fireproof safe.

They could not find a fireproof safe. They decided to make do with an oak wardrobe—homey and not as heavy as a safe, but a solidly symbolic enclosure still. On July 6, 2007, Voina waited for Prigov in a Moscow bookstore café. Prigov was two hours late.

The he called, laughing: "I have somehow landed in a hospital. I'm in intensive care." Voina went to see him. He seemed to think the whole thing was pretty funny, and so did the young people who crowded around his bed: they were willing to think whatever Prigov thought. Ten days later, Dmitri Alexandrovich Prigov, aged sixty-six, died in the hospital.

Voina had a wake. Instead of ascending to the twenty-second floor, they descended into the Moscow Metro—another symbol of Soviet monumentalism and architectural gigantism. They boarded the circle line at the scarcely inhabited midnight hour and quickly set up red plastic picnic tables, which fit perfectly between the benches that run along each side of the subway car. They covered the tables with white tablecloths and rapidly distributed place settings, bottles of wine and vodka, and traditional Russian bitter and sweet wake fare. Anton the Crazy One approached other passengers to offer them food and drink (all declined). Oleg Vorotnikov recited an early Prigov poem:

My ambition is serving as compost
For the future, more rational sort,
So a youth, full of merit and purpose,
Grows tall in my fertilized dirt,

So a youth, incorruptibly, proudly
Has disdained shady foreigners' pay,
Realizes all madness around him,
*Yet declares "I love you," come what may.**

"It was a total installation," Petya told me, using a term coined by the émigré Russian artist Ilya Kabakov to describe installations that represent segments of a larger narrative. "It was our first experience of working with public space, intended to bring life into it. The Conceptualists pushed the boundaries of language and we pushed the boundaries of public space."

The Wake, or *The Feast*, as Voina named it, is my favorite among their actions because it was heartbreaking. There were about a dozen people at the picnic tables. They were very young and amped up, like kids who are having a party while their parents are out of the house. They looked shaken, small, and alone—exactly the way people feel when someone they love has died. They succeeded in capturing the very essence of a Russian wake, a party of maudlin abandon. Or rather, they captured the spirit of the post-Soviet wake, which, like most post-Soviet rituals, combined a memory of Russian traditions

---

*Translation by Gregory Zlotin

with bits of Soviet officialdom. It was a perfect tribute to Prigov. It was also a perfect preview of the future of Voina, which would become best known for making the private public.

Voina videotaped the action and, as it would do with all its actions in the future, edited it into a short clip with an accompanying text narrative. The video made it into a show in Kiev, and Voina went there and even restaged *The Feast* on the Kiev Metro. They were a bona fide art group now.

ONCE THEY RETURNED FROM KIEV, they launched a series of actions that had the cumulative effect of making people feel as if Voina had been around for a while, commenting on Russian life and politics without mercy. On February 29, 2008, five couples had sex in the Biology Museum and videotaped it. The action was called *Fuck for the Heir Puppy Bear*, a play on Dmitry Medvedev's last name, which derives from the Russian word for bear. Medvedev, a tiny man who looked like a cross between a third grader and his favorite stuffed toy, had been anointed Putin's successor; the day after the action, he was elected to the office of president so he could keep the chair warm for Putin for four years. The location for the action was chosen for its animal associations, while the form was meant to communicate that Russian political life was like pornography: the commercialized imitation of passion.

In May, Voina staged *The Humiliation of a Cop in His Home*: pretending to be students delegated by local high schools, they entered police precincts and replaced portraits of Putin with ones of Medvedev. Policemen watched, mortified at having to witness what felt like an affront to the regime but unable to act because formally the "high school students" were doing the right thing: Medvedev was being inaugurated that very day.

In June, Oleg Vorotnikov donned the long black robe of a Russian Orthodox priest and a police officer's hat, entered a supermarket, and left with a full cart of groceries but without paying—to demonstrate that both priests and cops were robbers. This was called *Cop in a Priest's Cassock*.

In September, Voina staged one of its most loaded and confusing actions, which was also destined to be among its best remembered. Called *In Memory of the Decembrists*, the action referenced Russia's nineteenth-century would-be revolutionaries in a decidedly obscure way. Five of the Decembrists had been hanged, so Voina staged the hanging of five men—three representing, in costume and makeup, migrant laborers and two representing homosexuals (one of whom was also Jewish in real life)—in the aisles of the Auchan hypermarket, which represented itself, unbridled consumerism, and a signature accomplishment of Moscow's mayor, who was known for his xenophobic remarks. Auchan customers were handed "hunting licenses," cards that purported to grant them the right to shoot migrant workers.

In November, on the anniversary of the October Revolution (which also happened to be Nadya's nineteenth birthday), they staged their *Storming of the White House*. Voina smuggled a powerful laser projector into the attic of the Ukraine Hotel (another Stalin skyscraper) and used it to project an enormous skull-and-crossbones across the Moscow River onto the White House, seat of the Russian government.

They closed out the year on December 28 by welding shut

the doors of Oprichnik, one of Moscow's most ridiculously expensive restaurants, whose name referred to members of Ivan the Terrible's shock troops. A message nailed to the door said: "For the security of our citizens the doors of the elite club Oprichnik have been reinforced." Voina members had thought a New Year's celebration was under way inside when they welded the club shut. In fact, Oprichnik was empty that night.

———

THEY PROVED TO BE TALENTED RECRUITERS. They would attend shows at Moscow's Rodchenko School of Photography and invite gifted students to come and play—this was how a short, boyish young woman who called herself Kat became a regular participant. They would go to established artists for counsel and involve them as well: Kulik joined them occasionally, and a writer named Alexei Plutser-Sarno became the group's quasi-official blogger and the leading source of information on their actions. A filmmaker named Tasya Krugovykh came to them when she needed a consult on shoplifting for a film she was planning—and they came back to her with a request for scripting one of their actions. She agreed.

Shoplifting was an essential part of the Voina ethos. They rejected consumption; more to the point, they had no money but liked to eat well and often—so they raised stealing food to an art form. They could hold forth for hours on the theory and practice of stealing to eat, including the finer details of stores' unsuccessful shoplifting-prevention strategies.

Petya, Nadya, Oleg, Natalia, and a shifting number of other Voina members formed what amounted to a commune. They generally lived together—in a two-room apartment Petya was able to rent for a while, in Kulik's basement studio where Anton the Crazy One lived, in a squat, in a rehearsal space. They traveled together when they had shows. They talked all the time, usually about art and politics. Eventually they tired one another out. In late 2009, they split acrimoniously—Oleg and Natalia and their allies on the one hand and Petya and Nadya and theirs on the other. Both groups continued to call themselves Voina. Oleg's claim appeared to have more credence: his Voina continued to generate remarkable actions, including the group's simplest and wittiest one, the laconic opposite of their early excesses. In June 2010, they painted the giant outline of a penis on half of a drawbridge outside the regional secret police headquarters in St. Petersburg. When the bridge was raised, the penis erected itself right into headquarters windows. The action was called *Fuck the FSB*. From this, Oleg's Voina graduated to damaging and destroying police vehicles, then to getting arrested briefly, and finally to fleeing the country. Oleg and Natalia went into hiding in 2011 and eventually reemerged in Venice, Italy.

Nadya and Petya did not do anything as decisive or dramatic. They had had a baby: Gera happened to them much the way Nadya had happened to her own parents—Nadya was pregnant within months of meeting Petya. They scheduled a meeting with Andrei, Nadya's father, in the Metro to tell him the news. He remembered sitting on a train pulling out of the station and realizing "there would be a baby and this character named Petya would now be a part of my life." Once Nadya turned eighteen, she and Petya got a marriage license. Nadya was nine months pregnant when they "fucked for the heir puppy bear." Gera was born four days later. The baby spent much of her time at Petya's mother's apartment while her parents were out making political art.

But by the time Gera was two, her parents—aged twenty and twenty-three—were a bit like art-world retirees. Their best or at least most dramatic work appeared to be behind them. Petya took to referring to Voina's 2008 actions as "classics." It seemed they had been a part of creating something much bigger than they had realized—and much bigger than they themselves were. But the moment in which that work had been created was over. The outrage was gone. The Marches of the Disagreeable had devolved into small protests in one of Moscow's central squares, held every other month. The 2008 financial crisis had tamed Moscow's consumerist extravagance. Medvedev kept spouting somewhat believable liberal rhetoric. What had been black and white turned an indecisive shade of gray—a color not conducive to making radical art.

Nadya studied. She looked for Russian translations of essential works of philosophy written during the last forty years; sometimes she found self-published or unpublished translations, and sometimes she found none at all and became a translator herself. Petya was restless.

THREE

Kat

"MY CHILDHOOD WAS not particularly ordinary before it became ordinary." Yekaterina Samutsevich had an indirect relationship to language; I had noticed this in spending time in her company even before we sat down for our first formal interview. She aimed to be precise, her word choice was always intentional, but she seemed unaware of images or associations that her words called forth in others, and as a result her speech often served to obscure rather than to illuminate. Now I had told her I wanted to hear her whole story from the beginning, and she started by saying her childhood had become ordinary after it had been extraordinary.

"It was extraordinary at first because I was always in hospitals, in some sort of institution, like an orphanage but actually a hospital. I must have had serious health problems of some sort, as I was told later. So when I was a child, I never saw my parents. I don't remember how old I was when I first saw them—it's hard to tell the age from the memory. I remember Mother and Father came. Mother was wearing a black fur coat—I remember that. I was told, 'This woman and this man are your parents. They waited for you and now they have come to take you.' And I remember that I had been in hospitals and also there were other women I didn't know. I lived at a woman's home once and she gave me treatment potions. I had been spending all my time with strangers. So the first time I was shown my mother and father, it made no impression on me: I didn't care who they were. I was just sad I had to go to some strange place. And they took me to the apartment where I still live."

"Did you ever ask your parents what was wrong with you?"

"Of course I did. They told me I was a biological child, I was not adopted, but I had been very seriously ill. I don't know what it was—maybe there was something wrong with my heart. So they'd had to keep sending me away to make sure I could survive."

Here was the only central character in this story to whom I could have unfettered access, and we seemed to have encountered a fundamental problem at the very beginning of its telling. From everything I could see, she had told me a classic adoption story, and now she was telling me it was not what it seemed. We all deal in personal and family myths and legends, we conspire to exaggerate and obliterate, but usually we make adjustments to the stories to make them believable (indeed, often true stories must be systematically altered in order to actually be believed). Never before had I been told a story that appeared to represent one event and been instructed to take it on faith that it actually represented another. This was going to happen again and again in my conversations with Yekaterina and her father.

Stanislav Samutsevich was a very tall man who looked younger than his seventy-four years. He also looked remarkably un-Russian: in a short-sleeved blue oxford shirt, gray belted slacks, and black loafers, he looked more like a retired American insurance salesman or midlevel IBM employee than a Russian engineer. We sat on a park bench in central Moscow; like many Russians his age, he had not adopted the Western habit of meeting in cafés.

"She had a problem with her kidneys," he said when I asked him about Yekaterina's early childhood. "She was in working condition by the time she was five, so that was when we collected her. It was possible to take care of her, and now she is a physically healthy child."

He was talking about a thirty-year-old woman.

"Sure, she is physically underdeveloped," he continued.

If I was able to stifle my reaction when Samutsevich called his grown daughter "a healthy child," I must have failed now: he clearly noticed I had cringed at the word *underdeveloped*. Yekaterina was five feet tall and had broad hips that made her look stockier than she was. She had an angular way about her and could sometimes look awkward, but she was by no means "underdeveloped."

"It's just that everyone in my family is large," explained Stanislav Samutsevich.

ONCE SHE WAS HOME, Yekaterina had an ordinary childhood. She was a lonely girl growing up in a lonely family of lonely people, a late-Soviet version of any American novel of suburban desolation. Her parents had an old-fashioned sort of mismatch: the father hailed from an educated and well-placed Moscow family, while the mother came from the Ukrainian countryside. He felt embarrassed by her and she felt oppressed by him. She spent her days teaching drawing at the school Yekaterina attended—a regular neighborhood school, like scores of other schools around Moscow—and her evenings and summers in the kitchen.

"She was brought up conservatively—that the woman's place was in the kitchen," Yekaterina told me. "And my mother really did work at home her whole life. I mean, she worked around the house. Always cooking, cleaning. My father never did a thing, from what I understand. And she was always resenting him for that. She would say, 'He is an intellectual, what are you going to do.' In the summers we lived at the dacha, and I would see it: the summer, the heat, and she and my aunt are always cooking. Making preserves too, and other strange things. I didn't understand what it was all for. But she told me, 'Your life is going to be like this. You'll spend it in the kitchen.' I looked at it all in horror. And I view it negatively now."

Stanislav had other ideas for his only child: he steered Yekaterina toward his own field of computer programming. She graduated high school with a gold medal, given to straight-A students. "It was easy enough," she told me. "I was surprised other people didn't have gold medals." She paused. "And then they started pressuring me to go to college." The Moscow Institute of Power Engineering seemed as good a choice as any. It also took Yekaterina out of her dreary southeastern Moscow neighborhood for the first time since she landed there at the age of five; at least during the daytime hours she spent at the institute, she saw something other than the permanent traffic jam that had been the view from her apartment and school windows throughout her childhood.

The summer after her first year of college, Yekaterina lived at the dacha with her mother; her father worked, splitting his time between Moscow and the countryside. One day her mother, who was standing at the stove as usual, collapsed with a massive heart attack. Yekaterina called her father and her aunt and an ambulance, but by the time anyone came, her mother was dead. Yekaterina tried not to go to the dacha after that.

She spent six years at the institute, getting a master's degree, and then left instead of pursuing a Ph.D. "I was disappointed to a certain extent. The department had outdated equipment, my adviser was ninety years old, and I didn't think this was a very good sign. Naturally, he died soon, and there was no one left, literally, except for a single professor. The state just did not want to invest in attracting people to working in research. So I decided to get a job. And since I didn't have any work experience, I just started going around from one research institute to another, looking for someplace willing to let a student in." This was the mid-2000s; young Russians with Yekaterina's credentials were getting jobs at Google, its hip Russian competitor Yandex, or any number of other high-tech firms that were actively recruiting engineers. But that was in a different, contemporary Moscow: Yekaterina was, like her father, still living in the Soviet city of her childhood, where engineers toiled at research institutes. Or rather, they usually worked at Ministry of Defense outfits behind the facades of research institutes—and that is exactly the kind of place where she found work.

The Agat Institute was a God- and state-forsaken outfit inhabited by dead souls and a few disoriented live ones like

Yekaterina, who was put to work developing software for the weapons-control system of a nuclear submarine. This particular submarine had been under construction in fits and starts since Yekaterina was nine years old and the USSR still in existence. Now, ten years past its original deadline, it was earmarked to be leased by the Indian navy—if and when it was ever completed.

In 2007, construction of the submarine was largely finished and engineers were needed on site for the final adjustment and testing process, which was expected to last about a year and a half. Russian authorities were haggling with India—the price tag kept growing and the deadline kept getting pushed back—and the engineers were coming under pressure too. This was when Yekaterina quit.

"I was completely disappointed there too," she told me. "For all the same reasons: corruption, the state's lack of desire to invest in quality military equipment. Programmers got very low pay, while project leaders, who weren't doing anything, just watching the security clearances, got a hundred thousand rubles [about three thousand dollars] a month. And the people who never showed up but were making sixty thousand. And you went to work and you didn't know who you reported to or what you were supposed to do."

What Yekaterina remembered as her first stern act of rebellion, her father remembered differently: "When she was supposed to go to the Far East for equipment testing, I wouldn't let her go."

"What do you mean, you wouldn't let her go?"

"Well, would you have? She was twenty-five years old, a little girl—what kind of father would let a child go to the Far East for one and a half to two years? And I've served in the military myself. I have been to those parts—they are crawling with criminals. So I didn't let her go. And a good thing I didn't too."

Yekaterina quit the defense institute and started taking on freelance software-writing assignments, or so her father thought. Her actual first act of rebellion was responding to an ad for a new school of photography, named for the Constructivist artist Alexander Rodchenko. The ad was a message from the other Moscow, a modern, cosmopolitan city Yekaterina had barely suspected existed. She had been to a couple of photo exhibits, and once she had been struck by the work of Boris Mikhailov, a Ukrainian-born photographer living in Berlin, one of a handful of living, world-renowned artists who hail from the former Soviet Union. Yekaterina saw a couple of pictures from his famous Red series, over-the-top romantic images flooded with Communist red. "I liked them. I didn't know why."

She had the summer to turn herself into a Rodchenko applicant. "I tried to make pictures that would be conceptual and not just pretty. I realized they were no good, they needed to be smarter. So I started studying books by photographers—I don't remember who. And then, unexpectedly, I got in." The school was free for those who were admitted on the basis of their portfolios, and Yekaterina decided not to tell her father about it. Every day she would slip out of the apartment and enter the world of contemporary art critics, curators, and photographers: the best of Moscow's best taught at Rodchenko.

In November 2008, the fire-extinguishing system on the nuclear submarine on which Yekaterina had worked malfunctioned while the vessel was en route to a weapons-testing exercise. Twenty people aboard died, including seventeen civilian engineers. Stanislav Samutsevich felt his instincts had been good and his strictness had been vindicated; it was a good thing his daughter was a freelancer now.

WHEN YEKATERINA EVENTUALLY ADMITTED she was studying photography, Stanislav Samutsevich tried to be understanding and asked to see her work. "She was making pictures of abstract things, and I told her, 'Take pictures of life around you and the way people live, and that way you will have psychology in your work.' That went right over her head."

In fact, she did take pictures of life around her. The class assignment for the 2007–2008 academic year was photographing elections. During the parliamentary election in December 2007, members of the class, armed with credentials issued by the mayor's office, went to different polling stations—and got roughed up, detained, or chased away. At one point Yekaterina and her closest friend at the school, a tall, pale, skinny young woman named Natasha, decided to photograph Yekaterina voting at her own old school. Natasha shot her walking toward the building—and discovering that it was locked. "Then these people in civilian clothing showed up and said the election was over and the building was closed." It was an hour before the polls were scheduled to close.

Yekaterina's political education intensified in March, when she and Natasha set out to photograph the presidential election. Putin's anointed successor, Dmitry Medvedev, was running essentially unopposed. From a list of polling stations, Yekaterina and Natasha picked an address that seemed odd to them. They found a psychiatric hospital—as it turned out, it was one of a number of ghost precincts created for the counting of dead-soul votes. They took pictures of themselves look-ing for a place to cast their votes inside a psychiatric ward—until they got kicked out.

That spring the Rodchenko School had a student show. When Yekaterina and Natasha arrived, someone told them a group of people was looking for Natasha—they had liked her video installation and asked to meet the artist. The two women found Petya, Nadya, Oleg, and Natalia standing by Na-tasha's work. The visitors introduced themselves as Voina and were surprised to hear that Rodchenko students had dis-cussed their work in class. They exchanged phone numbers. A month later, Voina called, and Natasha and Yekaterina joined. Yekaterina now called herself Kat. They took part in *Humiliating a Cop in His Home* and helped to prepare the *Cop in a Priest's Cassock*, *Storming the White House*, and the hang-ing of the Decembrists in Auchon. More important, they be-came part of the fabric of Voina, the arguing, the organizing, and the endless purposeful hanging out. Toward the end of that year, the inherent tensions started getting the better of the group. Soon after Voina welded shut the empty Oprichnik restaurant, Natasha left in a huff. The remaining five people traveled to Kiev and broke up there.

Nadya, Petya, and Kat returned to Moscow intent on con-tinuing Voina. This was when they called Tasya Krugovykh, the filmmaker they had instructed on shoplifting, and asked her to help them conceive and script an action. Tasya's idea was, naturally, cinematic: she was fascinated with the idea of filming the stereotypes and fears resident in the collective un-conscious. She scripted an action in which members of Voina hid out by the side of the highway where traffic policemen were stopping cars with the intention of extracting bribes. Once the cop had his potential victim with the window rolled down, Voina emerged from the shadows, impersonating the cop's family. Kat would be wearing a housecoat and carrying a platter with a chicken on it (eight chickens had been shoplifted for the occasion). Nadya played a pouty teenager. All of them implored the cop to extract a larger amount. "Five hundred is not enough! Look at the number of mouths we have to feed! Get more!" The cops, mortified, would try to tell drivers that the group was not their real family.

It made a great roadside show—the visualization of a general stereotype and the well-known premise of many jokes, traffic cops extracting bribes in order to feed their large families and to keep their overbearing wives out of the workplace—and Voina staged it a number of times. But the resulting video clip, the ultimate product of their work, disappointed them. Their previous actions, captured on video, had been essentially one-liners. This one was a story, and it came across like a miniature movie, which lacked the Voina edge. It felt like they themselves lacked an edge now. The Moscow faction of Voina fizzled.

Kat and Nadya continued to spend a lot of time together. Natasha had gone home to Siberia, and Kat, who had found she was most comfortable next to someone more willful and driven than she was, became a sort of Sancho Panza to Nadya's Don Quixote, who was obsessively trying to figure out how she was going to confront the world next.

"They were always in my apartment," Stanislav Samutsevich complained on the park bench. "They were always in Yekaterina's room. Doing girl stuff, I thought. I didn't realize what they were up to until I got a phone call from the police."

FOUR

Wee Wee Riot

On December 5, 2011, Violetta Volkova and Nikolai Polozov met up a bit before seven. They had never met in person before—they had been following each other on Twitter for a couple of months, since Volkova's teenage daughter dragged her mother into the era of social media by starting an account for her. Polozov and Volkova had exchanged a few messages because they seemed to have a couple of things in common: they were both in their late thirties, they both worked as criminal defense attorneys, and they both held, as Volkova put it a year and a half later, "views not in favor of the authorities." This was an awkward but surprisingly precise definition; in a country where there was no political opposition, either in parliament or in the street, a few people discovered their commonality online because they produced similarly disaffected 140-character comments on the Russian government.

As criminal defense lawyers, Volkova and Polozov did not

enjoy the kind of social status an American might associate with this profession. The Russian court system, never a sterling example of justice, fairness, or competition, had regressed in the Putin years—and Volkova and Polozov were too young to remember anything else. With an acquittal rate of less than one percent and judges drawn largely from the courts' secretarial pool, the courts had turned into an arena for technocratic bargaining at best and systematic bribery at worst. Volkova's and Polozov's more ambitious law school classmates had gone into corporate or tax law and had over time come to imitate the style of their City of London counterparts—and to make a lot more money than they did. Volkova and Polozov, on the other hand, wore polyester suits and held as low an opinion of their profession as anyone else did.

But it had occurred to Volkova that they could do something important, or at least something different. Another man she had followed on Twitter had posted about a protest planned for this evening. Volkova had never gone to a protest, or even seen one anywhere but on TV—and that had been the protests in Cairo; it had been years since anything of any magnitude had happened in Moscow. But for some reason she felt moved to Tweet a response to the virtual acquaintance who had posted about the protest. She said she would be willing to help if anyone got arrested. Someone suggested she take up a watch post somewhere near the protest site. She found a café with a good view out a second-floor window. She figured she would spend at least a couple of hours there straining to see anything in the wintery darkness outside. She messaged Polozov, suggesting he keep her company.

Whatever it was that brought Volkova and Polozov out that

night had worked on thousands of other people as well. In a city where for years no protest had drawn more than a few hundred people—not pensioners coming out against drastic cuts in benefits, nor journalists coming out to mourn their slain colleague Anna Politkovskaya, nor the varied crowd who came out to protest the continued imprisonment of a pregnant woman who had worked for jailed oil tycoon Mikhail Khodorkovsky—suddenly, almost without warning, between seven thousand and ten thousand people took to the streets to protest yet another rigged election.

Nadya and Petya and Kat and many others had been waiting for this day for a long time. For Nadya and Petya, the waiting had commenced years earlier, when they dreamed that the Marches of the Disagreeable might lead to change. Kat had been waiting for four years—since the time she and Natasha were roughed up when they tried to take pictures at a polling station. Many Russians had been surprised and inspired in the summer of 2010, when scores of people led by a young woman named Yevgeniya Chirikova waged a battle to save the forest in Khimki, just outside Moscow, where a new toll road was to be built. Many others began waiting for Russian protests six months earlier, when they watched the Arab Spring explode in hope. And hundreds of thousands felt they could wait no longer when, on September 24, 2011, they watched Vladimir Putin and Dmitry Medvedev appear together to announce they had decided to swap seats again, with the former retaking the office of president and the latter becoming prime minister again, in a sham presidential election to be held in half a year's time. They had announced this and blithely begun preparations for an equally bogus parliamentary election that was held on December 4. And on December 5, the people finally came out.

Nadya and Kat and some of their friends, old and new, had been preparing for this. They were ready. Sort of. Maybe. Almost.

IN THE COUPLE OF YEARS since Voina fizzled, they had occasionally tried to create actions. At one point Nadya and Kat asked Tasya Krugovykh, the filmmaker, to videotape them wrapping evidence tape around groups of trees; the imprint on the tape said STABILITY—the buzzword of the Putin years. Cinematically, however, the action once again turned out unimpressive and they never released it. After a while, they had another idea: they would kiss cops. They would kill them with kindness, smother them with love. The action was tied to another in a long line of President Medvedev's symbolic but substanceless actions: he had ordered that the Russian police, which had since the early days of the Soviet Union been known as *militsiya*, or militia, be renamed *politsiya*, or police. As though that would magically render the police less corrupt and brutal, less likely to rape, pillage, and terrorize, and more likely to protect. As though it would magically make them human. To test this transformation, Nadya and assorted Rodchenko students they drafted would approach police officers and ask them for simple directions. If the officer responded helpfully, one of the actors would go into paroxysms of gratitude, culminating in a kiss—on the lips, when possible. The kisses, it was decided at the outset, should be same-sex. The reasoning behind this decision was, as often happened with Voina, opaque, but the organizing itself proved an interesting experiment: the men of Voina turned out to be no more capable of administering same-sex kisses than the men of *militsiya/politsiya* were of receiving them. They would abort the action a day or a few hours before it was planned, pleading exhaustion, ill health, or nothing at all. So it was by accident that *Buss the Buzz* became Voina's first women-only action.

Or perhaps it was not entirely accidental. Nadya's self-education course had taken her into feminist theory. During the production of *Buss the Buzz*, Nadya carried Julia Kristeva's *Revolt, She Said* with her—to read on the Metro and, it turned out, to quote from when the unhappy object of an unwanted kiss searched her. "We are happy because we are revolting," Nadya proclaimed, but the attempt to quote Kristeva fell flat, in part because the play on words was lost in translation, so it came out simply "rebelling," or "rioting."

Since *Buss the Buzz* had turned into a women-only action, it made sense to release the video clip on the eve of International Women's Day, March 8, 2011. It went viral and was generally liked, though some people—I was among them—found the nonconsensual physical interaction disturbing. Two years later, Kat assured me there had been no force or coercion involved and only the choppy video editing had made it look like the women of Voina had forced themselves on unsuspecting cops. At the time of the action, though, Kat had sounded pretty aggressive: "A cop's face is communal property, just like his or her nightstick or your personal belongings, of which he can conduct an illegal search," she told a reporter. "A cop's face, as long as he is wearing a uniform and a badge, is but a tool for communicating with citizens. He can use it to demand your documents and . . . to tell you to come to the precinct. And you have only one way of responding: 'Yes, sir/ma'am, officer, I obey you and I am coming.' We are proposing a new way of interacting with this tool, we are introducing variety into the relationship between the people and the police."

Nadya's message to the same reporter was simpler: "The decision to become a cop is a hugely serious decision, and it should be made responsibly . . . I say to her, 'Madame Officer, have you heard your boss the mayor's speech in which he said that 'Moscow does not need gays'? No? That's reason enough for me to suck your face."

Queer theory and feminist theory was teaching Nadya, and Nadya was teaching Kat, that things should be done differently—not just differently from the way they were done in Russia but also differently from the way they had been done in Voina. It had been a group of men aided by their wives. It had also been a group in which the women had jealously watched their husbands. Both conditions now felt a bit embarrassing, as did the serious regard Voina accorded itself. The more Kat and Nadya and occasional others argued—this method of creating actions had remained unchanged—the more they agreed that their new strategy should not involve Art with a capital *A*; indeed, the fact that it was art should be concealed by a spirit of fun and mischief. Whatever they did should be easily understood, and if it was not, it should be simply explained. It should be as accessible as the Guerrilla Girls and as irreverent as Bikini Kill. If only Russia had something like these groups, or anything of Riot Grrrl culture, or, really, any legacy of twentieth-century feminism in its cultural background! But it did not. They had to make it up.

THE LAST WEEKEND of September 2011, Nadya was invited to speak at a conference called in the hopes of uniting the many small and disjointed Russian opposition groups. The organizers, who had met Nadya during the 2010 Khimki Forest protests, did not have much of an idea who she was or what they wanted her to say, but Nadya knew exactly what she wanted to tell them: She wanted to spread what she had been learning. She wanted to use her ninety minutes to compensate for Russia's lack of a feminist movement, a body of social theory, or a Riot Grrrl legacy. She put together a set of thirty-seven slides.

Nadya and Kat sat in one of the front rows, by the projector, with their backs to the mostly male audience.

"Since our schools and universities do not yet have gender studies departments, we lack the opportunity to offer a complete theory course," Nadya began. "Our presentation today will be fragmentary; it will contain a number of separate clips; it will be, essentially, an advertisement."

They began with Bikini Kill, sped through 1970s feminist activism in the United States and Europe, described separatism without saying the word, paused to summarize Shulamith Firestone's *The Dialectic of Sex: The Case for Feminist Revolution*, transitioned to the French artist Niki de Saint Phalle's visual critique of the view of women as consisting only of their reproductive organs, and jumped back over to contemporary Russia, where Vladimir Putin had responded to a female speaker at a conference of his United Russia party by saying, "Natasha, I have only one wish: please do not forget about fulfilling your obligations with regards to solving our demographic issues."

This got them as far as the 1980s in the United States; they talked about the Guerrilla Girls as a way of getting into issues of race in feminist art; described the Guerrilla Girls breaking into art museums wearing gorilla masks and eating bananas— and pointed out that "today the banana remains a preferred racist tool for insulting people; take, for instance, repeated instances of Russian soccer fans throwing bananas at black players." While bell hooks, they explained, had shown people it was possible to be doubly oppressed, the Austrian artist Valie Export had demonstrated that the naked female body could not only please but also frighten and haunt. They showed a two-minute video about Valie Export's work, including her 1968 *Genital Panic*, featuring her genitals and a machine gun in a Munich movie theater. This took them back to Russia, where a spokesman for the Russian Orthodox Church had suggested, recently and repeatedly, that a dress code be imposed on Russian women. They showed Cuban artist Ernesto Pujol's *The Nun*, featuring a young man in a habit, and suggested a dress code for men might be in order. Over to French artist Orlan's image *Skai and Sky*, featuring two crosses held by a woman wearing a black rubber habitlike dress, with her right breast exposed. Martha Rosler's 1975 *Semiotics of the Kitchen*, a black-and-white send-up of cooking shows, followed. Cut to British artist Sarah Lucas in an armchair, denimed legs spread, a fried egg on each of her breasts. Her *Get Off Your Horse and Drink Your Milk* showed the (nearly prostrate) Russian men in the audience a naked man, for a change, holding between his legs a milk bottle in place of a penis and two cookies in place of testicles. But pictures of Russian artist Elena Kovylina were even more shocking: using hypodermic needles, she had affixed to her naked body pictures of girls cut out of magazines—and demanded that people attending the show in Moscow remove the pinups while she sat impassively until the last of the images was gone. And as though that were not enough, Nadya and Kat followed up with images from more of Kovylina's works: Kovylina boxing, in red; Kovylina naked, lying immobile atop a grand piano interminably, symbolizing woman as we are used to seeing her in art.

After that, they headed back to the West and more theoretical work addressing obscure topics, which provided much-needed relief for the audience: the French performance artist Orlan's work on plastic surgery and diatribes against stereotypes and fixed identities. To relax the viewers further, they introduced Marcel Duchamp's gender-altered *Mona Lisa*, with the penciled-on mustache and beard, and Man Ray's portrait of Duchamp as a female movie star. Duchamp's urinal made it into the slide show too, possibly to provide the audience with at least one familiar image in addition to the *Mona Lisa*. Then there was Diane Arbus's portrait of a transvestite, Yasumasa Morimura's portrait of an Audrey Hepburn impersonator, and Morimura himself as the model in a Vermeer painting. And back to Russia, where the male artist Vladislav Mamyshev had made a career out of being Marilyn Monroe. Was that all that Russia had to offer to cap this tour of contemporary feminist art? A gay male artist who had risen to prominence twenty years earlier and had invented nothing new since?

They had probably given the audience as good an introduction to feminist art as any undergraduate seminar in feminist art might offer in a country where such seminars are offered. But the last thing Nadya and Kat wanted to do was deliver what amounted to a lecture on how things were done "over there." They were, after all, activist artists at an activist conference, and that kind of abstract presentation makes bad activism and bad art.

The fact, though, was that feminism had never taken root in Russia. It had been part of Bolshevik ideology in the 1920s, when "revolutionary morality" replaced bourgeois morality, abolishing marriage and monogamy and introducing free love, communal children, and full gender equality. The USSR even introduced the world's very first laws against sexual harassment in the workplace. But the egalitarian spirit did not last. Starting in the 1930s, laws against homosexual conduct were restored, as was marriage; abortion was banned (to be legalized a few decades later, and to become the country's sole method of birth control); a child's legitimacy once again became paramount in establishing social standing; and Communist Party organizations commenced close watch over the integrity and moral purity of families. "If he cheats on his wife, he will cheat on his country" became a catchphrase.

Bourgeois morality was, in other words, fully restored, but in keeping with the principle of calling things by the names of their opposites, it was called "Soviet morality" while feminist thought was branded bourgeois. Virtually all Soviet women held two full-time jobs—one for pay and one, at home, for nothing but hardship, which, in light of constant food shortages, could be extreme—and this was called "full gender equality." Even after the Soviet Union collapsed, the tradition of reviling and ridiculing feminism proved surprisingly resilient. A few feminist organizations that appeared in the late 1980s, on the glasnost-and-perestroika wave, either stayed small or disappeared. Feminism was an academic pursuit, and an unpopular one. Combined with the general paucity of political content on the Russian art scene, that meant that Nadya and Kat had only Kovylina's (problematically commercial) work to show. If they wanted to show something radical, feminist, independent, street-based, and Russian, they would have to make it up.

"It is worth noting," Nadya said importantly, "that punk feminist art is being produced in Russia today. Here is an example. The Pisya Riot collective works in a great variety of genres, including both visual and musical compositions."

Pisya is a kid's word for genitals of either sex; it is most like wee-wee or pee-pee.

Nadya brought up a slide of Titian's *Madonna with Child and Saints*, where the male saints had been replaced with a woman, a clothesline from which a variety of boxer shorts were hanging had been placed in the background, and piles of anachronistic dirty dishes occupied the foreground. The reproduction and the alteration were flawless. The audience observed respectfully.

Then Nadya pushed a button on a boom box. A sound like the scraping of a thousand rusty nails started up. Nadya and Kat rose and quickly but calmly left the audience alone with Pisya Riot's first and only musical composition, "Kill the Sexist."

BEING A FICTIONAL GROUP, Pisya Riot could not write its own music. Neither of the real-life members of the phantom group could; Nadya had taken music lessons as a child and had not

done well, and Kat had no musical background. So they borrowed a track from the British punk group Cockney Rejects
and used a handheld Dictaphone to record their lyrics over
the sampling:

You are sick and tired of stinky socks,
Your daddy's stinky socks.
Your entire life will be stinky socks.
Your mother is all in dirty dishes,
Stinky food remains in dirty dishes.
Using refried chicken to wash the floor,
Your mother lives in a prison.
In prison she's washing pots like a sucker.
No freedom to be had in prison.
Life from hell where man is the master.
Come out in the street and free the women!
Suck on your own stinky socks,
Don't forget to scratch your ass while you're at it,
Burp, spit, drink, shit,
While we happily become lesbians!
Envy your own stupid penis
Or your drinking buddy's huge dick,
Or the guy on TV's huge dick,
While shit piles up and rises to the ceiling.

Become a feminist, become a feminist
Peace to the world and death to the men.
Become a feminist, kill the sexist!
Kill the sexist and wash off his blood.

Become a feminist, kill the sexist!
Kill the sexist and wash off his blood.

They found they liked being Pisya Riot. Maybe they even really wanted to be Pisya Riot. To become a punk rock group, though, they would need musicians. They thought of N, a woman Nadya's age who had come to Voina with her boyfriend; they were both anarchists. Nadya sought her out. N was with another boyfriend now, a cool older guy who collected and fixed antique bicycles, and she was no longer an anarchist—she was making a living as a computer programmer and apparently maintaining a perfectly respectable middle-class existence, though she was still serious about her music. N found Nadya changed too: "In Voina, she had been this chubby-cheeked child, and now her cheeks had thinned and her voice took on a certainty. She had chosen her issues, and she may even have chosen them at random, but now she was serious and her topics were LGBT and feminism. And the choice had changed her: she no longer saw herself as an appendage to Petya and Vorotnikov, even if she had once been a willing appendage. It had still limited her. When you are with someone, you are not flying through the cosmos, because your soul always has its home in another person—you may need it sometimes, but it is limiting and it keeps you from taking flight. Nadya got this at some point and took flight." Pisya Riot, on the other hand, seemed to N almost pure silliness, but she envied whatever it was Nadya felt. She took on the music.

They would need other participants too, but that did not seem like a big issue; what they had in mind could be done by three or five or seven or eleven people, and they had friends and the Rodchenko School had students to be recruited. They also needed a stage. At first, playgrounds, with their platforms and slides, looked pretty good. They had recorded "Kill the Sexist" at a playground. It was raining. It was also nighttime, which meant there were no children at the playground, but there were beer-drinking and cigarette-smoking young people, who grew concerned when they heard young women screaming their heads off about stinky socks.

They said, "What happened? Did someone hurt you? Do you need help?"

Nadya and Kat had said, "Don't worry, we are just making a record." But now that they were planning on making videos, they needed a different stage, something more spectacular. One day, as they got off the Metro, they spotted it: some stations had towers made of scaffolding, with platforms at the very top, for changing lightbulbs or painting ceilings, or performing punk rock, perhaps. Moscow Metro stations are, for the most part, grand architectural affairs, all marble and granite and ostentatiously spanning arches and dramatic lighting; they look like classical concert halls, and the crude scaffolding towers, viewed from the right angle, look very much like a punk affront of a stage.

They performed a number of reconnaissance missions and identified several stations where the towers were particularly tall and well placed, which is to say, placed close to the center of the hall. Then they began rehearsing. If they were going to be a feminist punk rock group, they were going to have to have instruments—Kat picked up a bass—and they were going to have to climb up the tower and unpack their instruments and mics and amplifier and take up positions fast, faster than the Metro police knew what was happening.

They practiced at playgrounds.

As they rehearsed, it became clear they needed staging and visuals and costumes. "Because if we just got up there and started screaming, everyone would think we were stupid," Kat explained to me. "Stupid chicks just standing there screaming." First they came up with wearing balaclavas, which would make them anonymous—but not like Russian special forces, who kept their identities hidden behind black knit face masks with slits for the eyes and mouth, but like the opposite of that: their balaclavas would be neon-colored. Then they would need dresses and multicolored stockings, to show that the whole getup was intentional. Bright, exaggerated makeup showed surprisingly well through the slits in the balaclavas. And the pillow—the pillow appeared because parliament members had begun talking about banning abortion and Putin kept talking about Russia's so-called demographic problem, by which he meant that Russian women were not getting pregnant often enough, and so Nadya stuck a pillow under her green dress. And then she tried taking it out during the screaming, or the singing, and ripping it open. The feathers created a sort of snow effect, in addition to the birth effect and the abortion effect. That worked.

They spent a month filming their first clip. This was now a complicated production, and it opened the door for Petya—who had been itching to join them—to actually do so. Nadya was good at putting together lectures, Kat was good at helping her, N was good at the music, Tasya was good at filming, but all of them were a nightmare when it came to logistics—at which Petya, with his rare combination of manic energy and attention to detail, was incomparable. There was one time they climbed atop a Moscow electric bus and performed—it turned out the feather-letting worked outdoors as well—but mostly they filmed at Metro stations, as many as fifteen of them in all. A couple of times, they got detained. Once, Tasya, who was filming, got beaten up by police. This was before many Russians came to think of being beaten up by police as a regular part of their existence. There was the time when the police tried to beat up Petya, and Nadya wedged herself between him and them and literally shielded him with her body, and there was probably no one, not even Nadya, who appreciated the beauty of her doing this after screaming about stinky socks and penis envy.

And there was the time when the police called Stanislav Samutsevich. "They would not let me see them," he recalled. "They were in a holding pen. I had a conversation with two interesting young men. They talked to me about contemporary art and activism. I asked them who they were, and they said, 'We are art critics in civilian clothing.'" It was an unfunny joke that Stanislav Samutsevich did not get: *art critic in civilian clothing* was a term used to denote KGB agents whose job it was to inform on dissidents in the Soviet Union; just like their predecessors in the 1970s, Pisya Riot had developed a following among these "art critics" before the broader public ever heard of them. That is, the secret police had literally started following them around—there were more of them with each consecutive taping.

Stanislav Samutsevich would not have known, or wanted to know, anything about dissidents in the Soviet Union, or about those whose job it had been to spy on them or jail them. "So I shared with them my views on contemporary art." What were they? "Well, I am an old man." The ones in civilian clothing were more knowledgeable about contemporary art. "The girls had really wreaked havoc there and the police didn't know what to do with them. Then a big police vehicle came for them and Yekaterina told me to go home. She came home later, on the last train. I had a talk with her after that, but I am a dinosaur and I don't understand anything about anything, so that was the last time she ever told me anything." From that point on, Stanislav Samutsevich learned about performances from the media—or from police. He did try to protect the girls from themselves. "One time they were in the hallway, painting posters of some sort, and I came out and said to them, 'Look, you've already been to the police station once, and no one knows how things could end.' Nadya stopped coming over to the house after that."

After that particular detention, the media got wind of the tower climbing and the screaming and the feathers flying in the Metro. They assumed Voina was back in action. Petya and Nadya were invited to the studios of the lone independent cable television channel, Dozhd ("Rain"). They denied it had been a Voina action. They said they had been detained while attending a performance of a new, different art group. They said it was called Pussy Riot.

FIFTEEN SHOOTING DAYS, a month of organizing, rehearsing, and editing, one night spent at a police station, several police chases, and a few skirmishes later, Pussy Riot had its name, its identity, and its first video. On November 7, 2011, the ninety-fourth anniversary of the October Revolution and Nadya's twenty-second birthday, Pussy Riot launched its blog with the publication of its first clip, "Free the Cobblestones." The music

was borrowed from the British punk rock band Angelic Up-
starts and arranged by N, and the voices, now declaiming
more than singing or screaming, were clearly pronouncing
lyrics that no longer sounded like a caricature of what a feminist punk group might say if it existed in Russia but were
making a serious attempt at what Pussy Riot would master
in the next couple of months: painting a portrait of Russia in
words that could mean nothing else:

> *Voters are stuffed into classrooms,*
> *Polling booths stink up stifling rooms,*
> *It smells of sweat and it smells of control,*
> *The floors have been swept and stability has been served.*

> *Free the cobblestones! Free the cobblestones!*
> *Free the cobblestones! Free the cobblestones!*

> *Toilets have been shined, chicks dressed in civvies,*
> *The ghost of Žižek flushed down the drain,*
> *The Khimki forest has been cut down, Chirikova kicked off*
>   *the ballot,*
> *Feminists dispatched on maternity leave.*

> *Free the cobblestones! Free the cobblestones!*
> *Free the cobblestones! Free the cobblestones!*

> *It's never too late to take charge.*
> *Nightsticks are loaded, the shouts get louder.*
> *Stretch your arm and leg muscles*
> *And the policeman will lick you between your legs.*

Free the cobblestones! Free the cobblestones!
Free the cobblestones! Free the cobblestones!

Egyptian air is good for the lungs,
Turn Red Square into Tahrir,
Spend a full day among strong women,
Find an ice pick on your balcony and free the cobblestones.

Tahrir! Tahrir! Tahrir! Benghazi!
Tahrir! Tahrir! Tahrir! Tripoli!
The feminist whip is good for Russia.

The clip went viral. Pussy Riot got press. A typical item read, "It appears a new sort of urban nutcases are on the loose in the country. A feminist group calling itself Pussy Riot consists of five girls in face masks with bad voices that they use to shout out songs 'about the tyranny of housework, a triple workday for women, contemporary trends in revolutions, and the right ways to subjugate men.' And they perform their songs only in places where it is illegal, like on the roof of a bus or on the Metro." Pussy Riot thought this was perfect.

Three weeks later, they produced their second clip. This time they focused on the Putin era's obsession with luxury. Most of the performances that made up the clip were shot along Stoleshnikov Lane, a pedestrian street lined with designer boutiques. They stormed into these boutiques, unpacked their equipment, and performed until security guards got their bearings and removed them. One time, they climbed atop a glass display case surrounding a luxury car—or at least they thought it was a glass case; it turned out to be made of Plexiglas, which

bowed perilously beneath their feet. They were terrified of falling in and onto the car, but that did not happen, and their fear
and discomfort were not visible in the resulting video, which
showed them strong and confident atop the display case, spray-
ing from a fire extinguisher and screaming:

> *Use your frying pan to occupy the city.*
> *Come out with your vacuum cleaner and reach orgasm.*
> *Seduce battalions of policewomen.*
> *Naked cops are happy about the latest reforms.*
>
> *Fuck the sexists fucking Putinists!*
>
> *Kropotkin vodka is swilling in their stomachs,*
> *You feel good while the Kremlin bastards*
> *Face a toilet riot, a deathly poison.*
> *No flashing lights will help them. Kennedy is waiting.*
>
> *Fuck the sexists fucking Putinists!*
>
> *Sleep it off, another day comes, time to subjugate again.*
> *Brass knuckles in your pocket, feminism sharpened.*
> *Take your bowl of soup to eastern Siberia*
> *To make the riot really truly crude.*
> *Fuck the sexists fucking Putinists!*

The song was called "Kropotkin-Vodka": Kropotkin for Peter Kropotkin, Russia's anarchist prince, and vodka for unbridled consumption. In the process of filming "Kropotkin-Vodka,"
Pussy Riot got pretty good at talking to the police. They devel-

oped rules. Rule Number One: Do not give your real name. They found an old online database and memorized random names and addresses. It would turn out this was not the most brilliant idea ever—the database had been compiled by the police, and some of the people on the list were wanted for more than outstanding traffic tickets. In addition, Pussy Riot often could not manage to keep their stories, names, and addresses straight, and this infuriated the cops. Still, it was probably better than accumulating an arrest record. Rule Number Two: Tell a good story. The story was, they were applying to theater school and needed to make a clip and wanted something both original and brave in order to really stand out. It was not a particularly convincing story, but it seemed to work, and perhaps it worked precisely because it was so absurd. Neither the police nor any of the boutique owners ever pressed charges. And Pussy Riot never really damaged any property—except one time.

They crashed a fashion show. They had this idea of creating visual effects with white flour, which they sprinkled on the floor, and balloons, which they let float up off the floor. But after they had unpacked their equipment and started singing, the flour on the floor caught fire from candles that the show organizers had placed along the walls. Fire spread instantly along the floor and up the balloon strings, singeing and burning garments. Miraculously, no one was hurt. But everyone was terrified. Pussy Riot finished their song and ran out, with one of the show's organizers in pursuit. "Stop them, stop them!" she yelled to the bouncers, who stood flabbergasted. Then she addressed Pussy Riot themselves: "What did you do? You just burned us down."

"We are sorry," Pussy Riot said.

"Who are you?" the woman screamed.

"Here, have a phone," Pussy Riot said, pressing a cheap cell phone into her palm. They always bought these cell phones for actions: the devices had SIM cards that the security services did not have on file and presumably could not start tracking in the space of one night.

"All right," the woman said, unaware, in her state, that the gadget was of no use or worth. Pussy Riot walked away, and then they pulled off their balaclavas and started running, up the street, then down, down, down, all the way into the Metro. On the train they started laughing.

"We are burning up!"

"Hot!"

"Let's call this one 'Pussy Riot Burns Down Putin's Glamour'!"

They got off two stops later, at Kropotkinskaya—not because it was named for Peter Kropotkin but because this was where the Metro line turned and ran alongside the Moscow River away from the center, which created a kind of psychological boundary. It was dark, cold, unseasonably snowless, and damp, as it had been for days and would be for another couple of weeks. It was late—nearing midnight—but the area around Kropotkinskaya was full of people: tens, possibly hundreds of thousands standing quietly in line outside the Cathedral of Christ the Savior. The people, most of them women, were waiting to see the Holy Girdle—that is, a fragment of what was said to have been the Virgin's undergarment. The relic, which normally resided in a monastery in Greece, was winding up its tour of Russia. More than three million had come to see the Girdle as it toured the country, more than a million of them in Moscow, spending long days and nights in the freezing rain, waiting their turn.

What a strange city this was, with its alternating rituals of glitter and Girdle. And how in the world was Pussy Riot going to fit it all into their performances, finally to point up the frightful absurdity of the land? This was what they wanted to do, but now that the adrenaline from the run was ebbing, the task seemed just about impossible. Because the city, and the country as a whole, seemed endlessly willing to accept whatever it was handed: the enormous income discrepancy, the rampant corruption that fed both the boutiques and the Cathedral of Christ the Savior, and the lies that underlay it all.

UNTIL DECEMBER 5, that is. "Kropotkin-Vodka" was published on December 1. Three days later, there was the parliamentary election that was no less but also perhaps no more rigged than the ones four and eight years earlier, but it drew more attention from Russian citizens than any election in a decade and a half. They came out to vote and, more important, they signed up in droves to become independent election monitors. And on December 5 criminal defense attorneys Violetta Volkova and Nikolai Polozov sat drinking their cappuccinos in a second-floor café and watching as Russians came out into the street. The space allotted for a three-hundred-person rally, for which a city permit had been issued, filled up in a matter of minutes. And then they watched as ten times that many people arrived from every direction in the space of ten minutes. And, in another ten minutes, there were three times that many again. More than seven thousand in all, and perhaps as many as ten thousand. They watched prisoner transports pull up, and water cannons, and buses with special forces troops. They watched a peaceful rally proceed, as the police looked on without interfering. They watched the rally starting to break up and the police opening up only a very narrow passage in the direction of the Kremlin and secret police headquarters at Lubyanka. They saw several thousand leave easily, through wide passageways open in other directions, and they saw nearly half of those present squeezing into the bottleneck in the direction of the Kremlin.

"It's going to start now," said Volkova.

And it did.

The people who had turned toward the Kremlin tried to organize a march. The police started to sweep them up. More than five hundred were detained. Volkova and Polozov spent the night going from police precinct to police precinct to holding facility. They got scores of people released on the spot, and they met a lot of new people in addition to each other. In the morning, when it seemed they were done, Polozov told Volkova it was his birthday and went home to grab some sleep before his party. Just after he left, Volkova got a phone call—her number had gotten around through the night—asking her to come to a holding facility in northern Moscow, where several dozen prominent activists had been taken. She was slightly awestruck when she saw Boris Nemtsov, a former cabinet member now in opposition to Putin: he was there to deliver McDonald's hamburgers to the high-profile detainees. "I had never seen him in person. Actually, I had never been interested in politics." Volkova was not familiar with most of the names of her new clients, who had been separated from the rest of the night's detainees because they had arrest records. A skinny bearded guy named Petya Verzilov was among them.

WHAT STARTED THAT NIGHT was the Russian protest movement, what came to be called the Snow Revolution; the name appeared the following day. A lot of patterns were set that night. People would be getting arrested in the coming months, almost every day. A small team of young men would be tracking the arrests and helping coordinate legal help (the tracking system was born that night at my apartment, near the protest site, when one of the young men came there to warm up and started Tweeting information about detentions—I watched it start but did not know what I was seeing). Volkova and Polozov would be the two lawyers at police stations at all hours, defending those who got detained. It did not matter that they had never done this before. Everyone in the protest movement was making it up as things developed. Including, of course, the women who had become the group they had made up a couple of months earlier. Now that the revolution had started, Pussy Riot would be heard.

FIVE

Maria

"LAWLESSNESS, THE DENIAL OF RIGHTS, and forced mutual de-
pendence that results from collective responsibility are all
things to which we have become accustomed." The courtroom
was stuffy—and stuffed with people. Most of us had spent a
day or so getting here: take the red-eye from Moscow to Perm;
brush your teeth in the airport bathroom, where the chipped,
muddy-colored tile and an entire collection of filled-to-bursting
black trash bags were somehow made bearable by piped-in
seventies disco music; then catch a transport to Berezniki—a
four- to six-hour drive, depending on the snow—then line up
outside the Civic Collegium of the People's Court, one of dozens of identical gray five-story buildings on Five-Year-Plan
Street in this city of scores of identical five-story buildings,
which house all of its 150,000 residents and all the courts,
polyclinics, and residential authorities that rule their lives.

IT WAS MINUS-TWENTY DEGREES CELSIUS (minus-four Fahrenheit) in Berezniki, the kind of weather against which any sort of clothing can provide protection for only minutes, not for a stationary wait of a couple of hours. The court marshals allowed journalists and activists into the building one at a time, conducting thorough searches of every frozen person. In the end, about a hundred people filed into the courtroom and another fifty or so had to stay in the lobby and watch the proceedings on a video monitor set up especially for this uniquely media-worthy occasion. The courthouse, or at least a part of it, had been given a fresh paint job and a glass-and-plastic aquarium to hold Maria Alyokhina in the courtroom. Her high-pitched voice bounced off its smooth new walls, so to the audience in the courtroom she sounded like a dodgy telephone connection, coming in loud and fading out.

All day, the court had been reviewing Alyokhina's motion to postpone the serving of her prison sentence until her son turned fourteen—a measure sometimes applied in cases of nonviolent offenses, and, in cases of the well connected, not just the nonviolent ones. "This is our unfreedom, which, as we all recall, is worse than freedom," said Alyokhina, referring to former president Dmitry Medvedev's awkward declaration that "freedom is better than unfreedom." He had been talking up his economic policy.

"This is the way we are forever serving life rather than living life. I want to live life. My freedom is this: Here I stand, I can do no other, as Martin Luther said. My cause may be hopeless, but I find my freedom in the responsibility I take on, and to retreat for me would be to die a little, to use the words of the students protesting at the Sorbonne in 1968." I thought there were probably only three or four people in the crowded courtroom who got Maria's references and appreciated their proximity to one another, and to Martin Heidegger, whom she had quoted earlier in the hearing. Two of those people were Petya and I.

MOST THINGS MARIA HAD SAID in her life were addressed to people who did not even try to understand them. Her mother, Natalya, had discovered the chasm that separated her way of thinking from her daughter's when Maria was thirteen. "After seventh grade, I had her change schools to go to one with a concentration in mathematics," Natalya told me, chain-smoking in an overpriced Moscow coffee shop. Here was another parent who would not receive me at home—it was too big a mess for visitors, she claimed. I found this easy to believe: Natalya had the air of someone who struggled, probably unsuccessfully, with the daily requirements of homemaking and family life. She was a software engineer who had always lived with her own mother—a perfectly normal pattern for Russian women of her generation—and had never married, which was unusual. She had given birth to Maria at thirty-five, an almost impossibly advanced age for first-time motherhood in Russia, even in 1988. Maria's father was a mathematician who did not stick around to see the baby born—or show any other sign of life until Maria was a teenager, at which time Natalya shot down his sudden attempt to communicate with his daughter.

The daughter, meanwhile, had spent seven years at a decent

school near their apartment building in the relatively scenic bedroom suburb of Kuntsevo (unlike most of noncentral Moscow, Kuntsevo had a variety of buildings—some brick and some concrete, some five and some nine stories tall). It was a boarding school with intensive instruction in English, and Maria was a day student, which meant she took all her meals at school and came home after seven o'clock in the evening. In grade school, she was a bit of a bully, regularly beating up her enemies and occasionally swinging at her friends. As she grew into a teenager, her aggressive streak vanished. And Natalya decided it was time to transfer to a math school, as she herself had done at that age—and as she thought only natural.

Maria rebelled. Natalya was surprised. "I don't understand the word 'humanities,'" she complained when she talked to me. She started a frantic search for a suitable new school. She finally placed Maria at a school where she knew the principal—but not before conceding that she would probably never understand what her only daughter said, read, or wanted. When it came time to look for a college, Natalya said, "I can't give you any advice on this: I don't even know anyone in the humanities."

What might have made another child feel abandoned and misunderstood made Maria feel independent and respected. When I asked her to sketch her autobiography in a letter from the penal colony, she began as follows: "You might say I was raised at home: I never went to preschool, and I spent my time in the building's yard. I loved climbing trees, getting to the very tops of oak trees and birch trees and looking down at the way their branches intertwined beneath my feet. I lived with my mother and grandmother and I was always treated like an adult; no one fussed over me, and actions were always discussed. Probably the most important thing about my childhood is the absence of unmotivated prohibitions. If something was not allowed in our family, the reason was always transparent. Independent opinions and actions were respected."

Maria's grandmother died when the girl was nine, leaving Natalya feeling helpless in the face of the challenges of keeping house and raising her daughter. "Our relationship was chilly ever since the incident with the math school," she told me, and then corrected herself: "No, ever since my mother died. I guess it was my fault—it's always the parents' fault. I'm probably too aggressive when it comes to arguing. She always said, 'I don't want to argue with you.'" It seems once Maria got out of the habit of slugging her enemies and her friends, she developed a kind of private policy of nonconfrontation—as though, perhaps, she were saving her strength for fighting on a global scale. "It's the strangest thing," N, who was a lifelong friend, told me. "I can tell you anything at all about her because I just know she won't take it the wrong way."

EVEN AFTER ESCAPING from math school, Maria continued to perceive high school as an unfortunate obligation. When something caught her interest—usually this was a Russian literature lesson—she paid attention; the rest of the time she sat in a corner on the floor with a book, looking like a flower child out of place and out of time. Her reading list was unburdensome: Russian quasi-dissident science fiction that had been trendy in the seventies and mildly satirical popular fiction that had been trendy in the nineties. Her part-time job at a video rental store provided a slightly bigger intellectual challenge: there she watched her first David Lynch, Hitchcock, and Fellini films, as well as one movie each by Lars von Trier and Catherine Breillat. None of this made for common ground with her high school classmates—though once, when she ran into N in a pedestrian underpass near home, she told her about *Requiem for a Dream*, Darren Aronofsky's grim movie about addiction, and this rekindled their friendship. Though as N grew more sophisticated in her tastes, she poked fun at Maria for falling for Aronofsky's maudlin musings. Maria did not take offense.

Maria wandered to the Arbat, an historic area of Moscow that had served as the city's lyrical heart, then its counterculture center, then its first modern tourist attraction, and, finally, a caricature of itself. In the sixties, singer-songwriter Bulat Okudzhava crooned, "Ah, Arbat, my Arbat, you are my calling, my joy, and my sorrow." In the seventies, hippies would gather at the Gogol monument at the end of Arbat Street, where police would regularly sweep them up for loitering. In the late eighties, Arbat Street got a makeover as a pedestrian mall—just as the USSR was starting to lift the Iron Curtain. In the nineties, street vendors of everything from fur hats to handmade jewelry shared the street with street musicians, street artists, and fans of the once wildly popular singer Viktor Tsoi, who had died in a motorcycle crash in 1990 at the age of twenty-eight. The fans had constructed a tiled wall in the Arbat as a memorial to him and milled around it, mourning their idol 24/7, year after year. Tsoi's most famous song was "Change!" "Our hearts demand change! / Our eyes demand change!" went the refrain.

By the naughts, the Arbat had turned into the tackiest street in Moscow, lined with overpriced cafés with bad food and stores selling counterfeit antiques. Of the street vendors, only the fur hatters remained. Tsoi's wall drew a crowd only in August, on the anniversary of his death. The street musicians had gone on to get real educations and actual jobs as advertising executives, and the only trace of their existence were three or four men who continued to strum their guitars in "the Pipe," the pedestrian underpass at one end of the Arbat. Their audience was a semipermanent group of inebriated adolescents who had been drawn to the Arbat by its old reputation, in search of the counterculture or perhaps even a cause (Tsoi had represented one) or meaning (Okudzhava had promised it). This was where Maria met Nikita in 2006.

Nikita was older—twenty-two to Maria's seventeen—and had been drinking harder and longer. He had a backpack with his essential belongings, which included a slim volume of Immanuel Kant, and he had been wandering central Moscow for a few years, with only an occasional stopover at home, in the northern Moscow bedroom suburb of Otradnoye ("Delightful"), one of the most dreadfully gray and desolate areas in a city almost unremittingly gray and desolate around its edges. Maria and Nikita started wandering together. They were both slim, not very tall, and both had long, slightly frizzy chestnut hair. Perhaps together they felt like the ghosts of those long-ago Arbat hippies. "It was a marginal way of life," Nikita told me over tea in Moscow's first vegetarian café. "A megamarginal way of life."

Whatever it was that Nikita had been seeking when he drifted to the Arbat, he had long since stopped looking. Maria barely managed to graduate from high school; getting into college was out of the question. "When she did something, she threw herself into it fully," N told me. "And drinking was no exception." Most people I asked about Maria tried to skirt around the drinking issue—it seemed inappropriate, and disloyal, to discuss her teenage binges while she was struggling in jail—but found it difficult to tell the story without this part of it. "Should I be talking to you about this?" N asked me. I admitted I was not sure how I was going to handle the drinking in the writing, but told her this: I had been a teenage alcoholic myself; I nearly flunked out of high school because I was always either drunk or hungover; and I had no real explanation for what it was that enabled me to stop drinking. Nor did anyone really understand what gave Maria the strength and vision to quit: Nikita thought it was the Art of Living, a prepackaged yoga outfit that provided her with daily exercises that anchored her better than daily drinking; N thought it was getting pregnant—which Maria did in the fall after she did not go to college. She was eighteen.

"We got very inspired when she got pregnant," Nikita told me. "We started researching birth, going to classes. She made plans. She has this ecological bent, she tries to lead an ethical life without the killing of animals, so she wanted to give birth at home and we made plans." A home birth would indeed have required planning, as well as money, and trying to make and keep either with an alcoholic is a lost cause, so when Philip was born in May 2007, it was on the gray sheets and within the yellow walls of a regular neighborhood "birthing home," where giving birth is rough and free. The only item on Nikita and Maria's to-do list that they could actually check off was putting up new wallpaper in one of the rooms in Natalya's apartment in Kuntsevo, where all four of them were now resident. Maria and Nikita, though, maintained a regular schedule of breakups, so most of the time the Kuntsevo apartment housed only the child, his mother, and grandmother—just as it had two decades earlier.

Philip was not yet three months old when Maria and Nikita took him to Utrish, a national park in southern Russia. Nikita had been hitchhiking to camp there for many summers; Maria fell in love with the place her first time there.

I had asked Maria to tell me what had led her to become an activist, and the path stopped here. "Looking at this list of facts, neither you nor I can tell how I became an activist or why I continuously changed the focus of my activism," she wrote. "I acted intuitively—I generally tend to trust myself when I take steps that I later realize were important. In 2008, when I was in my first or second year of college, I read the news that Utrish, one of the places I hold dearest in Russia, would be cut down. I found two telephone numbers and addresses on the Internet, packed a knapsack, and, straight from college, went to the offices of the World Wildlife Fund and Greenpeace. I met some of their staff members. The people at Greenpeace counseled me to start collecting signatures and printed out sign-up sheets for me."

I could visualize this scene. Moscow nonprofits do not get a lot of foot traffic—they are usually staffed by seasoned activists, many of whom have spent time living, working, or studying abroad, in countries where one might get the idea to become an activist. The appearance of a starry-eyed young woman looking like a throwback to some imaginary 1970s—wearing a hand-sewn skirt, a wide-brimmed hat over frizzy long hair, and a backpack, as though she were planning to hike to battle without delay—and speaking (in the high-pitched voice that tends to crack when she is excited) of how much she loved Utrish was definitely odd and quite possibly comical. Handing her a stack of sign-up sheets may have been an attempt to test her or just to get rid of her.

"So this was all I had—a bunch of blank sign-up sheets and not a single activist among my friends. I collected forty-three hundred signatures in one week and met wonderful people: artists, students who belonged to the environmental group at Moscow State University—I can't even list them all. Many people wanted to help." Pretty soon Maria was in charge of the grassroots organizing effort for the defense of Utrish, though she modestly omitted that fact from her letter to me. She helped organize rallies and pickets and, when the illegal clear-cutting of the national forest began in November 2008, she joined dozens of activists who traveled to Utrish to shield the trees with their own bodies. "I did everything with my son in a sling. When it got cold, family members would take him while I was at rallies or pickets." Five years later, at the hearing in Berezniki, having involved her toddler son in political activities would be cited as one of the reasons to deny her early release.

EVENTUALLY MARIA DID DECIDE to go to college, and the college she chose, the Institute of Journalism and Literature, was a tiny, almost quaint private undertaking, unknown to virtually anyone who did not study or teach there. I had been an editor actively recruiting young journalists in Moscow for years, and I had never heard of it, nor had anyone I asked. Its workshop-based system drew the kind of kids Maria had been: the ones who had spent their high school years sitting in a corner with a book. The institute offered a scheduling option perfectly suited to working people or young mothers: attending classes on weekends only. Maria spent the week with Philip and doing her activism, and the weekends, when her mother could take the baby, at seminars at the institute, only about a block from her old Arbat haunts. This was the first school where she actually made friends; by her second year there, a tight group had formed. They studied together and, in the evenings, attended any of the many readings that constituted Moscow's poetry renaissance: by the mid-naughts, the city had more working, walking, and reading poets than it had had in decades. An annual poetry festival in May saw lines snaking down the block from any of several cafés that hosted readings. Most of the city, of course, was entirely unaware of the poetry or the poets: the reading and writing community was small but loyal and fiercely active. Maria and her friends represented a minority faction in the audience: people who were not poets themselves and did not know most of the poets personally.

Most members of the group planned a career in writing. One of Maria's closest friends, a quiet, diminutive young woman named Olya Vinogradova, got a job writing book reviews for Moscow's central children's library. "I thought she would make a very good journalist writing about social issues," Olya said of Maria. "She is very good at getting into places. But she really was undetermined, because—this would sound weird if not for what has transpired—she had this idea that she would change the world. She was always saying, 'What is the point of all these prose exercises, how do they contribute to world change?'" Institute friends were sharply aware of Maria's activism but foggy on its substance: Utrish seemed important but far away, and anyway, soon enough Maria seemed to start shifting focus. For all her passion and ability to "get into places," she was no proselytizer, so aside from the fact that she was now concerned with both electoral politics and contemporary art, her institute friends knew almost nothing.

Maria had a bit more time now: when Philip was four or so, Nikita stopped drinking. He had had dry spells before, and she had always made use of them to get time for herself, but now he not only could pitch in with child care but craved time with Philip, because it turned out he was good at being the father of a small boy. They even went to a fitness club together three times a week: Nikita did yoga with the zeal of an addict, and Philip joined in kids' activities. Nikita was not nearly as good at being a companion for Maria, nor did he really try: their relationship maintained its drifty rhythm, but the distance between them grew larger.

"She often tried to tell me something, but I wasn't really interested," Nikita told me with a kind of righteous evenness. "She had a lot of interests, while my internal resources were few. There was Utrish, then there were birds, some sort of ecocamp for migratory birds, then soap-making and anarchists. Then Putin showed up, and this really was incomprehensible. I mean, look at it from my point of view: I had only begun my recovery, and I was paying attention to my immediate surroundings—that would be Philip. Philip was real, while with Putin I wasn't so sure. Maybe he was a doll of some sort. So by the time all those protests began, I had completely lost interest. And anyway, I didn't know her friends, so it's not like I listened to her when she told me where she was going and with whom."

"I was always an outsider everywhere," Maria wrote in her first letter to me, talking about the schools she had attended. By the time she was in her early twenties, she had, like many people who perpetually feel like outsiders, perfected the art of compartmentalizing her life. She made little effort to talk politics or literature to her mother or Nikita (Natalya and Nikita, meanwhile, had perfected the art of living as strangers under one roof). She kept politics largely out of conversations with her institute group: they discussed poetry. And she fell behind on her reading because it was not exactly compatible with her activism. "She had to cram Sartre when she needed to at the institute," Olya told me, apparently ashamed to be disclosing her friend's embarrassing circumstance. "She lacks the concentration necessary for reading: it's easier for her to watch movies." What was worse, N told me, Maria persisted in her unself-conscious admiration for Aronofsky's sentimental *Requiem for a Dream*.

Maria found the time and concentration to catch up on her reading in jail. Which was part of how she came to be quoting Heidegger, Martin Luther, and French student activists to an indifferent court in the faceless town of Berezniki.

PART 2

Prayer and Response

SIX

A Punk Prayer

THE FLOODGATES OPENED after December 5. It was like everyone had found his long-lost family, like daylight had broken after years of polar night. Opposition groups that had hobbled along with a dozen members on a good day now found they had hundreds and even thousands of volunteers. An ad hoc coordinating committee sprang up and people from opposite sides of the political spectrum sat down at the same table to try to channel the wellspring of human energy. People who had never thought of themselves as activists joined them, and everyone used the informal pronoun to address everyone, because everyone felt part of one great big impending revolution.

Pussy Riot did not know where they fit in at first, but then very soon they did. The day after the big December 5 protest, they went out into the street to protest again—because what else would they do? Several hundred people gathered to protest the previous night's arrests. Most of them got arrested.

This was the first time Nadya and Kat spent the night at a police station. A huge room with school desks was filled with detainees. In the morning, they were released, and they would not even have to go to court: the courts were choking on administrative arrests.

By the time they left the police station, it was clear that their next action would be where the action now was, at Special Detention Center Number One, where several dozen mostly young men were serving ten- and fifteen-day sentences in the aftermath of the protest. They included anticorruption blogger Alexei Navalny and a couple of other high-profile activists as well as men like Petya, who had been in and around the fight for several years, and other men who had stepped into the street for the first time. Petya had called and asked for food and Nadya and Kat went and stood in line at Special Detention Center Number One with a care package for him, which was a bit pointless because by that time Navalny's supporters had brought enough chocolate and tangerines to last the opposition all winter.

Inside Special Detention Center Number One, the revolution was in full swing. One large cell had set up a round-the-clock webcast of their detention, which was filled with passionate discussion of the future of protest and the motherland. Another cell was making banners out of bedsheets and hanging them out their grated windows. 15 DAYS OF FREEDOM read one, and to those looking from the outside, it did seem like the men had found liberty in their sentences.

Petya was in a cell with Navalny and many other men, and at one point someone—probably someone who had read memoirs of Stalin-era camps—suggested each of them deliver one lecture in his area of expertise; it would make the time go faster and each of them would come out of jail knowing more than he had going in. Lectures on business administration, tax law, and revolutionary philosophy went well, and then it was Petya's turn. He would speak on contemporary art. He got a late start—bad luck, and supper was delivered late, and Petya always got a late start on everything—and as soon as he began, the entire cell fell asleep. Except Navalny: Navalny stayed up for the duration of Petya's mistimed three-and-a-half-hour lecture, winning his political and personal support for all eternity.

Pussy Riot cased the joint. There was not much traffic behind the building, and there were garages there, low enough for the women to be able to climb up on the roof using the same ladder they had used for the "Kropotkin-Vodka" actions.

There were three of them on December 14. It so happened that no one except Kat and Nadya could make it that day, and they had left it pretty late—some of the men would be released the next day—but a woman came out of nowhere and said she could sing. She also said she was an anarchist, she would never tell them her real name, and she played the guitar. It was all true. They called her Seraphima.

When they mounted the garage, a traffic police car pulled up. An officer with a megaphone emerged and asked them to climb down. They pulled their ladder up onto the roof, threw off their coats to expose their neon-colored dresses, took out their microphones and their instruments, unfurled a large banner that said FREEDOM TO PROTEST, cast it over the fence so it hung on the barbed wire, lit three smoke bombs, and sang and shouted:

Time to learn to occupy squares,
Power to the masses, fuck the leaders.
Direct action is the future of humankind.
LGBT, feminists, stand up to the fatherland!

Death to the jails, freedom to the protests!

Make the cops work for freedom,
Protests serve to improve the weather,
Occupy the square, make the takeover peaceful,
Take all the guns away from cops.

Death to the jails, freedom to the protests!

Fill up the city, the streets, and the squares.
Lots to do in Russia, forget eating oysters.
Open the doors, throw off your epaulets,
Come and taste freedom with us.

Death to the jails, freedom to the protests!

The windows of Special Detention Center Number One filled up with faces. The second time Pussy Riot called out "Death to the jails!" the building roared "Freedom to the protests!" in response. The men rattled the bars on their windows, and it looked like the special detention center was going to explode. The cops who had gathered by the garage turned their backs on the performers and went into the building, closing the door behind them. Singing in broad daylight, performing an entire song in one go, to an audience that was not only captive

A Punk Prayer | 101

but receptive, Pussy Riot felt like performers for the first time. At the end, they joined the inmates in chanting "The people united will never be defeated!" Then they lowered their ladder and climbed down. No one tried to detain them; they put on their coats and went to their rehearsal space to edit the video.

They put up the clip that evening; the timing was good, but the clip itself was not. It felt raw, and not in a good way. It did not look like video art; it looked like an amateur video of three girls singing on a garage roof. At the end, their captive audience applauded and Kat, Nadya, and Seraphima took a deep, enjoyable bow and Kat blew a two-handed kiss. This was a performance rather than performance art. Maybe their mistake was in recording a single performance rather than a series before putting together a clip. Pussy Riot had declared seriality as one of its core principles, and at the age of two and a half months the group was too young to start screwing with its own foundation.

Truth be told, the crisis went deeper. In the space of two weeks, protest had gone mainstream in Russia, taking Pussy Riot with it. Creative direct action was not enough if everyone was doing it. And everyone was; there was even a clearing-house for direct action now, with hundreds of people coming to weekly meetings to propose dozens of actions, find collaborators, and start to organize on the spot. (I started the Protest Workshop, as it was called, and facilitated its meetings from December 2011 through June 2012.) These included flashmobs on the Metro, performative acts of art, and small-scale, un-sanctioned protests. What Pussy Riot had just done seemed to fit right in with the rest. Telling themselves they had been visionaries and had done it first seemed like cold comfort, and seriality alone was not going to save them from the predicament of having gone mainstream. Pussy Riot decided to take a creative hiatus until after the New Year.

WITH THE REVOLUTION UNDER WAY, people were finding their way to like-minded people. A woman who had taken part in a couple of Voina actions called; she was back after living abroad and was looking for work and calling everyone she knew to ask for leads. But she immediately agreed that an all-girl punk band sounded better than work. And when she came to a rehearsal, she said it felt right, it felt like her thing. They called her Seraphima because they had liked the first Seraphima, the anarchist who had never told them her name.

Petya met a woman at the Protest Workshop; they had both come to a meeting with their kids and struck up a conversation. The woman was smart, well educated, blond, and beautiful, and they decided her name would be Terminator.

N was around again, going by the nickname Morzh ("Seal"), and one day she brought her old school friend Maria, who everyone thought looked a little out of place with her hippie dresses and coquettish hats, but by the end of the conversation it was clear she would change the world.

There remained the question of how to change the world, or at least where to begin—or to resume—the process. With protests flaring up all over the city and administrative arrests becoming a daily occurrence, the location itself had to impress the imagination. Petya suggested the Duma, the Russian parliament. Then Terminator showed up and suggested the Duma. Like several other newly minted activists, she had just gotten a job as an unpaid aide to one of the opposition deputies, so she had a pass to the Duma and the ability to get more. The idea was to have Pussy Riot take up position in one of the press or spectator boxes in the main hall—they would get in posing as college students on a tour—then whip out climbing equipment and rappel down into the hall, their guitars strapped to their bodies, and singing. They did not know what they were going to sing, but at this point it mattered less than that everyone be trained in technical climbing. "I like being in a band," they started saying. "You get to learn to climb mountains."

Some women showed up and said they were also feminist artists. They suggested doing an action in Red Square. Pussy Riot thought that Red Square was overexposed; just about every Russian contemporary artist worthy of the title had done something there. Then again, if just about every Russian contemporary artist worthy of the title had done something there, why had Pussy Riot not done anything there? Pussy Riot became obsessed with Red Square.

The square contained a structure known as Lobnoye Mesto, a round stone platform about fourteen yards in diameter and eight feet high. Ivan the Terrible had used it to address Muscovites in 1547, and the czars' decrees were read from it in subsequent centuries, but contrary to popular lore, it had not been used for public executions. It did, however, beg to be exposed as a stage. A dozen steps led up to the top of the platform, but they were covered with snow, as was the stage itself, and one suspected that under the snow there was ice. Pussy Riot figured out a way to position themselves so they could not be removed. A stone barrier ran most of the perimeter of the platform, about a foot wide and about three feet high. If they climbed on the barrier, they would be more than ten feet off the ground and it would be virtually impossible to remove them forcibly without risking killing them in the process.

There was, in fact, ice on the barrier, and they discussed the need to wear nonslippery boots. They also needed a ladder, smaller than their old one, to get up onto the barrier quickly, and they bought that at the Auchan hypermarket. And then they rehearsed—a lot, because they knew this one had to be fast. Now was not like the old times, a couple of months ago, when no one suspected them of anything unusual until an action was already under way: now the police expected protest everywhere, and in Red Square they expected it most of all.

WHEN PUSSY RIOT WOKE UP on the morning of January 20, 2012, the day they planned to sing on Lobnoye Mesto, they found out that three gay activists had been detained in Red Square for coming out with a placard that said HOLD A GAY PRIDE PARADE IN RED SQUARE. Pussy Riot joked that they had been announced, and they went to Red Square.

> *A column of rebels is headed for the Kremlin.*
> *FSB windows are blowing out.*
> *The bitches piss themselves behind red walls.*
> *Riot is aborting the System!*
>
> *A Russian riot, the draw of protest.*
> *A Russian riot, Putin has pissed himself.*
> *A Russian riot means we exist.*
> *A Russian riot riot riot.*

Come out,
Live in the Red,
Show freedom,
Civic anger.

Fed up with the culture of male hysterics.
The cult of leadership is causing brain rot.
The Orthodox religion is a hard penis.
Patients are instructed to accept conformity.

The regime wants to censor your dreams.
Time to understand, time to confront.
A bunch of bitches from the sexist regime
Is begging the feminist army for forgiveness.

A Russian riot, the draw of protest.
A Russian riot, Putin has pissed himself.
A Russian riot means we exist.
A Russian riot riot riot.

Come out,
Live in the Red,
Show freedom,
Civic anger.

The Federal Guard—the presidential security service—
surrounded Lobnoye Mesto as soon as the eight women started
singing. But Pussy Riot's idea worked: the men in civilian
clothing dared not attempt to remove them, and just stood
around watching as the women threw down their backpacks,

which contained mostly warm clothing, sang, and even lit smoke bombs. It all took a while, and it was so cold it made some of the women wish the Federal Guard would move in on them just so they would not have to keep standing there with bare arms. Kat had worn her summer boots because they had a nonslip sole, and she was so cold that once the song was over, she started changing into her winter clothes right up there, on Ivan the Terrible's stone platform. Then they climbed down and the patient men in civilian clothing said, "Come with us."

They handed them over at the nearest police station. The cops leered at Pussy Riot's outfits and then put the women in a cage. Pussy Riot gave their fake names. The cops lazily debated who they were: prostitutes, protesters, or perhaps even performers. A while later the men in civvies returned carrying pictures; they had been photographing during the action, and they had now made prints. Pussy Riot asked to see. They looked good: a red, a purple, a white, a dark green, a lighter green, a brighter red, a blue, and a yellow dress, perfectly mismatched balaclavas, cross-matched tights, snow, smoke from the smoke bombs, with candylike St. Basil's Cathedral for their backdrop—they had never looked this good. There had never been so many of them either. They had waved a purple NO PASARAN flag with a fist in it. They had also had a portrait of Putin with Muammar Gaddafi, which Seraphima was supposed to douse with kerosene and set on fire, but she had bungled that part and failed to take out the portrait or to discover that kerosene is not particularly flammable—both the portrait and the liquid were in her backpack now. The portrait might have complicated the picture unduly. As it was,

Pussy Riot had just performed its clearest and most spectacular action, and this was what they saw in the photographs.

It all felt almost friendly, so when the cops pressed them, seven of the eight women gave their real names. They were released, but Seraphima, who had the kerosene, insisted on her fake identity and the police kept her back. They browbeat, threatened, and cajoled her for about six hours. They emptied out her backpack, took her cigarettes, and ritually broke each of them in half. If this was their idea of scare tactics, she found it pretty funny. Then they gave up and even made like they believed her fake-name story. They reprimanded her for driving her Porsche Cayenne while drunk—this was apparently the offense that had landed her alias in the police database—and let her go. Seraphima had been given a mild preview of future Pussy Riot interrogations.

———

PUSSY RIOT WAS FAMOUS. Moscow magazines were interviewing them and commissioning photo shoots of their rehearsals. The world seemed to say it wanted to know what they would do next. So did Pussy Riot.

The problem with Red Square is that nothing can top it—except, perhaps, the Kremlin itself. But even getting much closer to the Kremlin than they had been at Lobnoye Mesto—about two hundred yards from an entrance to the Kremlin grounds—was most likely impossible. The Duma was proving to be difficult: Kat, Nadya, and Petya were denied temporary passes for a planned reconnaissance mission; apparently, they were on a list. In the end, they used fake student IDs to

get in, but Terminator had gotten into trouble with her Duma
deputy and all of this promised more trouble for the action.
Plus, the Duma was no more than an approximation, a stand-in
for the Kremlin, at whose pleasure it served.

The protest movement continued to snowball, making the
Kremlin increasingly nervous. Putin had reshuffled his team,
evidently marshaling the troops—including the Russian Orthodox Church, a reliable ally of Russian dictators through
the centuries. On the eve of a large-scale opposition march
planned for February 4, priests around the country instructed
their parishioners to abstain from protesting. The patriarch
himself addressed throngs gathered for a liturgy at the Cathedral of Christ the Savior, that giant, gaudy structure where
the Virgin's Girdle had recently been displayed. "Orthodox
people know not how to attend demonstrations," said Patriarch Kirill. "They pray in the silence of monasteries, in their
monks' cells, in their homes, but their hearts are full of pain
for the turmoil among our people today, so clearly similar to
the desperate frenzy of the years immediately before the Revolution and the discord, disruption, and damage of the 1990s."
The patriarch, who, like many if not all highly placed clergy—
and like the once and future president himself—had served
in the KGB, was sending a two-part message. Putin, who became
president in 2000, had brought the country back from the
brink of disaster, and those who were rocking the boat now
would put the country back on a path to destruction. It followed that true believers should not only refrain from attending protest marches but should also attend a counterprotest
rally jointly organized by the Kremlin and the Church's youth

movements—and it went without saying that they should vote for Putin come March 4.

The following day—one of the coldest days of the year—more than fifty thousand people in Moscow came out to march against Putin. The protest movement was solidifying and becoming more clearly political; where earlier protests had called for fair elections, now people marched with explicit anti-Putin slogans. "Twelve more years?" asked one call-and-response chant. "No, thanks" was the answer. Another chant paraphrased a children's rhyme: "A storm is gathering once, a storm is gathering twice, a storm is gathering thrice—time for Putin to prepare for prison." Nadya marched with the rainbow flag contingent that day, and Petya tried, rather ineffectually, to help with organizing.

On February 8, Patriarch Kirill met with Putin. In the televised portion of their conversation, he described the flush aughts as "God's miracle, greatly aided by the country's leadership." The message was clear again: Putin was next to God, and this was not just Putin's election campaign—it was also the patriarch's and that of the Church itself. And this meant that Pussy Riot's next action should take place in the Cathedral of Christ the Savior, which was to the patriarch what the Kremlin was to Putin. It also represented the Putin era even better than the luxury boutiques did. This was where Putin and Medvedev came for holiday services, as seen on TV. It was a symbol of post-Soviet piousness, superficial and generously gilded. The cathedral was also home to some incongruous ventures, such as a luxury car wash and a banquet hall, the proceeds from which benefited the Cathedral of Christ the

Savior Foundation, which had not been known for its charitable contributions, or for anything at all. And at the same time, the cathedral had attracted a million to see the Girdle, a sign of Russia's ominous slide into the Dark Ages. Holding the next Pussy Riot action at the Cathedral of Christ the Savior was perfect and it was right.

AFTER LOBNOYE MESTO, Seraphima's astrologer told her to leave the country. She did not make much of an argument. She did not say, "Leave the country or else you will go to jail" or "Leave the country before things get bad," she just said, "Leave the country." Seraphima trusted her astrologer, but this was ridiculous. Seraphima was in the right place and she was doing the right thing. She had never felt this more than when Pussy Riot gave her the name Seraphima: she had a mystical certainty—she was not crazy, and she knew other people did not share it, but this knowledge just lived inside of her—that the Russian people had a special place and a special mission in the world, and she could feel that now was a time of transformation, and when she was given the very old-world Russian name Seraphima, she knew she had a special role to play in this transformation. Lobnoye Mesto, and her particular role at Lobnoye Mesto—even though the portrait had never gone up in flames—had felt like a part of her mission, perhaps only the beginning of it. But then again, she trusted her astrologer. So when at the first post–Lobnoye Mesto rehearsal, as Pussy Riot called it, the subject of their next location came up, Seraphima said, "Let's do it on an airplane. And leave the country at the same time."

Nadya and Kat said, "Let's do it in the Cathedral of Christ the Savior."

Terminator said, "Let's do it at the Duma."

Seraphima said, "We can't do it in the cathedral. They'll send us to jail." She mentioned the arts curators who had been convicted of inciting religious enmity for organizing visual arts shows that were critical of the Church.

Still, none of the curators had actually gone to jail: their sentences were suspended. And that was before! Now was a time of change. Nadya and Kat dismissed the worry. "This is different," said Kat. "And anyway, the authorities looked so bad in those cases, they know not to do that again." Between them, they called this the "first-detention effect": most women, after they were hauled into a police station for the first time, even if they were treated reasonably well and their alias was uncontested, would from that point on find a way to stay out of public actions. They would say things like "I'll help with the rehearsals." Seraphima was doing this now. She said, "I just can't go to jail. I mean, no one, no human being, can go to a Russian jail."

It was decided to hold the next action at the Cathedral of Christ the Savior.

The following day, Seraphima bought a plane ticket to India and left the country. It felt sad: Pussy Riot had felt like home, and Seraphima had felt a sort of love for each of the girls. Nadya, whom she had known the longest, was crazy. Crazy was not bad, and in Nadya's case it was definitely a light-filled kind of crazy, crazy as a force for good. Nadya was a born leader, but this also meant she had an inborn sense of self-importance, which made Serpahima weary. She took herself as seriously as Seraphima had been able to take only religion.

Seraphima had been a devout Orthodox for a couple of years a sort of long time ago, and she thought this was why now she had such a clear vision of how this action would end: it would end with jail. Sometimes Seraphima suspected that Nadya and Kat actually wanted to go to jail. At least they wanted to be the kind of people who had gone to jail. That said, Seraphima liked Kat. Maybe Kat just lacked the imagination to see what it would be like; she could probably visualize the solutions to mathematical equations a lot better than she could conjure up the reactions of people who would be deeply hurt by her actions and who had the power to do something about it.

And then there was Maria. She was new and no one knew much about her. She and Seraphima usually walked to the bus stop together, and Seraphima found herself thinking, *How did a girl like this end up with the likes of us?* There was something preternaturally pure about Maria. She probably had no idea what she was getting herself into either.

Nadya and Kat and, occasionally, some of the others, including Petya, began preparing for the action. They cased the cathedral. They discovered that security saw men and women through different optics: if a woman went in carrying a guitar case, she was stopped; a man was just a hippie or a weirdo with a guitar going to the cathedral. They set some ground rules. One, they would not disrupt the service. Showing such disrespect for parishioners would detract from Pussy Riot's message and expose them to unnecessary risk. They could be charged like those curators had been, and Pussy Riot did not want to risk arrest; in fact, they had grown pretty sick of detention. Sure, it would be spectacular to disrupt a service with a Pussy Riot action, but people just would not understand. But if Pussy Riot desecrated the space during hours when it was used solely for the activities of its corrupt foundation (and the car wash)—that is, when it was already being desecrated—the message would be clear.

Admittedly, this required compromise. The lights at the cathedral shone brightly—brightly enough to film—only during services; the rest of the time the place was dim. But they were adamant about not taking excessive risk, so they asked a couple of videographers and photographers to check the place out ahead of time and be sure to bring light-appropriate equipment. They chose the videographers carefully. This action had to be kept quiet.

There was a spot in the cathedral that looked like it had been created especially for Pussy Riot. They had no idea what it was called or what its purpose was, but it looked incongruously like a stage in the middle of the church. It was in front of and sort of beneath the altar—one could see it as forming part of its pedestal—but it did not seem to be protected like the altar. The altar had full-height gates that were locked in between services, and Pussy Riot noticed that no one went in casually. The platform had a low ornate fence around it, easily stepped over, and it seemed to inspire no particular piety; the cleaning lady marched up there with her equipment every day. Plus, it had a microphone on a stand, hooked up to easily visible amplifiers. Pussy Riot would most likely be unable to use this equipment, but the whole thing looked like somebody's television-inspired idea of a parliamentary pulpit imposed on somebody's television-inspired idea of a big official church. Pussy Riot laughed as they discussed this. Cathedral security gestured to them to stop laughing.

The fact was, there was a lot of security, burly guys, most of them without uniform but acting as they would in parliament, trailing anyone who seemed strange; this was, after all, the official church. Taking this in, Kat suggested the action would not work out: security would step in so soon, they would not even have time to set up.

The solution, once they hit on it, seemed simple enough: they would record the song ahead of time, then they would go to another, less central church and video-record there, and only then would they attempt an action at the Cathedral of Christ the Savior. Whatever they got at the cathedral—even if it was only a minute of footage—would be combined with previously recorded material to create a clip of an action at the Cathedral of Christ the Savior, even if the action itself existed mostly in their imaginations.

They recalled a cathedral near the contemporary arts center they frequented. It was appropriately grand and at the same time appropriately quiet, almost obscure. In fact, the Cathedral of the Apparition was the senior Orthodox church in Moscow, and the patriarch led important services there on occasion, but Pussy Riot did not know this. They knew that it contained enough gilt and opulence that in a fast-paced clip, if they interspersed the footage, it would pass for the Cathedral of Christ the Savior, just shot from a different angle.

Six Pussy Riot members took a mic with a stand, a floodlight—they had this idea of creating an illuminated-stage effect—and a couple of videographers and went to the Cathedral of the Apparition. They set up, only now discovering that the battery for the floodlight was backbreakingly heavy. They performed the moves they had choreographed and rehearsed for this song: frenetic dancing with kicking and boxing moves for the fast parts, kneeling and frantic bowing for the liturgical-chant parts. A woman appeared out of nowhere and grabbed the floodlight; she seemed to think that taking it away would get Pussy Riot to stop. They wrestled for the light. Pussy Riot won and left.

It did not feel great; there was none of the exhilaration they had felt during their previous filming sessions. They told each other this had been a technical day and they had accomplished what they needed.

MORZH COULD NOT SLEEP. This felt like too much. "I had had conflicting feelings about this from the beginning," she told me a year later, meaning Pussy Riot in general. "This was Nadya's project. I wasn't generating any ideas, I was just a participant—but the consequences could be serious." The group required total commitment: to be Pussy Riot you really had to live Pussy Riot. Otherwise, you felt like an extra in Nadya's show.

Plus, she did not really get this action. It seemed too simple somehow, more of a prank than art—and at the same time like they were protesting against the Church itself. In their early brainstorming sessions, they had discussed trying to fly the rainbow flag during the action—this had seemed fittingly spectacular and layered to Morzh—but Nadya had nixed the idea. So what was it about, then? Nadya had not made a very good case for needing to illuminate the obvious: the relationship between the Church and Putin. At eight in the morning, having slept not a wink, Morzh texted Nadya: "I can't do it." Nadya texted back: "Ok."

THE REMAINING FIVE of them gathered at a café not far from the cathedral, drank coffee, and talked, with long uncomfortable pauses. Kat did what she always did, in summer or in winter: she ordered a cup of café glacé and ate the ice cream, leaving the cold, milky coffee. For no reason they could pinpoint, they talked about calling off the action. But since they could not have explained such a decision even to themselves, as it got closer to eleven o'clock, they settled the bill and walked over to the Cathedral of Christ the Savior.

A high-pitched sound greeted them as they entered: *eeeeeeeeeee*. They all turned toward the source of the sound, which was just behind Nadya. "Whatever," said Nadya, and nonchalantly took off her backpack, opened it, and turned off the amplifier that had turned itself on. She put the bag back on, and all of Pussy Riot turned their heads to survey the cathedral. Something was wrong.

In the middle of the vast space, a small crowd lingered; about twenty people, most of them with cameras. Videographers. But Pussy Riot had told only three or four trusted documenters about the action and had given them strict instructions to keep their cameras concealed until the performance began. These were not videographers; they were journalists. There had been a leak.

The good news was, the guitar was inside. Because they had discovered that a woman could not enter the cathedral carrying a guitar case, Pussy Riot had asked a male friend to carry it in and leave it lying on a bench. It was waiting for them now. Picking it up, Kat discovered that whoever had packed it had gone to great lengths to disguise the fact that the package contained a guitar; it would take a while to unwrap it. Still, once Kat picked it up, the countdown began. They were now five women with a guitar, and they did not have much time to make their move.

Pussy Riot approached the elevated platform. Two men suddenly emerged from behind the altar and started rolling up the rugs on the platform. A security guard looked on. Something was definitely wrong. "Should we call it off?" one of the group whispered. "What are we doing?" whispered another a few moments later.

And then the cathedral was empty. The men with the rugs disappeared. The security guard walked off. The journalists did not seem as numerous as they had before. It was dim and very very quiet. Pussy Riot moved in.

Nadya commanded Kat to go first because she had to unpack the guitar. She did as she was instructed, and she put it on, and then she felt someone grabbing her. He pulled off her red balaclava, and she looked up: it was the security guard from a few minutes earlier. He carried her out of the cathedral and planted her just outside the door. As they exited, Kat heard the music begin:

Virgin Mary, Mother of God, chase Putin out,
Chase Putin out, chase Putin out.

Black robe, golden epaulets
All the parishioners are crawling to bow
The phantom of liberty is up in heaven
Gay pride sent to Siberia in a chain gang

Head of the KGB, their chief saint,
Leads protesters to jail under guard
So as not to offend the deity,
Women must give birth and love

Shit, shit, holy shit!
Shit, shit, holy shit!

Virgin Mary, Mother of God, become a feminist
Become a feminist, become a feminist
The Church sings the praises of rotten dictators
Black limousines form the procession of the Cross
A missionary is coming to your school
Go to class and bring your money!

Patriarch Gundyayev* believes in Putin
Bitch, better believe in God instead
The Virgin's Girdle can't replace the demos
The Virgin herself is with us in protest!

Virgin Mary, Mother of God, chase Putin out,
Chase Putin out, chase Putin out.

The "holy shit" line had been suggested by Andrei when his daughter told him they would be doing an action at the Cathedral of Christ the Savior. He would be very proud of this for years to come.

---

*Patriarch Kirill's worldly last name

SEVEN

Unmasked

THIS ONE REQUIRED a longer wind-down period. Kat had lingered just outside the entrance to the cathedral, and when she heard the guards radioing for police, she thought she should leave. She saw one of the other women walking out, and they fell into step, followed by the others. They walked across the plaza in front of the cathedral, down a couple of steps to the sidewalk, then picked up the pace, ran across the street and on and down into the Metro. At the next stop, they met up with two of the videographers, who handed over their memory cards. The videographers trailed along with the group for another stop or two and then everyone got off and went to a café. They grumbled about how poorly the action had gone. Nadya was cursing. A couple of photographers showed up, making the women tense. If things had gone right, the photographers would have had no way of finding them right now.

Then someone saw a Tweet: "Pussy Riot had an action

today, titled 'Holy Shit.'" This had never happened: they had never been exposed before they were ready, never lost control over their timing and orchestration. It was particularly upsetting because it was already clear that they did not have enough quality footage to put together a clip. To try to regain control, they called Mitya Aleshkovsky, an activist photographer who had said he had decent still shots despite the bad light, and asked him to publish the photographs with the correct title of the piece: *Mother of God, Get Rid of Putin*. And since it was clear that they needed to do further damage control, Nadya, Kat, and Maria went to an apartment—a semi-abandoned flat they had come to consider their headquarters—to see what they could salvage of the video footage. And also, perhaps, because they felt the need to be with each other. Something felt off among them, and each of them sensed it, the way each partner in a romantic relationship senses when it has started to crack, even though neither can say what went wrong and when. Whatever they had had during the Red Square action, that sense of lightness and righteousness, had left them; a sour sort of anxiety had set in. And just like lovers sensing those cracks often do, in their anxiety they clung together.

Looking at the video footage did not make them feel any better. A couple of the videographers had violated a cardinal Pussy Riot rule: they kept filming even after Kat's balaclava was off—which should have been their signal to turn their cameras off or away from her. Aside from the fact that Kat could be identified if an unedited copy of the video got out of Pussy Riot's hands, this also meant that the operators had not been filming the other four women while their cameras were trained on the unmasked Kat—missing a chunk of the too-brief performance. Nadya grew progressively angrier and kept cursing. Maria shifted into her we-can-do-it mode and forced them to finish editing the video. They needed nearly two minutes of video to fit the entire song, and even with the footage filmed at the Cathedral of the Apparition, they had to use the same sequences several times over and resort to including bits where the guards were stopping them or church employees were waving their hands at the camera. They all agreed it was the worst video they had ever published.

Publish it they did, though, with some explanatory notes. "Last Sunday Seraphima returned from church and demanded that all the Pussy Riot soloists urgently learn Byzantian Znamenny chant," they wrote, referring to a part of the Russian Orthodox liturgic tradition. "'During Morning Prayer today, I realized what we need to ask of the Mother of God and how to do it so that something might finally change in our spiritually bereft land,' Seraphima told us . . ." A detailed explication of the lyrics followed. "'Since peaceful demonstrations give no immediate result despite being hundreds of thousands strong, we will address Mother of God herself before Easter and ask her to get rid of Putin as soon as possible,' Seraphima, the most religious of the punk feminists, told the rest of the team as we headed toward the Cathedral on the cold February morning."

The video was up just after 7 p.m. They waited for the storm. *Moskovsky Komsomolets*, a popular tabloid, called first. Pussy Riot answered a couple of questions and then the journalist said, "You did good, girls! Everyone is going to be on your case now, but we support you." And for a little while, it felt better. Some more journalists called. Pussy Riot walked

down to the corner to don their balaclavas and give a couple
of on-camera interviews without giving up the exact location of their headquarters. Then they occupied themselves
with getting their equipment—an amplifier, a guitar, and a
microphone—out of captivity; security guards had taken them
when they broke up the show and now they were apparently
with the police. Pussy Riot hatched an insane plan. They
forged a couple of loan contracts and dispatched a male friend
to the police station to tell his tale: he had loaned the equipment to a virtual stranger, someone who had approached him
on the Metro.

Absurdly, it worked. The police fingerprinted the man and
then gave him the equipment. He brought it back to headquarters, and they celebrated. "We were euphoric," Kat told
me. "Despite the fact that the clip didn't work out, this felt like
a victory. And we even decided to set up some interviews for
the next day."

THE FOLLOWING DAY, they set up meetings at the Zverev Center of Contemporary Art, an off-the-beaten-path shared work
and exhibit space. The journalists seemed interested in the
group in general, asking only a couple of questions each about
the latest action. It was just the three of them—Maria, Nadya,
and Kat. Kat had brought food. Maria had brought a camp
stove, which amused the journalists. They talked to the journalists and to one another and drank tea in their balaclavas.
It felt normal, as long as one thinks that using a camp stove
indoors is normal. In the afternoon, they went home.

Maria picked up Philip from Nikita and took him to a playground in the neighborhood. It was late February, and it still got dark early, so they didn't stay long. They had barely stepped out of the tiny creaky elevator on their floor when they saw nine men crowded in the hallway, eight of them wearing civilian clothes and the ninth, her neighborhood cop, looking terrified.

"Please proceed with us. We need to talk with you," said one of the suits.

"I am not proceeding anywhere," Maria responded in her high-pitched voice. "I have my son with me. You'll have to serve me with a summons." And, back held straight, she marched into her apartment.

Nikita had gone to work. He had a job he loved now, working with predators at the Durov Center, an animal circus. He was not supposed to use his phone while he was feeding the tigers—if he did not want to be eaten himself, that is—but he did look at it when Maria's message came in, and then he wished he had not. The message said she needed to go into hiding "possibly for as long as a month" and he would have to take care of Philip.

NADYA, KAT, MARIA, PETYA, and one of the other participants in the cathedral action gathered late that night. Petya said he knew a lawyer. Nikolai Polozov had given him his card in late December, when the authorities had attempted to have Petya forcibly drafted. Polozov had shown up at the draft office where Petya had been delivered but was not actually allowed to enter and help; Petya had fought off conscription on his own. Now Polozov entered. He was a paunchy, balding man with glasses and a beard—he looked like a lawyer, in other words, and he talked like one as well. He said they should lie low. He said no charges had apparently been filed. He said that if charges were filed, he would help. Meanwhile, they left town.

Sort of. They left Moscow city limits. They knew other people generally left the country if they were hiding from police—Kiev was a favored destination because you did not need a visa, you could get there by train, and people spoke Russian. But that was for serious people in real trouble, not for intellectual pranksters who presented themselves as silly young girls. For them, the Moscow suburbs—atavistically rural, eerily quiet, apparently cut off from civilization—would be enough. In other words, they came up with an escape plan that served the purpose of displacing Pussy Riot but didn't necessarily get them out of sight of police and security services.

Which conducted a search of Nadya's dorm room that night. She had not lived there since before Gera was born, and the room had gradually turned into a storage unit for everything from Voina props and rally banners to compact discs and underwear. In the roughly seven hours that the search team spent there, they managed to turn the varied contents of the room into an undifferentiated pile in the middle of the floor.

Petya would learn this seven months later, when he would finally be given access to the room, which had been sealed as evidence until then. For now, the five of them found themselves in the white expanse of Moscow suburbs. Petya was high on their predicament and overproducing ideas; he had

Unmasked | 125

talked to someone who said he could arrange safe haven for
Pussy Riot members in the Perm region in the Urals. The
women brushed him off and grew increasingly annoyed. They
took long walks. They took turns sliding down a snowy hill.
They semi-adopted a stray dog. If they were trying to make
themselves feel like carefree kids, they failed; they felt ridiculous. There was no evidence that anyone was actually looking for them. All they had done was fail to stage a performance
in the Cathedral of Christ the Savior. Why were they fooling
themselves into thinking they needed to waste their time way
out here?

Especially when stuff was going on in Moscow. The presidential election was less than two weeks away. On Sunday,
February 26, protesters planned to come out onto the Garden
Ring—the avenue that circles central Moscow—and form an
unbroken "white ring" to symbolize their demand for fair
elections. Members of Pussy Riot should be among them, not
in this bland and silent snow-whiteness.

―――――――

IT WAS IN THE EARLY MORNING HOURS OF FEBRUARY 26, the day
known in the Orthodox tradition as Forgiveness Sunday, that
charges were filed in the case of unnamed women who had
attempted to stage a performance in the Cathedral of Christ
the Savior, thereby assaulting the feelings of Orthodox believers.

Maria texted Nikita from an unfamiliar number, giving
him Polozov's number and instructing him to get information
by calling it. Nikita called and asked what was going on.

"Who are you?" asked Polozov.

"I'm freaking Nikita," said Nikita.

"How do I know you are not the security services?" asked Polozov, reasonably enough.

Nikita texted Maria. Maria informed Polozov. Polozov called Nikita back and told him about the charges.

"What should we do?" asked Nikita. He meant himself and Philip, and he meant the question literally.

"Pray," said Polozov.

THEY MOVED TO ANOTHER PLACE in the suburbs. They realized they had to, because one of them had forgotten to use TOR, an anonymity protocol, when logging on to a Russian social network. Or perhaps they just needed to feel like they were doing something in response to the news of the charges. Then the other participant who had come with them left, so it was just Nadya, Maria, and Kat. Petya was drifting in and out.

After a couple of days, they decided to reenter the city. It was a strange city now, one where they could not go home. They oscillated between feeling scared, paranoid, energized, and just plain silly. Who could still be looking for them a week after the action at the cathedral? And if they were still looking, how long would they keep at it? Another week? A month? Longer? Polozov had said they should lie low until the presidential election. That was scheduled for March 4, ten days after they went into hiding.

Journalists kept e-mailing Pussy Riot and asking for interviews. The three of them would go to cafés in the center of Moscow with their laptops, answer e-mails, and set up a secure Skype connection. Then they would go into the bathroom, a laptop and three balaclavas in hand, crowd around the toilet, put on their balaclavas, and answer questions.

"What is your ultimate goal?"

"We have several of them. For example, we demand freedom for political prisoners. We heard some officials called for our imprisonment after the performance in the Cathedral of Christ the Savior. But we only wanted to stress there is far too much communication between the Church and the government. Our patriarch is not ashamed to wear a forty-thousand-dollar watch, and this is intolerable when so many families in Russia are on the edge of poverty."

"What do you think needs to be changed immediately in Russia?"

"We must reform the judicial system first. Democracy is impossible without an independent judiciary. Education reform and cultural reform are also needed. Putin pays attention to anything but culture—museums, libraries, cultural centers are in awful condition."

They sounded less like punks than like thousands of other members of the protest movement. It felt like the right line to take, with the election less than a week away and the anticipation of change stubbornly hanging in the air.

One time a waitress ran after them when they left a café. In her hands she had a balaclava they had left in the bathroom.

Evenings were the most difficult time. They were one another's household for now, and they needed to negotiate when and where this household changed locations. Petya's frequent appearances annoyed Kat, who felt he was careless about security; he kept his iPhone turned on all the time, while the women were religious about never using their old phones and switching cheap, effectively disposable ones every couple of days. But separating from one another felt unsafe as well, even if this fear itself felt absurd—and was illogical on the face of it. One evening Maria went to a reading given by one of her institute instructors, a neoromantic poet. Her friends already knew she was not living at home or using her phone. They went out for coffee after the reading, and she told them not to worry about her. They did not; they knew she could handle all sorts of frightening situations, like hitchhiking alone, for example.

The three of them went to stay at N's, or Morzh's, apartment. They discussed the issue of whether it was smart to stay with a Pussy Riot participant and decided that, since she had not been at the cathedral, it was all right. Perhaps they were just tired of strangers and strange homes: at N's place they could pretend they were just staying over at a friend's. It was a place out of time and space. On the eighth floor of a standard edge-of-Moscow concrete block, it had been remade with textured floors in zebra patterns, divided into sectors by pipes. A fur-lined corner in one room had an irregularly shaped built-in bed. N told Nadya she and Petya could take the bed and Kat and Maria could sleep on the floor in the same room, while N and her boyfriend slept in the smaller room, with the sound studio and all the vintage bicycles.

Petya was not there yet, and N put on a movie by Alexander Sokurov, a difficult Russian director; she was still working to reform Maria's taste in film. Halfway through the movie, Petya arrived with the news that the editor of a radio station that had aired an interview with Pussy Riot had been visited by investigators who had tried to cajole and coerce him into disclosing what he knew of the group's location. This was frightening. Really, it was the first truly scary sign since all those plainclothesmen had greeted Maria eight days before. (They did not yet know that Nadya's dorm room had been searched, or that the police had come to Kat's house as well— Kat had tried calling home once but no one had answered the phone.) They wondered if they should bolt. But then Petya said he had brought a napoleon cake, and they all crowded around the Formica table in the tiny kitchen, looking out over the black expanse of nighttime winter sky, pierced by tiny rectangles of illuminated windows, and they felt better.

———————

THEY LEFT N'S HOUSE the next day. Petya had given them the keys to a friend's apartment not far from the center of town. Of all the strange places they had stayed in the last week, this one was the strangest. It was in a pompous Stalin-era seven-story building with bay windows that looked across a busy avenue at the Moscow Hippodrome, a den of gambling, corruption, and horsiness that had miraculously survived there for nearly two centuries, through a succession of czars and other tyrants. With a quadriga atop the main building and a horse-topped weathervane on a tower, it looked like a slightly worn fairy-tale castle. The interior of the apartment, whose owner apparently lived abroad, was like nothing Nadya, Maria, or Kat had ever seen. It had an apparently endless number of rooms, two bathrooms, and a Jacuzzi. They spent the night there feeling lost in all the space.

The following day Petya arrived. His presence made Kat nervous again; his phone was on, and he was talking some kind of nonsense about celebrating Gera's fourth birthday the following day and maybe bringing her here or taking Nadya to her, and it was obvious to Kat that he was going to get them caught. This was all the more upsetting because, if Polozov could be believed, this might be the last day Pussy Riot had to be hiding: the election was tomorrow. They fought, and then they tried to find solace in their laptops. But there was a problem with one of the external hard drives, and to everyone's relief, Petya and Nadya resolved to go out to an electronics marketplace to try to get the thing fixed.

They stepped out. Begovaya ("Racing") Street, usually one of the most congested in Moscow, was almost empty on a Saturday afternoon. They looked left: the television tower, miles away, was clearly visible, but otherwise, there was not a soul or a suspicious vehicle in sight. They looked right: all clear as well. They headed right, in the direction of Moscow City, five high-rise towers in various stages of construction with a stairway-shaped, copper-colored one rising above the rest.

They passed a bank with a mortgage center, an Apple-authorized computer-repair shop, an old-fashioned Soviet-style art gallery with a mixture of sculptures and gaudy decorative objects such as plates, vanity tables, table lamps, and dolls in the display window; cheap 1980s-style light fixtures visible behind the mess of objects made the place look comically confused. They passed a cell-phone store on the right and, on the left, a flower shop and a sex shop with an illuminated, red-heart-shaped "24" sign. A newly built office tower stood at the end of the block, where the street gave way to a highway. They entered a narrow passageway that separated the tower from the road. The highway rose, forming a barrier on the left, steel bars cordoned off the tower on the right, and an arched, semitransparent roof made the passageway almost fully enclosed. The path was semicircular, so Petya and Nadya could not see more than fifteen feet ahead or behind them; they seemed to be completely alone.

They heard the stampede before they saw anyone. It sounded like a herd of horses had escaped from the hippodrome. It turned out to be a herd of men in suits and dress coats. Petya had enough time to think the scene would look good in a spy movie before about half a dozen of the men grabbed him and carried him forward. While four of them lifted him off the ground, two others forced his head down toward his chest so he could not see what was happening to Nadya, though he guessed that what was happening to her was the same thing that was happening to him.

The two groups of men ran for about a hundred yards, holding Petya and Nadya aloft, into an underpass that led to the Metro. Petya and Nadya were thrown against a marble wall and held pressed to it for a couple of minutes before being carried again—this time into a glass enclosure in the Metro lobby. It said POLICE in yellow-on-blue block letters on this structure, and there were a couple of transit cops inside. The men in suits shoved their IDs under the cops' noses, and the cops vanished.

There was a gray laminate desk in a corner, with two video screens sitting on top of it; three mismatched office armchairs; and an unusually deep but short bench that was bolted to the floor. Petya and Nadya were placed on the bench and the men in suits stuffed themselves into the space, which was large enough to accommodate perhaps six people comfortably.

They sat in silence for about twenty minutes. A man appeared, took a look at the detainees, and pronounced his verdict: "Verzilov and Tolokonnikova." He left. The rest of them stayed another two or three hours. Outside the glass, a trickle of people was coming in and out of the Metro. Past the turnstiles, a decorative tableau was visible: two copper horses with jockeys, a group of spectators, and an inappropriately heroic-looking race caller with a flag that looked more like a shovel in his hand.

This new period in Petya's, and Nadya's lives—as well as the lives of Maria and Kat and their families—would be characterized by endless, helpless, and often useless waiting. They waited inside a police car for about four hours. More men in suits appeared once in a while, looked at Petya and Nadya, and nodded. It was midnight by the time they were taken to a police precinct in central Moscow, where they were led to a block of offices in the basement. The place was buzzing as though it were a weekday afternoon and not the wee hours of Sunday morning. Polozov arrived, bringing Violetta Volkova with him. More and more police detectives kept showing up. Petya and Nadya were taken into separate rooms, and then into different separate rooms, passing each other in the hallway a couple of times. They were asked the same asinine questions by a succession of men.

"Who is the group's director?"

"Who is the group's producer?"

"Who is its costume designer?"

They kept saying, "I don't know."

Petya was asked, "What kind of music does your wife like?" and "Have you heard her sing lately?" Petya pleaded Article 51

of the Russian constitution, which guarantees the right to refuse to testify against oneself or one's immediate relatives. On
one of the desks in one of the offices, he spotted a thick pile of
documents showing that he had Canadian citizenship.

Around six in the morning, the police led both Petya and
Nadya out into the hallway. Kat and Maria were there. One of
the suits said Nadya and Maria were under arrest and Petya
and Kat were free to go "for now."

———————

KAT AND MARIA HAD LEFT the apartment for no particular
reason. They always just did; they would have taken the Metro
a couple of stops into the center of town and then one of them
would have suggested a café and the other would have agreed.
When they were pushed up against the steel-bar fence in the
same passageway where Petya and Nadya had been grabbed
a couple of hours earlier, the men had asked Kat who she was.
It appeared they had a visual ID on Maria and not on Kat. Co-
incidentally, Maria had her internal passport in her bag and
Kat did not. So Kat said she was Irina Loktina, a name she
had used during her previous detentions, and decided to pretend she did not know Maria. She stuck to her story at the police precinct, even when an investigator discovered a folder on
her laptop called "Pussy Riot Songs." She stuck to her story
when one of the investigators threatened to rape her, and
later, when he started twisting her arms. He stopped quickly,
as if realizing the maneuver was absurd, and resumed threatening her with rape. Then he fell asleep, and she and Maria
sat together in the basement hallway of the police precinct,
listening to him snore.

In the end, the police kept the laptop and told Kat she was free to go—for now. Polozov drove her to the building across from the hippodrome.

"You have a choice," said Polozov as he let her out of the car into the still-dark morning. "You can hide or not hide."

"I'm not going to hide," said Kat. "It doesn't make sense anymore."

"All right," said Polozov. "Although if I were you, I'd hide."

The polls were opening all around Moscow. Putin would be reelected president. Kat went upstairs to the most opulent apartment she had ever seen, retrieved the towel and change of clothes she had left there, stuffed them into her backpack, and went home. It was not that it no longer made sense to hide; if anything, now was exactly the time to stay away from the Samutsevich residence. It was just that she had no one to hide with. It would be the loneliest two weeks of her life.

EIGHT

Detention

Undated (early March)

Olya,
I have not yet seen your letter, though I know there is one.
My lawyer will come tomorrow and give it to me, and I will
hand over this response, which I am writing half blind.

Maria meant that she was writing the response without
having seen her friend's original letter.

I spent the last three days in quarantine, a very cold cell
where everyone lands upon first coming to pretrial
detention. It is a museum of conceptual art. The windows
are caulked up with bread crumbs; there are many many
many bread crumbs and it's not clear what holds them
there. There are 12 beds and they are welded to the floor.

*There are six bedside tables and they are welded to the
floor. It is cold all the time. We slept in our overcoats and
fur coats and the cold still woke us up.*

Do you remember the museum in Vilnius?

They had gone to the Genocide Museum in Vilnius together. The building had housed a succession of exterminating
governments' courts and police headquarters—the Russians,
the Germans, the Soviets, the Nazis, and the Soviets again,
with a KGB prison in the basement. The prison's nineteen
intact cells form part of the permanent exhibit; among them
is a cell where the floor is a pool of freezing water and the
prisoners had to balance on a tiny round platform in the middle until they nodded off and fell into the water.

*This place is like that museum, only more frightening. But
this fear mixes with incredible beauty—if only you can keep
looking at all times, if you can keep letting it all in—you
will feel a force capable of knocking out all the glass
windows, twisting the rusty grates, turning to dust the
concrete flooring of the inner courtyard where we are taken
for an hour a day and where the snow shines for a few
seconds after it falls through the squares of the ceiling
grate and then mixes with the gray-brown mass underfoot,
spotted with cigarette butts.*

*I am reading a book by Kuprin. It was the only thing
here. You cannot have your own books in pretrial detention,
and the library is a myth: to get anything out of it, you have
to go through utter hell. That is exactly what I am planning
to do in the next few days, and I hope to succeed.*

Forgive me for such an apolitical letter. There was a lot
that was good. Really. Really, really. I guess someone else
is fated to get a letter full of joy and calls to action. I miss
you. I miss you a lot. A lot.

Inmates had the right to correspond by e-mail—as long as
family or friends initiated the correspondence and paid for
their own letters and those they got in return; the rate was
fifty rubles, or just under two dollars a page. E-mail was read
by prison censors. The other way to correspond was to pass
paper letters through the defense attorney; this was officially
forbidden but tacitly tolerated, for the most part. Maria used
this uncensored route to correspond intensively with Olya Vinogradova, her institute friend.

March 28, 2012

Dear Olya,
First of all, please forgive me for writing about food
so much in my previous letters. It's just that I was
embarrassed that the girls, my cellmates, were always
treating me and I had nothing to offer them. Yesterday
volunteers sent so much food that all of us in this cell are
set for at least two weeks. Thank you so much!

As soon as word of Nadya's and Maria's arrests got out, a
spontaneous ragtag support group formed; it would stay together for much of the next couple of years, with friends and
strangers collecting money, food, and paperwork to help the
inmates. Once friends published the lists of foods the inmates

needed, there was a rush on the pretrial detention facility's online store, with people ordering food to be delivered to Maria's and Nadya's cells. It was particularly important in Maria's case since she was a vegetarian and could not eat most of what was delivered to the cell from the kitchen.

> *I really do feel all right here, and I think that if I have to spend half a year or a year behind bars, it will only make me stronger. There was a lot of misunderstanding at first, but now people support me even if they do think I am a little cuckoo. Among other things, the girls in the cell have been teaching me not to be naive and not to believe all the incarceration stories I hear. But I still believe everyone. I have always thought that all people are good and we need to separate their deeds (which are often not good) from the people themselves. To put it simply, everyone has a right to make mistakes. I know everything is not quite so simple and crude, but here, as I reiterate some basic things a hundred times over, I actually learn something.*

"Half a year or a year" sounded unimaginable to Olya. Maria's first arrest order was for two weeks, and this seemed like an impossibly long time. Then there was a hearing and the term of arrest was extended by a month, and this was shocking. In April, a judge ordered Pussy Riot held for another four months, and Olya started getting used to the idea that time behind bars could indeed be measured in months. By this time, the prosecution was talking about years.

Spring came yesterday. Pigeons are cooing by our window. The sky is slightly overcast right now, but when the sun is out, its rays paint a grate on the floor, lighting up bright oranges against the squares of worn floorboards. We have so many oranges now! A huge pail full plus a bucket! We also have a lot of pears. And a box of apples and kiwi and a pile of cheese. The metal shelves on the wall are buckling beneath the weight of all the cakes.

Continued on March 29, 2012:

Today is Naked Thursday. Inmates must go out into the hallway wrapped only in sheets or bathrobes and line up so that the doctor can examine each of them in turn, looking for bodily injuries. Cell #210 is different because I live here, so everything that the staff does with us must be recorded on video; the camera is either affixed to the breast pocket of one of the staff or held by hand, but it is always trained on me. For this reason we do not go out into the hallway naked; instead the doctor comes in and makes a notation on a piece of paper, indicating that no injuries were found on any of the bodies.

These cameras were a spontaneous and forced invention; they appeared after I had my first visit from the Community Monitoring Commission and complained that I had been treated rudely by the staff. The video recordings are meant to "monitor personnel behavior," but the camera is always looking in my direction, as though it were not the personnel at all but I who had to be "monitored." Ugh. I'll try to make a sketch.

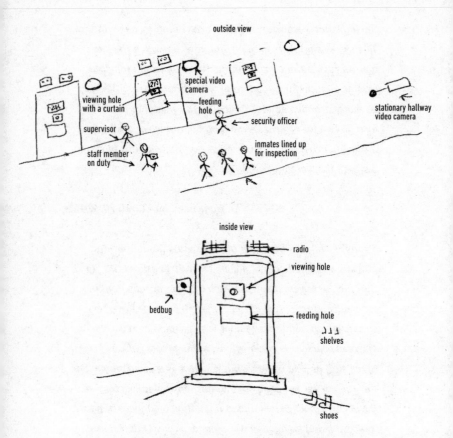

outside view

viewing hole with a curtain

special video camera

feeding hole

security officer

supervisor

staff member on duty

inmates lined up for inspection

stationary hallway video camera

inside view

radio

viewing hole

bedbug

feeding hole

shelves

shoes

Inmates and staff communicate mostly by means of the feeding hole. Food is delivered three times a day; correspondence is delivered once a day; a scissor knife for cutting bread and vegetables or fruit is also passed through the feeding hole. If you have a question, you have to "squash the bedbug," which means pressing a well-worn black button that turns on a light that the staff member on duty may see if she happens to be walking through the hallway, in which case she will open the feeding hole and ask, "What you want?" The door is thick and sturdy, made of metal and painted an odd shade of beige. The viewing hole has a curtain on the outside so inmates can't see what goes on in the hallway while staff members must monitor what goes on inside cells by regularly peeking in.

Olya, I think you know this, but just in case: you cannot put these descriptions up on the Internet or else very bad things will happen to me. Such are the rules of the institution that they can open the feeding hole at any moment to tell me I have 15 minutes to collect my things—and that goes for any of us here. They can transfer me from cell to cell once a week, forcing me to try to adjust to new people every time. A poorly made-up bed gets you solitary. Keeping letters gets you solitary. And so on. So I was thinking maybe someone else could make drawings according to my descriptions and eventually there would be enough for a show (if there is a need for such a thing). The rules here ban not just paints but pens other than blue (supposedly we could use them to make tattoos—as though we couldn't make a tattoo with a blue pen). When you write back, tell me whether you want detailed descriptions of everything (but only when you use this mail route—do not say anything about this by e-mail!).

I was just having lunch and thinking that if I wrote so much about food, I should write about what I do with it now that I have it . . . I make soup. So far I've made soup all of one time. This is forbidden, of course, and punishable by solitary, but that's a small detail. In the common cells, everyone makes soup; it's more difficult here in the specs [special cells] because the cell is smaller and it's easier to see what we are up to. I'll try to make a sketch.

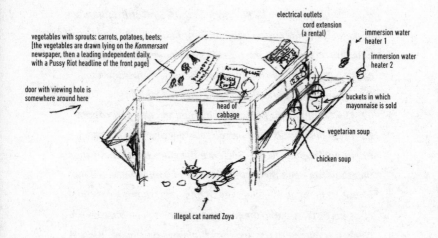

vegetables with sprouts: carrots, potatoes, beets; [the vegetables are drawn lying on the *Kommersant* newspaper, then a leading independent daily, with a Pussy Riot headline of the front page]

electrical outlets
cord extension (a rental)

immersion water heater 1

immersion water heater 2

door with viewing hole is somewhere around here

head of cabbage

buckets in which mayonnaise is sold

vegetarian soup

chicken soup

illegal cat named Zoya

Darn, it doesn't really look right. Immersion hot-water boilers are dangerous, but I have almost overcome my fear of them. They are allowed here, but only for the purpose of heating—cooking with them is forbidden. I still have not quite figured out at which point heating becomes cooking. So officially we heat up the vegetables in water with oil. But we have to keep mum about it at home.

I don't know how to continue this letter. Olya. Olya.

Continued on March 30, 2012:

I learned something last night that rendered me unable to write anymore. I've told you there are four of us in the special cell. To explain what has happened I will have to go back and write out some details that will allow you to understand it all, I hope. Most of the cells here are "generals," for 30 people; some are semispecs—for 12 people; and there are specs for 4 people. Living conditions in the specs are considered the best in this institution. I don't entirely understand how people end up here; some people—and now I think there are many of them—come here after signing a paper promising to work for the administration: to inform on other inmates, in other words. When I was transferred here from a general cell, the three women already in the cell had been "primed"—all of them. They had been told that I had acted as a provocateur in the general cell. This is why it was so difficult for me the first few days here, while they studied me to see whether I was as bad as they'd been told. What's worse, whenever I was taken out of the cell to meet with my lawyer or the detective, they were called in and told that I had gone to inform on them, that I was claiming that they were mean and bullying to me. And then we became friends and gradually I started learning all this bad stuff, and understanding what filthy, low approaches some staff members use in the work.

That was all prologue. There are three of us in the cell now because one girl has been transferred to a general. When I became friends with the other two women in the cell, this girl quietly wrote a request to be transferred, and once she was out, she gave me up. She reported that I had letters—your letters—which I had secretly brought to the cell, and said bad things about me. That I turned the other women against her and that now the whole cell is saying blasphemous things all the time and she supposedly can't stand to listen to all that. All night last night I couldn't believe it. When they were talking about this girl, I had

*been the only one who said she was good. I stood up
for her, you see? I am sorry, this probably makes for
uninteresting reading, Olya, but I just can't seem to come
to terms with what's happened. Anyway, now you have
learned a couple more things about this place.*

*I am going to do all I can to make sure you get this
letter, but I will no longer be able to take your response
back to my cell with me: it's too dangerous. I am going to
read it in my lawyer's presence and try to memorize it, so
please do not forget to write. And please forgive me if I
forgot to write about something or didn't have time to write
it. This quotidian filth has prevented me from writing much
about what I have been thinking. On the other hand, I just
wrote a big article about some of that, and I hope to be able
to get it out of here, and then you will read it. Thank you
again for everything, all of it. Please stick together, you
guys. I hope to see you soon.*

Maria

Greetings to everyone from Pretrial Detention Center #6!

*This is the detention center where they keep women
and former police staff. That would include the criminal
Major Yevsyukov.* But we are not criminals. We are punk
performers, activists, artists, and citizens. So we feel fine,
even when we are here. The innocent and the politicals*

---

*Denis Yevsyukov was a police major who, while intoxicated, opened fire in a Moscow supermarket, killing two people and wounding twenty-two in April 2009.

always have an easy time behind bars. I have given shout-outs to Maria and Kat out in the walking courtyard, and they are also fine.

I have been told that there will be a hearing on our arrest on April 19. The outcome of the hearing is clear in advance. But, try as those who put us here might, we are not going to commit the sin of gloom. They cannot take our selves away from us, and so we continue to understand and learn about the world here as anywhere else.

I am writing this in a hurry because my notes are taken away from me. My letters don't get to people, and letters don't get to me either. They are shamelessly shutting us up, denying us the right to take part in a public discussion and attempt to reach consensus with our opponents.

We hope that those of you on the outside continue your political activity, and ours.

Punk's not dead. [This line is written in English.]

Nadya
April 11, 2012

Nadya had been reading the New Testament, which happened to be available to her and her cellmates. She found it helped in talking to people. This had always been easy for her. Even when teachers and other authority figures turned a deaf ear, she made her peers curious and receptive, and they worked to understand her. Only in jail did she encounter people for whom her language was foreign and threatening, as was she herself. But one time she sat on her bunk reading the New Testament and one of her cellmates sat on the bunk opposite reading the same book, and they started saying verses back and forth to each other. And they seemed to reach an understanding of sorts. Plus, "sin of gloom" turned out to be a useful concept.

KAT DID NOT SLEEP all night because the women were talking. There were ten of them in this transit cell, where Kat's entire four-person quarantine cell had suddenly been transferred. Quarantine had hardly been comfortable, but with the exception of one woman, who was pregnant and went on and on about how she had taken the rap for her entire gypsy clan, her cellmates had kept quiet enough. In the transit cell, everyone talked. A Muslim woman kept praying, kneeling on her bunk. The rest chattered endlessly about the way things worked behind bars and, more generally, in their world. One of them had coffee grounds, but, this being a transit cell, there was no electric teakettle or portable water heater, so they made coffee with hot water from the tap and kept on and on talking about it. Then a couple of them started regaling the rest with the tale of a criminal case in which a young woman was raped repeatedly throughout the night and only in the morning light did it become clear that the victim was in the final stages of AIDS. "And then the guy who did the raping got really thin," finished one of the storytellers, and her audience roared with laughter.

I guess this is supposed to be funny, thought Kat, and this was the first time she felt despair overtaking her. She tried to tune the women out as they kept talking, and to concentrate on thinking about what had happened to her and what would happen now.

Thinking back was easier. When she was released on March 4, with Nadya and Maria staying behind bars, she had been handed a summons to report to the investigator in a few days' time; the summons was in Irina Loktina's name—the alias she had given. She went home that day, and the first thing her father said to her was, "Those friends of yours have been arrested. What were you doing at the cathedral?"

"I guess you've seen the clip by now. You know what we were doing there."

"The patriarch is despicable," said Stanislav. "But you still shouldn't have done what you did."

Kat was in no mood to argue. She just told her father he should plead Article 51 when the investigators came, and went to sleep.

She woke up with the awareness that she needed to prepare to be arrested. She messaged other Pussy Riot members—she wanted to meet up and hand over passwords to their blog, e-mail, and social-networking accounts; she was now the only keeper of the passwords who was not behind bars. No one was eager to meet. She went to see the investigator at the appointed time, accompanied by Violetta Volkova. Petya was there too—he had been summoned for the same day—but the investigator was not; an assistant handed them summonses to report back in a week, on March 15.

Even a week had not been enough to make sure that more than one other member of Pussy Riot had all the necessary passwords.

Volkova, Petya, and Kat met again. Volkova said her car had just been searched. As she drove them to the police, they called their media contacts to talk up the car search. Petya was agitated and apparently happy, as he always was when something dramatic was happening and he got to tell the media about it. Kat felt the world closing in.

Petya was the first to enter the investigator's office. He was out a few minutes later—"Another postponement, don't worry"— and he ran down the stairs, phone in hand. Kat went in. Artyom Ranchenkov, the head investigator in the case, was seated at his desk. At thirty-four, he was already a lieutenant colonel. He had a meaty, unmemorable face that bore a permanent stamp of displeasure. Volkova was sitting in one of the visitors' chairs in front of him.

"What is your name?" asked Ranchenkov.

"Irina Loktina."

"Are you sure? I am asking you again."

"Yes, I am sure."

"You don't want to tell me your real name?"

"It is my real name."

"All right, we will have to have a lineup." Two of the cathedral's security guards would have to pick Kat out.

Volkova and Ranchenkov haggled over the lineup for a long time. Volkova objected to the other women who had been chosen for it; they were dressed in feminine office garb and had manicured nails and nicely done hair. It was hours before all of the women were arranged to Volkova's satisfaction, with their stockinged legs and high-heeled shoes hidden behind desks, clothes concealed under identical police jackets, hands in pockets, and hair pulled back into ponytails, as Kat's had been the morning of the punk prayer. It was nighttime by the time Ranchenkov informed Kat she was under arrest. He was still calling her "Irina Loktina." Kat and Volkova stepped out into the hallway.

"Tell me your name," said the lawyer.

"Yekaterina Samutsevich."

"Where are your documents?"

Kat had left her internal passport with a friend so she could not be identified in her own home. She told Volkova the friend's address. Marshals came and took Kat away. The following day, at the arrest hearing, Volkova disclosed Kat's identity.

THE TRANSFER FROM THE transit cell in the basement to the special cell up on the first floor was just as abrupt as Kat's first transfer had been. The hazing in the "spec" lasted a full month. Kat's three cellmates would not talk to her except to scream about some offense, such as leaving a crumb of bread on the table. The monotony of hell was virtually unbroken: Volkova came to see Kat once, Polozov came twice, a strange lawyer she had never heard of came once, saying that her father wanted her to change attorneys—Kat sent him away—and her father came. In addition, every Monday Stanislav sent her food from the jail's commissary. She told him she did not like the candy, but he kept sending it anyway. Anonymous Pussy Riot supporters sent the things Kat asked for—cottage cheese and milk, which she now discovered she liked. She had to admit, she actually liked the prison food itself. No one had cooked at her house since her mother died eleven years before, and this food was cooked—overcooked—and homey: porridge in the morning, soup—she especially liked the pea soup—and barley or porridgelike peas with Spam for lunch. She liked the walks in the courtyard as well, even though they caused more contention in the "spec": Kat's cellmates did not usually like to go out for walks, and the guards opposed splitting up the cells. Still, Kat almost always managed to claim her hour in the ersatz outdoors. Otherwise, life was unremittingly and boringly dire.

She decided to break it up by declaring a hunger strike. She had heard that if you went on hunger strike, you were transferred to solitary. She would like that. Otherwise, she had no particular demands. That is, she was demanding attention from another human being, be it her lawyer or her father, who could not keep her preferences in candy straight; she would even have settled for attention from the jail staff, but she could not state that as a demand, so she just declared a hunger strike. She got the solitary and the attention. Her father came on Monday to order food for her, and an officer told him, "She is on hunger strike, you cannot send her food." Stanislav called the lawyers. Volkova came, bringing Mark Feigin, who had joined the defense team as Nadya's lawyer and immediately claimed the position of leader.

"You should have told us," the lawyers reproached her.

"How could I have told you if you don't come to see me?" Kat reproached the lawyers.

She quit the strike after five days. She felt refreshed; it had been worth it. Back in the special cell, the other inmates actually seemed to have warmed up to her.

MARIA AND NADYA HAD GONE on a hunger strike when they were first arrested, and held it for ten days, when Moscow City

Court rejected their appeal of their arrest. Their second hunger strike was a group one. On June 20, they were led into court in turn—first Nadya, then (after Nadya was taken out) Kat, and finally Maria. Wearing handcuffs, each in turn was placed in a metal cage, where each in turn made the claim that she needed more time to read the case against them—and heard the judge, a striking thirtyish blonde, reject the plea. Each of them then declared a hunger strike.

They had been "familiarizing" themselves with the case, as the process was officially called, for two weeks. The case consisted of seven volumes—piles of typing paper sewn together with thick white string. The volumes contained letters and transcripts and pictures and even discs—though the discs were in sealed white sleeves, and the defendants were apparently expected to familiarize themselves with their contents by reading descriptions: "The disc contains video footage of young women engaged in dance . . . A young woman, who in her appearance, movements, and voice resembles Tolokonnikova . . ." Kat was fascinated by the fact that the investigators created a record of watching their videos as they would have created a record of an apartment search: "In the presence of Such-and-Such and So-and-So as witnesses, the investigator clicked on the link . . ."

The case hardly made for a coherent narrative, but the reading process was further complicated because the staff shuffled the volumes as they saw fit and no one could be sure of being able to pick up where she had left off. The lawyers told them to take their time and hinted they should perhaps even stretch the "familiarization" process out, so they did not rush. Some days, Kat refused to leave her cell altogether, though for the most part she was grateful that the appearance of the seven volumes had finally broken up the monotony of her existence. Now, every day around lunchtime, an officer would come and fetch her to escort her to the investigative bloc, where she would be placed in a room with a pile of paper sewn together with white string.

One of the volumes contained her father's testimony. Kat discovered Stanislav had spoken to Ranchenkov within days of her arrest. He had said things she knew could harm them. Worst of all, he had named Nadya. Kat choked with shame and fury.

When I asked Stanislav about this nearly a year later, he told me he had not realized he was giving testimony. He wanted to tell Ranchenkov that Kat had barely taken part in the action, and he also knew he needed Ranchenkov's signature to be allowed to see Kat in jail, so he wanted to have a good, friendly talk with the investigator. And he felt he had one. "I told him she had always been a good student, and anyway, she had not been at the altar. I said, 'Let's watch the video—you will see that she had barely stepped on the soleas when two security guards in black grabbed her. While the others danced.' But he said, 'But it's an Orthodox church! I have a hundred and fifty letters here from believers.' But he could see I am a conservative man, an old-fashioned man, and this was why I was the first of the parents to get visitation rights. The others had to wait another month. But at the end of our conversation he asked me to sign the protocol, verifying that he had written everything down correctly. But I hadn't said any of the things people usually say when they are interrogated. So I signed, I affirmed that he had written it all down right. And then they made me into a witness for the prosecution. And yes, I had told him I'd had a falling-out with Nadya because I felt they might all end up in jail if they kept going."

Almost six months later, during the trial, Stanislav Samutsevich renounced his earlier testimony, claiming he had changed his opinion of the action and did not want to testify for the prosecution. But, to the extent anyone's testimony in the trial mattered, his mattered a lot: he had essentially said that the defendants had engaged in a conspiracy—one that he had perceived as a criminal one.

―――――――

NADYA AND MARIA ATE NOTHING for nineteen days. Maria grew so weak she could no longer walk; Nadya developed debilitating headaches. They gave up the strike on June 10. Kat held out for three more days. She felt great; she had gotten the second wind she had heard about from other inmates—when the weakness gives way to a new, light sort of energy. She was not even bothered by her cellmates—she was not moved to solitary this time—or by the smell of the food she had liked so much. But there seemed to be no point in holding out if Nadya and Maria were done. After that, perhaps to speed up the process, the three of them were taken to the courthouse to read the case together. They spent entire days in one another's company. They read all about themselves. Mostly, they read their own blog, which the investigators had diligently printed out. They laughed their heads off. They had written very funny stuff.

NINE

The Trial

Two days before the trial began, the British newspaper the *Guardian* came out with a huge story. "Pussy Riot aren't just the coolest revolutionaries you're ever likely to meet. They're also the nicest," gushed the writer, Carole Cadwalladr, who had reported the story during two packed days in Moscow. Her editor had dispatched her in a fit of sudden inspiration, after realizing something very big and very bizarre was about to unfold in Moscow. "They're the daughters that any parent would be proud to have. Smart, funny, sensitive, not afraid to stand up for their beliefs. One of them makes a point of telling me how 'kindness' is an important part of their ideology. They have also done more to expose the moral bankruptcy of the Putin regime than probably anybody else. No politician, nor journalist, nor opposition figure, nor public personality has created quite this much fuss. Nor sparked such potentially significant debate. The most amazing thing of all, perhaps—more amazing even than calling themselves feminists in the land women's rights forgot—is that they've done it with art." Petya called everyone. He ran around clutching the paper, with a very large and very beautiful picture from the Red Square action. He sensed, correctly, that this was a first taste of true fame.

MOSCOW WAS HOT, sunny, and empty as it gets when vacation season sucks the crowds and traffic jams out of it. Political trials were best conducted with no one around, and political verdicts were best rendered in August or just before the New Year—as Mikhail Khodorkovsky's second guilty verdict had been. Everything felt slowed down and unreal this time of year. The Muscovites called it "dead season." To get to a verdict before "dead season" was over, though, this trial would have to be speeded up.

THE POLICE CORDONED OFF the Khamovnichesky Courthouse. It had seen its share of vigils—Khodorkovsky's second trial had been held here—so the police knew how to keep the crowds dispersed, squeezed, and uncomfortable all at the same time. Only journalists were allowed to approach the courthouse, though few of them fit into the overcrowded courtroom. The prisoner transport pulled up to the back of the building, and the crowd behind the police cordon shouted as loud as they could to be heard half a block away: *"Svobodu!"* "Freedom!" Pussy Riot heard them; it sounded like a big crowd.

They had their own architecture within the sprawling

four-story building. Before and after the hearing and during breaks, they were held in isolation rooms in the basement; to get to the courtroom on the second floor, they had to be taken up the back stairway to the top floor, which was entirely closed off for the occasion, cross over using the empty hallway, and descend two floors. There, they were placed inside what everyone called an aquarium—a Plexiglas enclosure equipped with microphones for addressing the court and a small horizontal window for passing papers back and forth to the defense attorneys. The defense sat at two desks in front of the enclosure, with their backs to it. The prosecution, and the lawyers for the victims of Pussy Riot's alleged crime, sat facing the defense. The setup left room for benches to accommodate only about two dozen members of the public, including all the relatives and journalists. Petya sat in the front row closest to the enclosure. He wore a red-and-white-checked Ralph Lauren shirt; Nadya wore a purple-and-white-checked Ralph Lauren shirt, which looked like it was probably Petya's. Several friends sat in the front row as well, as did Natalya Alyokhina, Maria's mother; Stanislav Samutsevich sat just behind her.

A few minutes in, Violetta Volkova objected to the presence of witnesses in the courtroom. The judge, a woman in her midfifties with dyed brown hair, thin lips, and reading glasses, demanded to know whether there were any witnesses present, and none identified themselves. She then read out a roll call, and when she got to Stanislav Samutsevich, he stood up and said he was not aware of being a witness. "You are a witness for the prosecution," said the judge. "Leave the room. You will be called." He said something softly. "Leave," she repeated. She sounded testy.

Nine people identified themselves as victims of Pussy Riot's alleged act of hooliganism. Nadya, Maria, and Kat had seen
them all at the probable-cause hearing, and they had recognized some of them from the cathedral. Among them were the
security guards and the candle lady who had looked so
shocked by the performance. Nadya, Maria, and Kat remembered their faces and their hands as well, as they had dragged
and thrown the three of them out of the cathedral. Thinking
of these people as victims was funny. The three defendants
studied their ostensible victims from behind the Plexiglas
that was apparently meant to safeguard the public from them,
and them from the public, and laughed.

The prosecutor, a plump, prematurely balding red-haired
man wearing a summer uniform—a light blue shirt with dark
blue captain's epaulets—cringed, demonstrating that the public
really was afraid of them, he insisted. "In light of the heightened public attention to the case, we believe the lives of
witnesses, members of the court, and the accused may be in
danger," he said. He moved to direct video operators to stop
filming when victims and witnesses were testifying—
apparently to protect them from attack by Pussy Riot's crazed
supporters. The judge agreed.

The judge went around the room collecting other pretrial
motions. Maria asked to be provided with audio and video recordings that were described in the indictment but not actually included in the case. She also moved for a continuance
because the defendants had not had time to consult with their
attorneys. They had been promised a confidential meeting
with them the previous Friday but it never happened—instead,
they had been driven to the courthouse and around town and

back to jail, returning after visiting hours. Maria spoke confidently, with clear references to relevant laws and rules; she
had spent much of the last few months studying law books
and was well on her way to becoming a classic jailhouse lawyer. Nadya and Kat seconded whatever she said.

And then things got weird.

Volkova motioned to have an expansive list of witnesses
called, including the patriarch himself, "to shed light on economical issues of Russian Orthodoxy." She said the word
ekonomishesky (economical) several more times as she read
out her motions; presumably, she was mispronouncing *eku-
menichesky* (ecumenical). She said she also wanted to read out
loud—and into the record—the defendants' comments on the
charges. For a second, the judge sounded more surprised than
annoyed; the charges had not yet been read by the prosecution. Volkova pounced: "Do you have any basis for denying my
motion?" And as the judge fumbled, she continued, "In that
case I shall begin reading them into the record."

She began with Nadya's statement: "We believe that art
should be accessible to the public, and for this reason we perform in a variety of venues. We never mean any disrespect to
the audience at our concerts . . . The song 'Mother of God,
Chase Putin Out' reflected the reaction of many of our fellow
citizens to the patriarch's call for believers to vote for Putin in
the March 4 election. We share out compatriots' dislike for the
perfidy, treachery, hypocrisy, and bribery of which the current authorities are guilty . . . Our action was not motivated by
hatred for Russian Orthodoxy, which prizes the same qualities we do: charity, mercy, forgiveness. We value the opinion
of believers, and we want them on our side, in opposition to

authoritarian rule . . . If our performance appeared offensive to anyone, we regret that very much . . . We believe we have fallen victim to a misunderstanding."

Volkova had rushed to read the statements because she feared the judge might curtail videotaping at any point. Now the tens and possibly hundreds of thousands of people who were watching the live feed would at least hear Pussy Riot's position. But they would hear it out of order—the words to which Nadya was responding in her statement had not been said in the courtroom yet. And Volkova looked and sounded as different from Nadya as a woman could. Obese and wearing a clingy brown floral-patterned dress and a large gold cross, she read monotonously and stumbled over so many words, sometimes asking her colleagues to help her decipher the defendants' handwriting, that it seemed she might not fully comprehend what she was reading.

"I insist that the ethical and legal aspects of our case must be separated from each other," she continued. "My own ethical appraisal of our action is as follows: we made a mistake by taking the genre we have been developing, that of a sudden political punk performance, into the cathedral. But we did not think at the time that our action could be offensive to anyone. We have performed in many venues in Moscow since September 2011: on the roof of a bus, in the Metro, in front of Special Detention Center Number One, in clothing stores—and we were received with humor everywhere. If anyone was offended by our performance at the Cathedral of Christ the Savior, I am prepared to admit that we made an ethical mistake. But a mistake it was; we had no intent to offend . . . And I apologize for this mistake. But there is no criminal penalty for ethical mistakes of the sort we have committed . . . I shudder every time I read in the charges words to the effect that we came to the cathedral out of hatred and disdain for Orthodox believers. These are terribly strong words and terribly serious charges . . . Think about what hatred and enmity are. We did not have them in our heart. Claiming we did is bearing false witness. We are being libeled, and I cannot say it's been easy to bear being tarred like this, having attributed to me feelings of hatred that I have never experienced toward any living thing on the planet. The prosecution claims we have concealed our true motives. But we do not lie; this is one of the principles of Pussy Riot . . . We have repeatedly been told by investigators that if we admitted our guilt, we would be released, and yet we have refused to tell that lie about ourselves. Truth is even more important to us than freedom."

After barely a pause, Volkova began reading Maria's statement, in the same monotonous manner: "I am Russian Orthodox . . . I always thought the Church loved its children, but it seems to love only the children who believe in Putin . . . I see the charges as nonsensical, as I am a citizen of a secular state, which is where I thought I lived . . . I ask the independent court to conduct an impartial investigation and draw conclusions. I have never had any hatred for Orthodox believers, nor do I feel any now."

Kat's statement tried to deconstruct the logic of the charges. The charges indicated that Pussy Riot's guilt was proven by the fact that they rehearsed their performances. But did that fact prove the existence of hateful intent? It proved only the intent to perform, not the intent to perform a criminal act. "The prosecution knows that the main topic of

our group's work is not the Orthodox religion but the illegiti-
mately elected parliament and the authoritarian rule of President Putin."

It took Volkova nearly an hour to read all three statements.
When she was finished, the judge read out a written motion
Maria had submitted, asking that the case be returned to investigators because of numerous inaccuracies and omissions
in the documents. The defense attorneys looked surprised; it
seemed they did not know the motion was coming or indeed
the extent to which Maria had been teaching herself law. Maria was doing the lawyerly thing in court while the lawyers
made political speeches. None of this looked intentional;
rather, it looked like an amateur production in which the actors had mixed up their lines, or been badly misdirected.

The prosecutor was quick to ridicule Volkova's procedural
irregularities as ignorance and a violation of both the defendant's rights and the victims' rights to due process. "Maybe
they are just saying all these things to have them published
on the Internet right now," he said, suggesting the obvious.
And then he pointed out what might be considered a major
failing if the defense had actually been planning to mount a
defense: "Anyway, it is now clear that the women sitting on the
defendants' bench do consider themselves members of this
group."

The judge denied all of the motions filed by the defense.

The prosecutor read out the charges in rapid fire. Sometime before February 17, 2012, Nadya had entered into a conspiracy with Maria, Kat, "and other persons unknown to the
investigators for the purpose of rudely disrupting the social
order in a manner that would express a clear lack of regard

for societal norms, motivated by hatred and enmity, motivated by hatred for a particular social group, in the form of carrying out offensive actions inside a religious institution aimed at attracting the attention of a broad spectrum of citizen believers." The conspirators had "distributed roles among themselves and purposefully acquired clothing to be worn, clothes that clearly contradicted church norms, discipline, rules, and regulations inside the church." Being aware of the offensiveness of their attire "to the entire Russian Orthodox world" and "the criminality of their intent and the scale of the insult they planned to inflict," they used balaclavas to disguise their identities and thus make it more difficult for them to be charged. "This increases the gravity of their deed and makes it look like a well-planned act of malicious intent, meant to denigrate the feelings and beliefs of the numerous disciples of the Orthodox faith and diminish the spiritual foundation of the state."

"Do you understand the charges?" the judge asked, addressing Nadya.

"Yes."

"Do you understand the charges?" she asked Maria.

"No."

"What don't you understand?"

"I would like to make it clear that—"

"What don't you understand in the charges?" The judge was beginning to sound belligerent.

"I don't understand the ideological aspect." Now Maria sounded strident.

The judge was silent for a moment.

"I don't understand on what basis the prosecution is making

statements regarding my motives. And I don't understand why I'm not allowed to explain this."

"Don't rush things."

"I'm not rushing things."

"You'll have your say. Right now I'm asking you if you understand the charges."

"I don't."

"The prosecutor just read out the charges. What you are being charged with."

"I don't understand."

"What don't you understand? Please clarify."

"I just did."

"Do it again."

"I don't understand the ideological aspect of the charges. Pertaining to my and—pertaining to our motives."

"All right. Sit down. Samutsevich, do you understand the charges?"

"No, I don't."

"What don't you understand?"

"I don't really understand any of the charges. They strike me as unconvincing and unsubstantiated. It is not explained on what basis these assertions are made."

"Prosecutor, can you explain it to them?"

"Your honor, the charges are clear." He promised the basis for them would be laid out clear in the course of the court hearing. He then repeated the part about a rude disruption of the social order and hatred and enmity for a particular social group.

"Now do you understand?" the judge asked Maria.

"No, I do not understand, because the prosecutor has just

read out a small excerpt out of more than a hundred and forty pages."

"The prosecutor has just outlined the charges. All the evidence will be reviewed in the course of the court hearing."

"I still don't understand. I insist the entire indictment be read out."

"The prosecutor has outlined the charges. He is not supposed to present evidence at this stage."

"But I don't understand what the charges are based on."

"He'll explain what they are based on in the course of the hearing."

"That doesn't help me understand."

The lawyers laughed. They looked very pleased with themselves and their defendants. Feigin tightened his tie.

"The prosecutor has outlined the charges," the judge repeated.

"I've said everything I had to say. I have nothing to add, I'm sorry."

"The charges are not fully formulated," said Kat, standing up.

"All right, so that's what you think. Do you plead guilty? Tolokonnikova?"

"No, I do not plead guilty. Can I explain?"

"You'll explain later."

"But I want everyone to understand."

"You have pled not guilty. Sit down. Samutsevich, do you plead guilty? Stand up and respond."

"No, I do not."

"Alyokhina, do you plead guilty to the charges?"

"I can't plead, I don't understand the charges."

Pause.

"You are college-educated! You know Russian."

"First of all, I have not yet finished college. Second, I am being educated as a journalist. I am not a lawyer. I don't understand what I am being accused of. I can't plead guilty or not guilty. I don't understand."

"Prosecutor, please be so kind as to outline the charges again. They don't understand."

"The defendants are being charged with committing an act of hooliganism, which is a rude disruption of the social order showing a clear disregard for society, committed for reasons of religious hatred and enmity, for reasons of hatred toward a particular social group, committed by a group of people as a result of a conspiracy . . ."

"The prosecutor has mentioned that I have three defense attorneys to help me understand the charges. But I was denied the opportunity to meet with them prior to trial. As a result, I do not understand. I insist that they be allowed to explain the charges to me."

"Calm down, we are talking about something else."

"This is very important for me to say."

"Do you plead guilty to the charges?" the judge screamed.

"I don't understand the charges."

"The charges were perfectly clearly, eh, er, rendered. All right, please, Tolokonnikova, do you want to comment on the charges?"

Nadya quickly summarized the commentary Volkova had read into the record a couple of hours earlier. She said she felt no hatred for anyone. She also admitted she had been in the cathedral performing, but this had had nothing to do with hatred. "I do not really understand what I am doing in court, facing criminal charges."

Kat followed suit, in her characteristically indirect way: "I admit the occurrences in the cathedral, and I admit that I participated," she said, but she had never experienced hatred or enmity based on religion or membership in a social or ethnic group.

When the judge asked Maria whether she wanted to comment on the charges, Maria finally entered her plea:

"I plead not guilty to the crimes described in Article 213, Part 2. I also believe that in reviewing a case filed under this article, ideological aspects are as important as facts, because the arguments rest on motivation and the motives of our actions stem from our ideologies. The prosecution is trying to play down the political and creative components, which are in fact key here. I am also grateful to our lawyers for making sure our comments were sounded out here today. Contrary to what we have already been accused of, they were not written for the media. They were written so that believers, including those identified as victims here today, would hear us. I realize this is difficult within the framework of a court hearing, but there is something greater, and in the space of this greatness, where there is neither slave nor free, we shall hear one another."

The judge surely did not hear Maria quoting Galatians, but she did hear her letting the court off the hook by pleading not guilty—not to the charges she claimed not to understand but to the crime described in the article of the criminal code that was holding her here: felony hooliganism.

The lawyers were much less articulate. Polozov said the charges were absurd. Feigin started saying the charges

characterized their author as incompetent. The judge interrupted him, asking him to stick to the topic at hand. "Don't tell
me what to do," said Feigin.

It was four in the afternoon on the first day of hearings,
and the tone and pattern of the trial had been established: it
would be a Soviet political trial repeated as farce. About a
dozen trials of groups of Soviet dissidents took place from the
early 1960s until the mid-1980s; the transcripts of these trials
formed an important part of the dissident literary canon, and
the experience of these trials was, for a long time, the Soviet
Union's only living memory of something that resembled public political debate.

Each participant in a Soviet political trial had a clearly
defined role. It was the prosecutor's job to present the state's
position, which amounted to creating a legal pretext for jailing
people for exercising rights guaranteed to them by the Soviet
constitution. For example, when seven people were tried for
staging a demonstration in Red Square (in the very same spot
where Pussy Riot performed forty-four years later), they were
charged not with demonstrating—for the right to public assembly was guaranteed to Soviet citizens—but with disrupting traffic, no matter that it had been a Sunday, there had
been no traffic, and Red Square had been closed off to cars
that day anyway, to facilitate pedestrian access to the Lenin
Mausoleum. So was Pussy Riot charged not with praying or
even dancing in a church but with committing an act of hooliganism and hatred toward Orthodox believers.

The judge in a Soviet political trial played the role of a bureaucrat with a rubber stamp; his job was to facilitate a smooth
and speedy hearing, denying most motions filed by the de-

fense, and to issue a preordained verdict when the time came. There were trials the KGB wanted finished quickly, and in these cases, it was the judge's job to stretch the workday, compress the cross-examinations, and eliminate as much of the procedure as his idea of process would allow. The role of the judge had not changed in half a century.

Defense attorneys in a Soviet political trial, if they did not want to be disbarred, had to distance themselves from their clients. Traditionally, in their closing arguments they would state that they did not share the defendants' political views and condemned them as anti-Soviet and immature—while also arguing that the defendants should be acquitted and released. To this end, they made a close study of all the evidence and made painstaking legal arguments—despite knowing the sentence had been written before the trial ever began. The defendants themselves, on the other hand, had a choice to make: they could either engage with the court, making arguments and helping their lawyers poke momentarily satisfying but useless holes in the prosecution's case, or they could refuse to recognize the court's authority altogether and use the court hearing solely to try to make a political speech. Anatoly (Natan) Sharansky, given a chance to make a final statement to a Moscow court, turned to his brother and dictated a speech for distribution in samizdat, then turned back to the court to say, "And as for this court, I have nothing to say to it."

The motivation of Pussy Riot and their lawyers was exactly the same as that of their predecessors half a century earlier: they aimed, on the one hand, to act as one would in a courtroom, and a country, where laws were meaningful and respected, and on the other hand, they wanted to use the forum of the court to make political declarations that would be heard. Except that, as if they had heard only a distorted account of the traditional division of labor in Soviet political trials, defense and defendants switched roles. By accident and as a result of poor communication rather than by prior arrangement, it was the lawyers who demonstratively refused to recognize the court, while Maria spent her time detailing exquisite if futile legal arguments.

IF THIS HAD BEEN A NORMAL TRIAL, the judge, having finished with the preliminaries at four in the afternoon, would have broken until the following morning. But this was not a normal trial; this was a fast one. The judge announced a thirty-minute break. Victims' testimony would follow.

The first victim was Lyubov Sokologorskaya, a fifty-two-year-old woman with a tired, apologetic face. After eliciting her identifying information, the judge started the questioning rather than allowing the prosecution to proceed.

"Tell me, please, are you an Orthodox believer and an Orthodox Christian?" asked the judge.

"Yes," Sokologorskaya said apologetically. "I try to observe all the rituals. I have been fasting as prescribed for several years."

"Tell me, please, what in your understanding and in that of your religion, is God?"

The defendants gasped. Having read the prosecution's case, they had realized that the trial would focus not on their actions but on their attitudes toward religion. And after the probable-cause hearing, they had a bad feeling about its likely trajectory and about their lawyers' level of expertise. But nothing had prepared them for such an opening.

"In my religion, God is all that is, and we are all in His image and likeness," responded the victim. "These are not idle thoughts on my part. I have examined myself and learned how a person can change for the better if he strives. I am deeply convinced that God the Lord is the source of all change."

"The source of all change?" echoed the judge.

"Is God the Lord. I can explain." She cleared her throat. "Where our Orthodox religion is concerned, God's mercy is in the sacrament of repentance for all the sins we commit. This is the exact opposite of self-love. In other words, it's being liberated of all the passions with which we are contaminated."

"Tell me, what does the place where the sacrament happens mean to you?" Now it was the prosecutor speaking. "I don't mean only the Cathedral of Christ the Savior."

"We can't hear the prosecutor at all!" Maria shouted. "We are behind bulletproof glass."

No one seemed to hear what she said, though her words, carried by the microphone in their stall, were audible to everyone in the courtroom.

"What does the cathedral mean to you?" the prosecutor continued. "What do its walls mean to you as an Orthodox believer?"

"Actually, I would like to begin by stating that the Church, in our Orthodox religion, is the union that Jesus Christ led when He came onto this earth as God who was personified in the human image. This is the essence of Orthodox faith." What she meant was not entirely clear, but this did not discourage the judge from questioning her further.

After some more theological fumbling, the judge finally asked Sokologorskaya to describe what happened on February 21. Sokologorskaya said she came to work that morning, performed her usual duties of lighting oil lamps and cleaning candle holders and other ritual objects, and saw visitors enter the cathedral starting around ten in the morning. Those who came in an hour later made her suspicious. She described seeing Nadya, Kat, and someone she could not identify forcing open a gate to the soleas, the elevated platform surrounding the sanctuary. "I especially would like to underscore that to open this gate they had to use their bodies—I will show this now here at the podium—like so, they had to shove aside the ark which housed part of the Lord's robe. This is probably the first pain I felt. This ark had not been on display there for very long, and everyone approached it with reverence, one by one, and people would line up for the chance to pay their respects to it. So this was a show of disdain, at least for the Russian-speaking people, and every time I think about it, a bitterness wells up."

Haltingly Sokologorskaya described seeing the group force open a second gate and run up on the soleas. "I finally went up to the barrier and rose on the first two steps—and then I could not take another step; I could not step onto the soleas. This may mean nothing to other people, but I was like a pillar on those steps."

"God wouldn't let her up there," a chorus of whispers in the courtroom explained.

"Please tell me, did you try to use words to explain to them that parishioners of the female sex cannot go up on the soleas?" the judge asked helpfully.

"I told them, I begged them, I pleaded."

"Did they listen to you or did they ignore you?"

The defense might have objected that the witness was being led, but it was the judge doing the leading.

"They absolutely ignored me. More than that, the actions they undertook after that showed just how much they ignored me."

"Did you try to stop them physically? Did you try to use your hands or body to shield the sanctuary?"

"I had tried to do it at the first gate, but they closed it in front of me. I tried to grab them, tried not to let them in, but one of them slipped away, she waved me off, she was sly."

"Please tell me, after this group of girls stepped onto the soleas, onto the pulpit, how did events develop and what was the reaction of other people present in the cathedral?" The judge continued calmly and with great care to steer her nervous witness.

"At the first moment my inner reaction was, 'What are they planning to do next?' . . . The most frightening and unpleasant part of the situation was feeling, yes, that I was being held still by the Lord and I cannot raise my foot and take even a single step . . . The most frightening thing would be if, God forbid, they try to force their way into the sanctuary—well, then I wouldn't just stand there! Let me explain something to you. The Lord's gate, the gate to the Kingdom of the Lord, is the actual gate to the sanctuary. When a cathedral is built, the sanctuary is blessed first, along with everything inside it. In fact this is the place of Christ's presence. And as far as we Orthodox Christians are concerned, Christ has risen . . . Moreover, at that moment the sanctuary housed a nail with which Christ had been nailed to the cross. And when people come to the cathedral, I tell them about this with special trepidation, I tell them that this is God's trace on this earth. This very nail was used to nail the demigod who is everything and everyone for us Orthodox believers. So this was another relic. Plus there was the Lord's robe, which had been given to us by a member of the Muslim faith. He had acquired it in his battles way back when and then he gave it to us in the seventeenth century, when the Romanov dynasty ascended to the throne."

The defense appeared to be in a stupor while Sokologorskaya continued to cite random episodes of Russian history, returning periodically to the unremitting heartache caused by Pussy Riot's action. Finally, when the victim seemed to run out of breath, the judge asked her to return to the story of what happened in the cathedral on February 21. Sokologorskaya looked confused.

"What were they wearing?" asked the prosecutor. "Was their clothing the sort that would be permissible in church?"

Sokologorskaya responded by telling the court the group apparently had a leader and she thought it was Tolokonnikova.

"The clothing that remained on them—how would you describe it?" The judge would not abandon her efforts to get the testimony she needed. "Was it modest, vulgar, permissible in a church?"

"The clothing they had on was not permissible for being in a church. It was vulgar. One of the unidentified persons even had a bare shoulder. I quickly thought, 'Oh my God, make it so they don't strip!'"

"Please tell us what they did then," asked the judge.

"They began to don masks with slits for the eyes and

mouth. I was caused further anxiety by the fact that a guitar was being taken out."

"A regular guitar?"

"No no no, not a regular guitar. It was an electric guitar."

"Were they standing still?"

"They began bodily movements and those shouts."

"Please describe their bodily movements."

"I am not going to look for a description now. As far as I am concerned, these were devilish jerkings."

"Were they jumping and skipping?" asked the judge.

"They were jumping and skipping and making arm movements with their hands in fists. They raised their legs so high that you could practically see everything below the waist. Doing this in front of the sanctuary, at the Lord's gate, at the pulpit, this sort of jumping—how can anyone say this was just a small ethical transgression? And I felt like they were showing off to one another, to see who can raise her leg higher."

"Please tell us, were these actions accompanied by shouts of any sort that were of an offensive and sacrilegious nature with regards to the Orthodox faith, Jesus Christ, the Virgin Mary, the Russian Orthodox Church, and Russian saints?"

"That was their whole nature. It was offensive. There was no other nature to them."

"Please tell us, did the actions of the defendants and of unidentified persons cause moral damage to you?"

"They caused huge moral damage to me. The pain will not go away."

"In your opinion, did their video clip offend the feelings and souls of believers? Did it provoke them to retaliate in kind, and did it, as well, provoke those who are not Orthodox believers to view the Orthodox negatively?"

By Russian law, a witness or a victim of an alleged crime can testify only to the facts; witness opinions must be disallowed when offered and must never be solicited. But those who testified as witnesses against Soviet dissidents were often asked to render their opinions on the anti-Soviet nature of actions or materials attributed to defendants—and their opinions, scripted by the KGB, often made it into the wording of the courts' verdicts.

"It did both," Sokologorskaya obliged, adding that the impact was exacerbated by timing: it had been the week before Lent.

"And if we abstract ourselves from what happened in the cathedral, in your opinion, would this kind of behavior be acceptable from a moral standpoint in any other public space, or are these immoral acts of hooliganism?" the judge asked the candle lady.

"Naturally and without a doubt, this kind of behavior would be unacceptable anywhere. From my point of view, it is simply immoral."

At length the judge, having preempted the role of the prosecution, invited the defense to cross-examine the witness.

"You said you heard what the participants said, but you cannot repeat it because of your religious convictions," said Mark Feigin. "Is this correct?"

"Yes."

"In that case, I am going to read out several phrases myself and you'll tell me whether you heard them. Did you hear them sing 'Mother of God, chase Putin out'?"

"No."

"All right. Did they say, 'Mother of God, become a feminist'?"

"It's all mixed up with the video clip now. You know, I don't remember."

"Did they mention Patriarch Kirill's last name?"

"I was standing there and praying as hard as I could so I wouldn't hear these words. I definitely heard the word 'patriarch.' And we only have the one patriarch."

"You said you were praying. When you pray, do you hear what other people are saying to you? Do you take in information, wholly or in part?"

"I didn't say that and I won't. I want to say that praying normally and praying in that setting are different things. It was enough that I heard the word 'patriarch.' I'm not going to tell you which grammatical case it was used in."

"So you can't say what you heard exactly?"

"No."

"So you didn't hear anything!"

"Sure I didn't!"

"You keep asking the victim the same question," said the judge. "She's already answered. I'm disallowing it."

"You mean the court doesn't need to know what the victim heard?" asked Volkova.

"I said, I'm disallowing the question!" the judge squealed.

"Tell me then what kind of moral suffering you experienced when you heard their show," said Feigin.

"I am disallowing the question!" the judge screamed again. "The victim already answered it. You should have been paying attention."

"I didn't get an answer."

"But everyone else did," said the judge.

"All right. Who told you that the young women you saw at the Cathedral of Christ the Savior and the women in the clip you watched were the same people? They were wearing balaclavas."

"I can put two and two together," said Sokologorskaya. "I'm not the stupidest person there is."

"You said the defendants performed bodily movements that you called 'devilish jerkings.' Could you explain what devilish jerkings are?"

"I am disallowing the question."

"Why?" Volkova stood up again. "Is the court curtailing our rights?"

"No one is curtailing anything," said the judge.

"The victim's statement is part of the record," insisted Volkova. "We would like to know what 'devilish jerkings' are. How does the victim know how the devil jerks? Has she seen the devil?"

"I demand respect for the victim," said the judge. "I am reprimanding you."

"We would like to know why the court is disallowing our questions. On what basis?"

"Continue the cross-examination," said the judge.

The lawyers had run out of questions. The defendants themselves stepped in.

"We stand accused of publicly expressing hatred and enmity toward Orthodox believers," said Maria. "I want to understand the difference between a personal insult and the public expression of hatred for believers."

"I said that what happened in the Cathedral of Christ the

Savior was a personal insult for everyone who came there with deep pain," responded Sokologorskaya. "Your behavior showed that you want publicity, that's all."

"Do you believe a personal insult of that sort is a crime punishable by law?" asked Kat.

"I am disallowing the question," said the judge.

"Was my clothing inappropriate for being in a church?" asked Kat.

"You had on the longest dress, and your shoulders were covered," admitted Sokologorskaya. "But you had bright stripes and a mask."

"I am aware that the cathedral's internal rules dictate that women should cover their heads," said Volkova, "but I don't know that they say women can't wear masks. Do they say that?"

"I am disallowing the question," said the judge, visibly angry. "Stop this mockery!"

"What mockery? I insist that if this is part of the charges, then we need to see the rules that forbid it."

"Continue with the cross-examination."

Kat rose again. "I would like to know what you heard me say, if I said anything."

"You are lucky that you were detained by security right away and didn't have time to say anything!"

"Oh my God," said Nikolai Polozov.

"So did Samutsevich say anything or not?" asked Volkova.

"At first they were all saying stuff and then I don't remember," said the victim.

"Why do you think that if I break the cathedral's internal rules of behavior, that means I do it out of hatred and enmity toward believers?" Kat insisted. "What makes you say that?"

"I am disallowing the question!" said the judge.

"Still, I would like to know what you heard me say, if you think I was expressing hatred toward believers."

"You are trying to force me to say bad words and curse words. I'm not going to do it."

"By law they cannot be said in court," added the judge.

"But unprintable words and 'bad words' are two different things," said Volkova. "If we don't know what she said, we cannot tell whether the charges are warranted."

"The victim has already informed us that her religious convictions preclude her from saying these words," said the judge. "She has that right. I have disallowed the question. Continue the cross-examination."

"I have no more questions until I get answers to the ones I already asked," said Kat.

"Is it only the defendants who are not allowed to be in the cathedral dressed like this?" asked Volkova. "Considering that the parts of the body that women tend to cover—they had those covered. And their dresses were below the knee."

"But that is why they tried to raise their legs as high as possible—because their skirts weren't short enough. Plus I'd like to note that the length of the dress is not the only criterion of appropriateness."

"Not short enough?" Volkova said. "With all due respect to the court, I studied logic in college, and the responses we are getting today seem to me entirely unconnected to the questions. I want to know all the criteria of appropriateness, and I would also like to understand if other women, women who are not on trial today, are allowed to enter the Cathedral of Christ the Savior wearing a brightly colored dress. I am wearing a dress right now, and it has flowers on it. Would I be able to enter a church in it?"

"Now that you mention it, your dress is kind of like that color." The brownness of Volkova's dress notwithstanding, the exchange had already exceeded the limits of absurdity.

"You are being asked to define the criteria of appropriate dress," said Polozov.

"I want to hear you address the length of every individual dress," said Volkova. "You are not answering our questions."

"Appropriateness of dress is determined by a set of criteria, including length and extent of exposure. I noticed that Alyokhina's dress was a bit long as well, and this must be why she was trying to raise her legs so high."

"Any other questions?" asked the judge.

The defense huddled for a minute.

"We have no more questions," said Feigin, "because our clients require a break."

"You have given them no food or water since five in the morning," added Volkova.

"By international law, this constitutes torture," said Polozov.

The journalists present scribbled furiously; this was the first quotable quote from the defense all afternoon. The judge called a break.

CALLING IT "TORTURE" was not an overstatement. They had been up at five; on days when they had hearings, inmates had to be dressed and ready before breakfast because the order to report to the door could come at any point in the morning.

Some days, the call came before breakfast and this meant they got none. Once out of the building, they were placed in a prisoner transport equipped with what they called "glasses"—vertical enclosures about three feet square and five feet three inches high (that is, high enough for Kat and Maria but not for Nadya to stand up straight) that served to isolate them from one another. There were stools in the glasses to sit on, uncomfortably. Nadya, Maria, and Kat had food with them, if you could call it that, a plastic box that contained several packets of soup, tea bags, some crackers, and several plastic cups. During breaks, they could ask the marshals for hot water—and they did, and they ate the soups, but the soups turned out to be absurdly salty and they wanted to ask for water, but, mindful of the fact that the marshals did not always heed their requests to be taken to the bathroom, they thought better of it. So in the afternoon, they were dehydrated and still hungry.

Their aquarium was an airless stall; it had been built in retaliation after Khodorkovsky's lawyers secured a European Court of Human Rights ruling that deemed holding defendants in steel cages inside courtrooms inhumane. For their second trial, Khodorkovsky and his codefendant got a shiny new unventilated Plexiglas cube. This was the very enclosure in which Pussy Riot sat now. It engulfed them like a nightmare; now the picture was clear and now it was obscured by the fogged-up walls of the aquarium, the heavy air inside, the haze of hunger and sleep deprivation, and the general sense that none of this could be real.

The judge denied their request for a break. "We'll stay here until morning if we need to," she declared. She called Denis Istomin to the stand. He was a tall handsome blond

young man with a gym body. An activist of a Russian Orthodox nationalist movement, he had testified a couple of years
earlier at the trial of a curator accused of organizing a show
that offended the believers; Istomin had seen Nadya protesting during that trial, and his testimony had been essential to
the women's arrest. Now he testified that what he saw on February 21 had hurt his feelings so much that he cried. He said
he had come to the cathedral that morning to buy a ring at the
gift shop, but, happening upon the kerfuffle, had helped remove Maria from the cathedral.

"You said you were in a state of shock as a result of our
performance. Tell me, what did you do after you handed me
over to the police?" Maria said, likely meaning security.

"I went back inside the cathedral. I wanted to leave, because
I had done a good deed, I'd helped clean up the cathedral, so I
could leave, but there was a force holding me back. So I went
inside and into the shop."

"You were in a state of shock and you went into the shop.
I see, thank you. One more question. Did you hear that after
lunch today I apologized for our ethical violation?"

"Yes, I heard." Istomin sighed. "But all things should be
done in their time. As Stanislavsky used to say, I don't believe
you. I don't believe you have repented."

"Let's discuss their apologies later," said the judge. "Maybe
they'll find a more repentant way of saying them."

After Istomin testified that he had found the words *holy
shit* offensive and sacrilegious, Volkova asked him what else
struck him the same way.

"The phrase 'Mother of God, become a feminist.' I believe
this is unacceptable disparagement."

"Disparagement of Jesus Christ?"

"Disparagement of Jesus Christ."

It was after eight when Istomin finished testifying. The judge called a ten-minute break, enough to go to the bathroom but not enough to get anything to eat.

AT HALF-PAST EIGHT, the judge was livid. "I called a ten-minute break! Ten minutes! Why is everyone here except for the defense attorneys? What do they need, a special invitation?"

"Your honor, this kind of attitude is called contempt of court," the prosecutor suggested helpfully.

"Let's not talk about attitude," said Volkova, the only defense attorney in the room. "We see who's got attitude."

"Where are your colleagues?" the judge demanded to know.

"And so we return to the scene of our disgrace," said Polozov to Feigin as they walked in.

"I am reprimanding the defense," said the judge. "Whom are you going to cross-examine now?"

"We are not going to cross-examine anyone," said Volkova. "We are demanding that the judge recuse herself. The judge is clearly prejudiced against the defendants."

An hour later, after everyone had weighed in on Volkova's motion, the judge refused to recuse herself and called the next victim, Vasily Tsyganyuk, an altar man. He was wearing a black T-shirt emblazoned with a large Dolce & Gabbana logo. He also testified that he had been deeply hurt by the performance and that he had heard no political statements, only sacrilegious and hateful ones. He stopped testifying at ten, the hour past which Russian law forbids conducting court hearings.

With the waiting in the basement isolation rooms, the requisite searches, and the circuitous routes prisoner transports always seemed to take, Nadya, Maria, and Kat would be back in their cells at two in the morning. Three hours later, they would need to be ready to begin a new day of their trial.

All the days would be similar to the first one. They would be interminable. The lawyers would veer from fumbling to speechifying, and there would be no time or opportunity to discuss, much less change, their defense strategy. Feigin, Polozov, and Volkova had decided they would focus their efforts only on drawing attention to the outrages of the trial and would not speak to the court on the court's terms. Indeed, they would sometimes act in ways that exacerbated the travesty to make it that much more obvious. Months later, after things had gone wrong and then very wrong, they still believed they had chosen the right approach; there was, after all, no waging battle against a judge who clearly relished running a witch trial. The lawyers believed their public statements, endless Tweets, and tireless media work had mobilized unparalleled support for the women on trial, and this, in turn, gave them the best chance they had of going free.

"But what made you think the Russian authorities would listen to these people?" I asked them much later. "You'd seen them put Khodorkovsky away for ten years—and there had been a major international campaign to support him."

"This was different," said Polozov. "These were the very people they invite to sing at their parties!"

This was not entirely illogical; at least the Russian elite listened to these people when they sang.

Faith No More had invited Pussy Riot members to join

them onstage during a July concert in Moscow—and five women in balaclavas did and lit sparklers and chanted that "Putin pissed himself." The Red Hot Chili Peppers spoke out when they came to town three weeks later. Franz Ferdinand and Sting issued statements of support. Then came Radiohead, Paul McCartney, Bruce Springsteen, U2, Arcade Fire, Portishead, Björk, and hundreds of others. Never had the worldwide music industry mobilized on this scale and at this speed to support a colleague—especially colleagues who were not, in fact, musicians in any traditional sense.

Judge Syrova's court plowed on. A small crowd continued to keep vigil in front of the courthouse. A middle-aged man in glasses stood at the entrance with a sign that read YOUR HONOR, WHAT HAPPENED TO YOUR HONOR? Whenever Nadya, Maria, and Kat were delivered to the courthouse, the crowd managed to let them know they were there. When the victims walked in and out of the building, the crowd shouted, "Shame!" Some of the victims responded by making the sign of the cross toward the crowd.

On Day Two, altar man Tsyganyuk testified that Pussy Riot had acted as though they were possessed.

"Those who are possessed can act in a variety of ways," he explained. "They can scream, thrash around on the floor, sometimes they jump."

"Do they dance?" asked Polozov.

"Well, no."

"That's enough of this talk about who is possessed," said the judge. "Tsyganyuk is not a medical doctor and is not qualified to render a diagnosis."

Security guard Sergei Beloglazov testified he had been so

traumatized by the performance that he had been unable to work for the last two months (almost six months had passed since the performance).

"But as far as myself, I forgive them," he said. "I do not hold grudges. But as for God, the sanctuary, and other believers, I can't decide that—that would be God's will and the court's decision."

The court managed to fit all the victims into the first two days of hearings. Day Two even ended by nine, which meant Nadya, Maria, and Kat might be in their cells by midnight.

DAY THREE BEGAN with an ambulance. The hearing was scheduled to start at one, but Nadya, Maria, and Kat were installed in their basement rooms in the morning; such was the way of prison transports, which functioned a bit like buses, delivering inmates from various jails to different courts in the morning and taking them back in the evening. By midday, all three were close to fainting. Nadya was in her third day of debilitating headaches. Underweight Maria was simply depleted, as was Kat. They demanded a doctor repeatedly, until an ambulance was finally called. The doctors examined them and said they were fit to stand trial. Two hours later, Nadya moved for a continuance because she felt too ill to go on. The judge banged her gavel furiously and said the ambulance doctors had cleared them. It was so hot and stifling in the courtroom that day that at one point Volkova left the courtroom to get some air. In the late afternoon, ambulances were called again, this time for Volkova and the three defendants. In between, several witnesses for the prosecution testified that they had seen the defendants jumping, jerking, and insulting the Orthodox faith.

On Day Four, there was a bomb threat. The building was evacuated while the mine squad swept it, but Nadya, Maria, and Kat spent that time in the isolation rooms in the basement. Once the building was declared bomb-free, the court heard from the cathedral's cleaning lady, who testified that Pussy Riot had danced to music that was "neither classical nor Orthodox." Pressed by the defense, the cleaning lady admitted that she cleaned the soleas despite being female. The prosecutor grabbed his head with his hands. The judge directed the court marshals to remove anyone who laughed.

For its last witness, the prosecution called Stanislav Samutsevich. "I refuse to answer questions about my daughter," he said immediately, but the judge did not let him leave the stand. The prosecutor badgered him. "Did she go to the Rodchenko School? Did she meet contemporary artists there? Did she share their views? Did Tolokonnikova get her involved in various groups?" Stanislav looked pained and refused to answer. The prosecutor read aloud the testimony Stanislav had given back in March: "Tolokonnikova got her involved in the feminist movement. I told Katya that women already had all the rights, but she would not listen to me . . . I have banned Tolokonnikova from our home. I believed it's Tolokonnikova's fault that Katya took part in the action at the Cathedral of Christ the Savior . . . Sometimes I felt like she was under a spell. She did not want to listen to logic, she lived in a made-up world. But I am sure my daughter did not use drugs or alcohol; she was under the influence of Tolokonnikova."

"I was upset," said Stanislav. "I wanted to make things better for my daughter . . . I said many things that aren't true. Please don't take my testimony into account."

That evening the judge read aloud the conclusions of a committee of psychiatrists and psychologists who had examined the defendants. They had found them sane and fit for trial but had nonetheless diagnosed each with a personality disorder. Maria, they said, suffered from emotional distress brought on by her desire to protest. Nadya and Kat were both labeled with something called "mixed personality disorder." Nadya's symptoms were her "active position in life" and "heightened ambitions," while Kat exhibited an abnormal "insistence on her own point of view."

They left the courthouse at ten.

President Putin spent that day in London, meeting with the British prime minister and confronting questions, protests, and letters in support of Pussy Riot everywhere he went. He finally made a statement: "If those girls had defiled something in Israel, they'd have to deal with burly guys over there," he said wistfully. "They wouldn't have gotten out of there alive. Or if they'd gone to the Caucasus, even closer to home. We wouldn't have even had time to arrest them. But I still don't think they should be judged too harshly. I hope that they draw their own conclusions." The more optimistic among Putin's listeners concluded that Pussy Riot would get a suspended sentence; the more realistic thought this meant they might get less than the possible maximum of seven years.

ON DAY FIVE, the prosecutor began opening evidence boxes. He pulled out a yellow dress and a blue balaclava and then a black one. To show the court that the masks had slits, he pulled one of them onto his rubber-gloved hand. A journalist was removed from the courtroom for smiling.

That afternoon three men in balaclavas showed up on the roof of a storefront across the street, level with the courtroom window. They chanted, "Free Pussy Riot!" Three policemen climbed up there, but the roof was too small for them to risk a scuffle in trying to force the men down. While the police-men huddled at one end of the roof, trying to figure out what to do, the masked men began singing "Mother of God, chase Putin out." Everyone in the courtroom was transfixed on the roof across the street. "If you want to look, leave the court-room," a marshal barked. But Nadya, Maria, and Kat stretched to get a better look; no one was going to kick them out of the courtroom for rubbernecking. They were smiling, too.

An hour and a half later, a crane finally took the men down.

That day, the defense called Maria and Kat's professors to testify to their character. Both said they were wonderful young women who harbored no hatred toward the Russian Orthodox religion. The defense called Olya Vinogradova to the stand.

"We were going to school together," said Olya. "We have been together for three years." She smiled at her friend be-hind the Plexiglas.

"You'll do your laughing when you leave here!" the judge shouted. "This is not a circus or a movie theater."

"Don't pressure the witness," said Volkova.

"I am giving you a reprimand," said the judge.

"I want one too!" said Feigin.

"Reprimands for all the defense lawyers," said the judge. "Enter it into the record."

Maria asked her friend to describe her political views: "What is my attitude toward the Putin regime?"

"I am disallowing the question," said the judge.

"Why?" asked Maria.

"We are examining your character."

"And my character can't have an attitude toward Putin?"

"It can, but . . . " said the judge and trailed off.

"Did I make any statements about any political figures, and if so, then what did I say?"

"There you go," said the judge.

"I believe you made very negative statements about Vladimir Vladimirovich Putin," said Olya.

This was the only point in the trial when the defense managed, for a moment, to focus attention on the political nature of Pussy Riot, if not on the political nature of the action itself. The rest of the time the court successfully obscured the content of the song, as though Pussy Riot had indeed defiled the cathedral by asking the Virgin Mary to become a feminist. Those who knew of Pussy Riot only from the trial or from state television could be forgiven for not knowing this had been an action against Vladimir Putin; the court had managed even to play the recording in such a way so as to skip the refrain every time so that the Mother of God was never asked to get rid of the president.

They left the courthouse after ten that evening.

SATURDAY AND SUNDAY in pretrial detention felt almost like a vacation. The routine resumed on Monday, Day Six of the trial: up by five, in the courtroom by ten, out at ten, in their cells at two. On Monday morning, Volkova tried to engage the court in a discussion of the term *shoulder*. The prosecution claimed Pussy Riot members' shoulders had been exposed, but that would only be true of their shoulders in the anatomical sense, meaning the upper arms, and not shoulders in the vernacular sense, meaning the shoulder joint, anatomically speaking.

"If you look at me, your honor, I will show you what I mean."

"I am not looking at you!" screamed the judge, who lost her composure repeatedly that day. It seemed that while the defendants had gotten their second wind, the judge's nerves had been entirely worn out by the grueling hearing regimen.

The defense kept filing motions to call its witnesses; the judge kept shooting them down. Around eight in the evening, when yet another of these motions came up for discussion, Maria lashed out at the judge: "It seems to me you keep forgetting that this concerns us personally. We were brought here by force. And I have only one desire: I want to rest and I want to have a confidential meeting with my attorney, and I keep trying to ask for this for a week and a half. I absolutely cannot concentrate in order to write my closing statement. I have to write my testimony at night. I want to draw attention to this!"

"Are you done?" asked the judge.

"No! I also want to say that the things the prosecutor says make me suspect he is a provocateur. And I can't even respond to him because I don't have that right."

"You want to talk about it?" asked the judge.

"Yes!" said Maria. "It hurts being unable to say anything!"

The judge said it was now Kat's turn to speak.

ON DAY SEVEN, the prosecutor gave his summation.

"The defendants' claims that their action was politically motivated are specious. Not a single politician's name was pronounced in the cathedral. An analysis of the song showed that the phrase 'Mother of God, chase Putin out!' was inserted artificially and the true purpose of the lyrics was to insult the feelings of Orthodox believers. Putin's last name was included for the sole purpose of creating a pretext for publicizing the action as a protest against the authorities." He asked for three years behind bars for each of them.

"I am incredibly ashamed to be listening to the prosecutor's speech," said Volkova in her own summation. "It's like we are not in Russia in the twenty-first century but have gone through the looking glass. It's like all of this will fall apart and the three imprisoned girls will go home. In what legal book did the prosecutor find such terms as 'blasphemy,' 'sacrilege,' and 'legs hiked up in a vulgar manner'? . . . The girls have been in jail for many months. They have not seen their families, their children, they have not seen the light of day, they have been tortured. And what are they accused of? They stood in the wrong place, they prayed the wrong way, they crossed themselves too fast and in the wrong direction, they turned their behinds to the sacred nail—and they ruined the foundation of foundations!"

"The girls are being asked not just to apologize—for they have apologized," said Feigin. "They are being told to lick the judge's boots, to humiliate themselves, to cry, to give the state the opportunity to rip them to shreds. Nothing has changed since the Soviet period: a defendant can hope for forgiveness, for humanity, only once he is destroyed."

Polozov lectured the court on the Russian constitution, listing those of its articles that had been violated during the course of the trial, starting with Article 13—guaranteeing a variety of ideologies and banning a single, state-enforced ideology—and ending with Article 123, which guarantees equal treatment for both sides in court hearings.

That night, Madonna performed in Moscow. At one point, she turned her back to the audience and pulled off her jacket, exposing the word PUSSY over the black strap of her bra and the word RIOT beneath it. She then pulled on a balaclava. Petya and Tasya had VIP seats. Tasya was filming. "Imagine them getting real jail time after this," said Petya. "Just imagine!" They both laughed so hard Tasya's camera shook.

THEY HAD BEEN TALKING about their closing statements. Rather, Nadya and Maria had been talking—and writing. Nadya had spent at least several of their short nights writing. She showed Maria entire notebooks she had filled with theses and with passages she had copied out of the New Testament. Maria wrote right after returning from court but still tried to get some sleep. When Maria asked her if she had written much, Kat said, "Nah, just a few words." She told herself she was not going to kill herself over the closing statement. She would write at night if she felt up to it, until sleep took over, or in the morning, in that no-man's-land period after she was taken out of her cell but not yet placed in the transport.

Once, Kat heard Nadya rehearsing her speech. She found

this odd and slightly irritating: Didn't responding to this rigged, empty ritual so earnestly only validate it? Didn't engaging the religious argument legitimize the very idea that religious issues could be taken up in court? But Nadya was determined to accomplish something for which she had never before striven: she wanted, desperately, to be understood.

On Day Eight, Nadya was the first to make her closing statement.* She was wearing a blue T-shirt emblazoned with a yellow fist and the words NO PASARAN.

In the great scheme of things it's not the three Pussy Riot singers who are on trial here. If it were, what happens here would be of no consequence whatsoever. But it is the entire Russian state system that is on trial here, a system that, to its own detriment, is so enamored of quoting its own cruelty toward the human being, its own indifference toward his honor and integrity—all the bad things that have ever happened in Russian history. The process of imitating justice is beginning to resemble closely that of Stalinist *troikas*, I am very sorry to say. We see the same thing here: the investigator, the judge, and the prosecutor make up the court. And on top of it and above it all

*Unlike some versions of Pussy Riot's closing statements, these are the speeches as they were spoken during the trial, not as they had been written. I have translated them from transcripts prepared by Elena Kostyuchenko for *Novaya Gazeta*. I have intentionally kept the occasional repetitions, incomplete sentences, and ambiguous or factually incorrect statements (e.g., Putin does not hold international meetings daily or even weekly). These are the statements as Kat, Maria, and Nadya made them, sleep-deprived, drained, and almost entirely deprived of the benefit of one another's intellectual or editorial input.

stands the political demand for repression, which determines the words and actions of all three.

Who is responsible for the action in the Cathedral of Christ the Savior occurring and for the fact that this trial followed the concerts? It is the authoritarian political system. Pussy Riot does opposition art. In other words, it's politics that uses forms created by artists. In any case, it's civic activity that occurs in conditions where basic human rights, civil and political liberties are repressed by a corporate system of state power. Many people who have been having their skin stripped off by the systematic destruction of liberties since the beginning of the 2000s are starting to riot. We were seeking true sincerity and simplicity and we found them in the holy-fool aesthetic of punk performance. Passion, openness, and naiveté exist on a higher ground than do hypocrisy, lying, and false piety used to mask crimes. Top state officials go to church wearing the correct facial expression, but they lie, and in doing so they sin more than we ever did.

We staged our political punk performances because the Russian state system is so rigid, so closed, so caste-based, and its politics so subservient to narrow corporate interests, that it pains us to breathe the very air in this country. We cannot abide this at all, and it forces us to act and live politically. The use of force and coercion to regulate social processes. A situation where key political institutions, the disciplinary structures of the state—the uniformed services, the army, the police, the secret police, and the corresponding means of ensuring political stability: prisons, preventive detentions, the tools of exerting rigid control over citizens' behavior.

We also cannot abide the forced civic passivity of the majority of the population as well as the total domination of the executive branch over the legislative and judicial ones.

In addition, we are sincerely irritated by that which is based on fear and a scandalously low level of political culture, and this level is intentionally maintained by the state system and its helpers. Look at what Patriarch Kirill says: "The Russian Orthodox do not go to demonstrations." We are irritated by the scandalous weakness of horizontal links in society.

We object to the manipulation of public opinion, carried out with ease because the state controls the vast majority of media outlets. Take, for example, the blatant campaign against Pussy Riot, based on the perversion of all facts, undertaken by the mass media with the exception of the very few that manage to maintain independence in this political system, is a good example.

Nonetheless, I am now stating that this situation is authoritarian: this political system is authoritarian. Nonetheless, I am observing a sort of crash of this system where the three Pussy Riot participants are concerned. Because the result for which the system was aiming has not come to pass, unfortunately for the system. Russia has not condemned us. With each day more and more people come to believe in us and to believe us and to think that we should be free and not behind bars. I see that in the people I meet. I meet people who represent the system, who work for it. I see people who are serving time. And with every passing day there are more of them who wish us luck and wish us freedom and say that our political act was justified. People say, "At first we had doubts about whether you should have done what you did." But with every passing day there are more and more people who say to us, "Time has shown that your political act was right. You exposed the sores of this political system. You struck the serpent's nest that has now come back to attack you." These people are trying to do what they can to make our lives easier, and we are very grateful to them for this. We are grateful to the people who are speaking out in support of us on the other side of the fence. There are a huge number of them. I know this. And I know that at this point a huge number of Orthodox believers are speaking out on our behalf, including praying for us, praying for the members of Pussy Riot who are behind bars. We have seen the little book these Orthodox believers are handing out, a little book that contains a prayer for those who are behind bars. This one example is enough to show that there is not one unified group of Orthodox believers as the prosecution is trying to show. It does not exist. And more and more believers are now taking the side of Pussy Riot. They think that what we did should not have brought us five months in pretrial detention and certainly should not bring three years in prison as Mr. Prosecutor would have it.

With every passing day people understand more and more clearly that if the political system turns all its might

against three girls who spent a mere thirty seconds performing in the Cathedral of Christ the Savior, that means
only that this political system is afraid of the truth, afraid
of the sincerity and directness that we bring. We have not
lied for a second, we have not lied for one single moment
during this trial. Whereas the opposite side lies exces-
sively, and people sense this. People sense the truth.
Truth really does have an ontological, an existential ad-
vantage over lies. The Bible addresses this. In the Old
Testament, for example, the way of truth always triumphs
over the way of lies. And with every passing day, the way
of truth is triumphing more and more, despite the fact
that we are behind bars and will probably remain behind
bars for a very long time to come.

Madonna had a concert yesterday, and she performed
with the words PUSSY RIOT on her back. More and more
people are realizing that we are being held here illegally
and on the basis of thoroughly falsified charges. I am
struck by this. I am struck by the fact that truth really is
triumphing over lies even though physically we are here.
We have more freedom than the people who are sitting
opposite us, on the side of the accusers, because we can
say what we want and we do say what we want. Whereas
the people over there [Nadya pointed at the prosecutor],
they say only that which political censorship allows them
to say. They cannot say the words "'Mother of God, chase
Putin out,' a punk prayer," they cannot utter those lines in
the punk prayer that have to do with the political system.
Maybe they think that it would be good to send us to jail
because we have spoken out against Putin and his system.

But they cannot say that because they are forbidden. Their mouths are sewn shut, and here they are nothing but puppets, unfortunately. I hope that they realize this and that ultimately they too will choose the way of truth, the way of sincerity and freedom, because it exists on higher ground than rigidity and false piety and hypocrisy.

Rigidity is always the opposite of the search for truth. And in this case, at this trial, we see people who are trying to find some sort of truth on one side and, on the other side, people who want to shackle those who seek the truth. To be human is to err; humans are imperfect. Humans are always striving for wisdom, but it is always elusive. This is exactly how philosophy came to be. This is exactly why a philosopher is a person who loves wisdom and strives for it, but can never possess it. This is exactly what makes him think and act as he does. And this is exactly what moved us to enter the Cathedral of Christ the Savior. And I think that Christianity, as I have understood it studying the Old Testament but especially the New Testament, it supports the search for truth and the constant overcoming of one's self, of what you once were. There is a reason Christ was with the fallen women. He said, 'Help must go to those who have made mistakes, and I forgive them.' But I see none of this in our trial, which purports to represent Christianity. I think it's the prosecution that is affronting Christianity!

The victims' lawyers are starting to disown them. That's how I see it. Two days ago attorney Taratukhin gave a speech in this courtroom in which he said that people should understand that the lawyer does not by any means feel solidarity with people he represents. Apparently the attorney feels ethical unease at representing people who want to see three Pussy Riot participants go to jail. I don't know why they want to see us go to jail, but that's their right. I am just pointing out the fact that the attorney seems to feel shame. Hearing people shout "Shame!" and "Executioners!" at him has touched him after all. An attorney always has to stand for truth and goodness triumphing over evil and lies. It also seems to me that a higher power may be directing the speeches of our opponents: the lawyers keep misspeaking or making mistakes. They keep calling us "victims." They've all done this, including attorney Pavlova, who has a very negative view of us. And yet a higher power of some sort is forcing her to say "victims" about us, not about those whom she is representing. About us.

But I wouldn't affix any labels here. I don't think anyone here is winning or losing; there are no victims and no accused. We need to find a point of contact finally, start a dialogue and commence a joint search for the truth. Strive for wisdom together, be philosophers together rather than simply stigmatize and label people. This is the last thing a person should do, and Christ condemned it.

Here and now, in this court, we are being desecrated. Who would have thought that man and the state system he controls could commit utter, unmotivated evil over and over again. Who would have supposed that history, including the recent frightening experience of the Stalinist Great Terror, has taught us nothing. I want to cry looking at the way the methods of medieval inquisition take center stage in the law-enforcement and court systems of the Russian Federation, of my country. But ever since we were arrested we have lost our ability to cry. Back when we could stage our punk performances, we screamed as loud as we could and knew how to, about the lawlessness of the regime. But they have stolen our voices.

Throughout this trial, they have refused to hear us. I mean, hear. To hear is to listen and think, to strive for wisdom, to be a philosopher. I think every person should, in his heart, strive for this—not just the people who happened to major in some kind of philosophy. That means nothing. Formal education by itself means nothing, though attorney Pavlova keeps trying to accuse us of being insufficiently educated. I think that striving is the most important thing, striving to know and to understand. This is something a person can achieve on his own, without the help of an educational institution. No degree, no matter how advanced, can ensure this quality. A human being can possess a lot of knowledge but fail to be human. Pythagorus said that extensive knowledge does not breed wisdom.

I regret that we have to state this here. We serve merely as decorations, as inanimate objects, as bodies delivered to the courtroom. If our motions are even considered—and then only following days of requests, arguments, and struggle—they are invariably denied. But, unfortunately, regrettably for us and for this country, the court listens to the prosecutor, who misrepresents our words and statements over and over again with impunity, rendering them meaningless. The basic principle of equal justice is violated openly—indeed, this seems to be the point.

On July 30, on the first day of the trial, we presented our reaction to the charges. Our words were read aloud by attorney Volkova because the court would not then let us speak. This was our first opportunity to speak after five months in captivity. We had been in captivity, we had been behind bars, unable to do anything: we could not make statements, we could not make films, we did not have access to the Internet, and we could not even deliver a piece of paper to one of our lawyers because this is not allowed. On July 30, we spoke out for the first time. We called for contact and dialogue rather than confrontation. We extended a hand to those who have chosen to see us as the enemy. We were laughed at, and the hand we extended was spat upon. We were sincere in what we said, as we always are. We may be childishly naïve in insisting on our truth, but we nonetheless regret none of what we said, including what we said that day. And even as we are spoken ill of, we will not speak ill in return. Our circumstances are desperate, but we do not despair. We are persecuted, but we have not been abandoned. Those who are open are easy to humiliate and destroy, but "when I am weak then I am strong."

Listen to us. Listen to us and not to Arkady Mamontov* when he speaks about us. Do not distort every word we

---

*A prominent television journalist who made three consecutive films about Pussy Riot, aimed to show them as heretics and enemies of the Russian state. The films aired on state television in prime time.

say, and let us seek a dialogue, a point of contact with the country, which is our country too and not just Putin's and the patriarch's. Like Solzhenitsyn, I believe that in the end, words will break cement. Solzhenitsyn wrote, "So the word is more sincere than concrete? So the word is not a trifle? Then may noble people begin to grow, and their word will break cement."

Kat, Maria, and I are in jail. We are in a cage. But I don't think that we have been defeated. Just as the dissidents were not defeated. They were lost in psychiatric wards and the jails, but it was they who pronounced the regime's verdict. The art of creating the image of an era knows not winners and losers. The same way as the OBERIU* poets remained artists, truly inexplicable and incomprehensible, even after being purged in 1937. [The poet] Alexander Vvedensky wrote, "The inexplicable pleases us, and the incomprehensible is our friend." According to his official death certificate, Vvedensky died December 20, 1941. Cause of death is not known. He may have caught dysentery in the prison transport, or he may have caught a bullet from one of the guards. It happened somewhere along the railroad line from Voronezh to Kazan. Pussy Riot are Vvedensky's students and disciples. We consider his principle of the bad rhyme to be our own. He wrote, "It happens that two possible rhymes come to mind, a good one and a bad one. I choose the bad one. It is sure to be the right one."

---

*The Union of Real Art, a collective of futurist artists, writers, and musicians in the 1920s and '30s.

"The incomprehensible is our friend." The OBERIUs' elevated and refined pursuits, their search for thought at the edge of meaning, ultimately cost them their lives, taken by the senseless and truly inexplicable Great Terror. They paid with their lives to show that they had been right to believe that senselessness and lack of logic expressed their era best. They made art into history. The price of taking part in making history is always disproportionately large for the individual and his life. But it is also the meaning of human existence. "To be poor but enrich many. To have nothing but possess everything." The OBERIU dissidents are considered dead, but they are living. They have been punished but not killed.

Do you happen to remember why the young Dostoyevsky was sentenced to death? He was guilty only of having immersed himself in socialist theory. A group of freethinkers who gathered at Petrashevsky's apartment on Fridays discussed the work of George Sand. Toward the end of these Friday gatherings Dostoyevsky recited [literary critic Vissarion] Belinsky's letter to Gogol, filled, according to the court's conclusion, with—and here I want you to pay attention—"impudent statements against the Orthodox Church and the executive power." Dostoyevsky prepared to die. He spent, as he later wrote, ten "terrible, endlessly frightening" minutes waiting to be executed. Then his sentence was commuted to four years of hard labor followed by military service.

Socrates was accused of exerting a bad influence on young people with his philosophical discussions and of failing to recognize the gods of Athens. Socrates had a strong sense of an inner divine voice and he was by no means an enemy of the gods, as he stated repeatedly. But what did it matter, when Socrates annoyed the influential citizens of Athens with his critical, dialectical, and unbiased thinking? Socrates was sentenced to death. He declined his students' offers to help him escape and coolly drank the horn of poison, of hemlock, and died.

And have you perhaps forgotten how Stephen, the disciple of the apostles, ended his earthly life? "Then they secretly induced men to say, 'We have heard him speak blasphemous words against Moses and against God.' And they stirred up the people, the elders and the scribes, and they came up to him and dragged him away and brought him before the Council. They put forward false witnesses who said, 'This man incessantly speaks against this holy place and the Law.'" He was found guilty and stoned to death.

I also hope that you all remember well how the Jews answered Christ: "It is not for good works that we are going to stone you but for blasphemy." And finally we would do well to keep in mind the following characterization of Christ: "He is demon-possessed and raving mad."

I think that if the czars, the elders, the presidents, the premiers, the people, and the judges of this world knew well and understood the meaning of the phrase "I desire mercy, not sacrifice," they would not judge the innocent. But our rulers are in a rush to judge, never to show mercy. We should, incidentally, thank Dmitry Anatolyevich Medvedev for another in a series of remarkable aphorisms. He defined his term as president with the slogan "Freedom is better than unfreedom." Now Putin's third term may come to be characterized by a new aphorism: "Jail is better than stoning."

I ask you to think carefully about the following idea. Montaigne expressed it in his *Essays* in the sixteenth century. He wrote, "It is putting a very high value on one's conjectures, to have a man roasted alive because of them." And should flesh-and-blood people be tried and sent to jail based merely on the prosecution's suppositions, ones that have no basis in fact? We never have nor do we now have feelings of hatred or enmity on the basis of religion. As a result, our accusers have had to find people willing to bear false witness. One of them, Matilda Ivashchenko, felt ashamed and did not show up for court. That left the false testimony of Messrs. Troitsky and Ponkin as well as Ms. Abramenkova. There is no other evidence of enmity or hatred. If the court were honest and truthful, it would have to rule inadmissible the opinion of so-called experts, simply because it is not an objective scholarly text but a filthy, fraudulent scrap of paper that harkens back to the Middle Ages and the Inquisition. There is no other evidence that in any way points to motive.

The prosecution shies away from citing Pussy Riot song lyrics, because they would present the most obvious evidence of the lack of motive. I am going to quote something I like very much. I think this is very important. This is an interview we gave to the newsweekly *Russkiy Reporter* after the performance at the Cathedral of Christ: "We have respect for religion, including the Orthodox religion. This is precisely why we are outraged that the great, kind Christian philosophy has been used in such a filthy manner. We are raging because we see the best and finest that exists today being violated." We are still raging. And we feel real pain looking at all of this.

Every single defense witness has testified to the lack of any expression of hatred or enmity on our parts, even when they were asked to speak only to our individual personalities. In addition, I ask you to consider the results of the psychological and psychiatric evaluation conducted at the investigator's request in pretrial detention. The expert testified that the central values of my life are "justice, mutual respect, humanity, equality, and liberty." This was his expert opinion. This was a man who does not know me personally. And I suspect that Detective Ranchenkov would have wanted the expert to write something different. But it seems that people who love and value the truth are in the majority after all. Just as the Bible says.

And in conclusion I would like to quote a Pussy Riot song. Strange as it may seem, all of their songs turned out to be prophetic. Among other things, we prophesied that "the head of the KGB and the chief saint march the protesters to pretrial detention under guard." But what I want to quote now is, "Open the doors, rip off your epaulettes, taste the smell of freedom with us!" That's all.

The courtroom applauded. "Respected audience," said the judge with uncharacteristic deference but with a familiar note of irritation in her voice. "You are not in a theater. Alyokhina, please, you have the floor." Maria, who was wearing a black dress, made her closing statement.

This trial has spoken volumes. The regime will be made to feel ashamed of it for years to come. Its every step has been the quintessence of lawlessness.

How did our performance, a small and somewhat absurd act to begin with, balloon into a full-fledged catastrophe? Obviously, this could not have happened in a healthy society. The Russian state has long resembled a body riddled with disease. This is the kind of disease that bursts loudly when you accidentally prick a boil. This is the kind of disease that is concealed at first but later always finds its way into conversation and finds resolution in it. Look, this is the kind of conversation of which the regime is capable. This trial is not merely a grotesque evil mask: it is the face of the state as it addresses the individual in this country.

For an issue to become the topic of public discussion, something has to serve as the trigger. It's worth noting that our situation was depersonalized to begin with. When we speak of Putin, we mean not so much Vladimir Vladimirovich Putin but the system he has created: a power vertical that requires the state to be managed personally at every level. And this vertical contains no mechanism whatsoever for considering the opinion of the masses. And what worries me most of all is that there is no mechanism for considering the opinions of young people. We believe that this system of management is ineffective and that this is clear in everything it does.

I want to use my closing statement to describe my immediate experience of confronting this system.

A person's integration into society begins with the education system, and this system is designed to ignore individuality. There is no such thing as personalized education. Culture is not taught, nor is philosophy or the most basic of information about civil society. On paper, these classes exist, but they are still taught as they were in the Soviet Union. As a result, contemporary art is marginalized, the impulse toward philosophical thought is repressed, gender is stereotyped, and civil opinion is swept under the rug.

Contemporary educational institutions teach people to live on autopilot from the time they are children. They never pose important questions, even taking age into consideration, and they impart cruelty and an intolerance for dissidence. A person learns to forget about his liberty starting at a young age.

I have spent time at a psychiatric live-in facility for minors. And I can tell you with certainty that any adolescent who expresses dissident opinion more or less vocally can end up in a place like that. Some of the children arrive there from orphanages. If a child tries to run away from an orphanage, it is considered normal in our country to commit him to a psychiatric facility and treat him with the strongest of sedatives, such as aminazine, used to suppress Soviet dissidents back in the 1970s. This is particularly shocking considering these institutions' general punitive trend and the absence of psychological help as such. All communication there is based on fear and the children's forced subjugation. They become exponentially more cruel as a result. Many of the children are illiterate, but no one makes an effort to do anything about that. On the contrary, they do everything to quash the last remnants of any motivation to grow. The children shut down and stop trusting words.

I would like to note that this approach to shaping children obviously stands in the way of affirming inner freedom, including the freedom of religion, and also that it is typical, unfortunately. The result is a sort of ontological humility, resignation as a state of being in society. This transition—this break, really—is remarkable, because if we look at it from the point of view of Christian culture, we will see that senses and symbols are being replaced by their very opposites. Thus humility, one of Christianity's most important values, is reinterpreted not as a path to enlightenment and ultimately to liberation but, on the contrary, as a means of enslavement. To quote Nikolai Berdyaev, I would say that "the ontology of humility is the ontology of the slaves of God." And not the sons of God.

When I was an environmental organizer, I came to think of inner freedom as the foundation for all action. I also came to recognize the importance of action itself, action for the sake of action. I am still amazed that several thousand people are needed to stop the lawlessness of one or a handful of bureaucrats in our country. I would like to note that this trial has clearly shown this. The voices of thousands of people all over the world are needed to prove the obvious: that the three of us are innocent. The whole world is talking about this! The whole world is talking about this in concerts, on the Internet, in the media. They are talking about it in the parliaments. The English prime minister greets our president not with talk about the Olympic games but with a question about why three innocent girls are in jail. This is a disgrace.

I am even more amazed that people do not believe they can influence the authorities in any way. When I was organizing pickets and demonstrations, when I was collecting signatures and organizing the collection of signatures, I would often be asked, and asked with a sincere sort of incredulity, why anyone should care about a forest that may be unique in Russia, may be unparalleled, but still small, still just a spot on the map of the Krasnodar region? Why should anyone care that prime minister Dmitry Medvedev's wife is planning to build a residence there and destroy the only juniper preserve in Russia? These people—

This is further proof that in this country people no longer feel that the country's territory belongs to them, to the citizenry. These people no longer feel like citizens. They feel themselves to be a mass of automatons. They don't even feel that the forest that comes up right to their house belongs to them. I even doubt that they feel that they own their own home. Because if an excavator drives up to their door and these people are told that they have to evacuate the premises because, sorry, we are razing your house and building a residence for a bureaucrat, these people will humbly collect their things, pack their bags, and go out into the street. And they will sit out there in the street right up until the moment when the authorities tell them what to do next. They are totally spineless. This is very sad.

I have been in jail for almost six months, and I have realized that jail is Russia in miniature. You can start with the management: it's the same power vertical, where action is possible only when the boss himself intervenes. There is no horizontal distribution of responsibility, though this would make everyone's life a lot easier. There is no such thing as individual initiative. Snitching and mutual distrust are endemic. Just like in the country as a whole, in pretrial detention everything is done to dehumanize the individual, to turn him into a function, be it the function of an inmate or a guard. One quickly gets used to the restrictive daily routine because it resembles the restricted routine of life to which a person is subjected from birth. People start to treasure the little things. In jail it's things like a tablecloth or plastic dishes, which can only be procured with the personal permission of the boss. Out of jail, it's standing in society that people treasure just as much, and this is something I, for one, have never understood.

One more thing: the regime is a show that conceals what in reality is chaos. What looks orderly and restrictive is in fact disorganized and inefficient. Obviously, this does not lead to order. On the contrary, people feel acutely lost, in time and space among other things. As everywhere in the country, a person does not know where to go with a particular problem. So he goes to the head of the detention facility. That's like taking your problem to Putin outside of jail.

When we describe the system in our lyrics—

I guess you could say we are not really opposed—

We are in opposition to Putinist chaos, which is a regime in name only.

When we describe the system in our lyrics, we aim to convey our opinion that virtually all institutions are mutating, that while outwardly they remain intact, civil society, which we value so highly, is being destroyed, yet we do not make a direct statement. We merely utilize the form of a direct statement. We use it as an art form. The only thing that remains identical is motivation. Our motivation is identical to the motivation of a speaker making a direct statement. This motivation is described very well in the Gospels: "For everyone who asks receives; the one who seeks finds; and to the one who knocks, the door will be opened." I believe and we all believe that the door will be opened to us. But, alas, for now we have been shut in jail. It is very strange that in reacting to our actions, the authorities neglected to take into account the history of dissident expression.

"Woe unto the country where simple honesty is perceived as an act of heroism at best and a mental disorder at worst," wrote the dissident [Vladimir] Bukovsky in the 1970s. Not much time has passed, but it's like there was no Great Terror and no efforts to oppose it. I believe we stand accused by people who have no memory.

Many of them have said, "He is possessed by a demon and insane. Why do you listen to Him?" Those were words spoken by Jews who accused Jesus Christ of blasphemy. They said, "We are stoning you for blasphemy" [John 10:33]. It's remarkable that it is this verse that the Russian

Orthodox Church uses to express its own view of blasphemy. This view has been put down on paper and admitted into evidence as part of the case against us. In expressing this view the Russian Orthodox Church cites the Gospels as static religious truth. The Gospels are no longer seen as the revelations they were from the beginning. They are seen as a monolith that can be broken up into quotes to be stuffed anywhere, into any document, used for any purpose whatsoever. The Russian Orthodox Church did not even bother to look at the context in which the word *blasphemy* was used—and did not note that in this particular case it was applied to Jesus Christ.

I believe that religious truth cannot be static. I believe it is essential to understand that contradiction and splintering are inherent to the development of the spirit. That these things must be lived through as an individual is shaped. That religious truth is a process and not a product that can be stuffed just anywhere. Art and philosophy strive to make sense of all the things, all the processes I have mentioned. That includes contemporary art. The artistic situation can and, I think, should contain its own internal conflict. And I am very irritated that the prosecution refers to contemporary art as "so-called art."

I would like to note that the same expression was used in the trial of the poet [Joseph] Brodsky.* His poetry was referred to as "so-called poetry" and the witnesses who

---

*Brodsky stood trial for the crime of "social parasitism" in Leningrad in 1964. His "so-called poetry" was judged not to be work and he served eighteen months in exile in the Far North.

testified against him had not read it. Just as some of those who testified against us did not witness what happened but only saw the video on the Internet.

In the collective prosecutorial mind our apologies are also apparently characterized as "so-called." Though I find this insulting. It causes me suffering and moral harm. Because our apologies were sincere. I am so sad that we have said so many words and you have not understood any of them. Or are you lying when you talk of our apologies as though they were insincere? I don't understand: What more do you need to hear? For me, only this trial can rightly be referred to as "so-called." And I am not afraid of you. I am not afraid of lies and fictions and of poorly coded deception in the verdict of this so-called court, because all you can do is take away my so-called freedom, the only sort that exists in the Russian Federation. But no one can take away my inner freedom. It lives in my words and it will survive thanks to the public nature of my statements, which will be heard and read by thousands. This freedom is already multiplying, thanks to every caring person who hears us in this country. Thanks to everyone who has found splinters of this trial in themselves, as Franz Kafka and Guy Debord once did. I believe that openness and public speech and a hunger for the truth make us all a little bit freeer.

We will see this yet.

The courtroom applauded again. A marshal blew up: "Keep your emotions to yourself! You were all told this." Then came Kat.

In their closing statements people are usually expected either to repent or to express regret for what they have done, or to list extenuating circumstances. In my case, as in the cases of my colleagues in the band, this is completely unnecessary. Instead, I would like to share my thoughts about the reasons what happened to us has happened.

Ever since Vladimir Putin's former colleague Kirill Gundyaev became the head of the Russian Orthodox Church, most thinking people in this country have known that the Cathedral of Christ the Savior has turned into an important symbol of political strategy. After this, the Cathedral of Christ the Savior started to be used as a colorful interior for the politics of the uniformed forces, which hold most of the power.

Why did Putin have to use the Orthodox religion and its aesthetics at all? He could instead have used the more secular instruments of authority, such as the state corporations or his frightful police force or his pliable judicial system. It's possible that the failed hard-line politics of the Putin project, including the sinking of the Kursk submarine, the explosions that claimed the lives of civilians in broad daylight, and other unpleasant episodes of his political career have made him think about recusing himself before the citizens of Russia decide to help him along in this. This must be when he decided he needed to have more convincing, transcendental guarantees of staying in power in Russia for a long time. This is when the need for using the aesthetics of the Orthodox religion, with its historical connection to the best times of the Russian empire, when authority was derived not from such earthly expressions as democratic elections and civil society but from God himself.

But how did he manage this, considering the state is supposed to be secular and any intersection of the religious and political spheres is meant to be curtailed by society, which is always on guard and thinking critically?

I guess the authorities were exploiting a certain absence of the Orthodox aesthetic in Soviet times, when the Orthodox religion had an air of lost history about it, something suppressed and harmed by the Soviet totalitarian regime, and that made it part of the culture of the opposition. The authorities decided to appropriate this historical sense of loss and present their new political project of restoring the lost spiritual values of Russia, which had a rather vague relationship to any sincere concern for preserving Orthodox history and culture. Logically enough, the Russian Orthodox Church, which has a longstanding mystical connection to the state, became the main agent of this project in the media. It was also decided that the Russian Orthodox Church should counteract all the detrimental influences of contemporary mass culture, with its concepts of diversity and tolerance, as opposed to the Soviet period, when the Church mainly opposed the violence done by the authorities against history itself.

This political project, interesting as it was from a variety of standpoints, required a large amount of multi-ton professional lighting and video equipment, air time on the central television channel for live broadcasts lasting many hours, and, subsequently, many more hours of filming for news stories aimed at reinforcing the moral fabric by means of transmitting the patriarch's seamless speeches, meant to help believers make the right choice at this difficult time in Putin's life, before the election. The filming had to be ongoing, the necessary images had to be burned into memory and continuously renewed, creating the impression of something that is natural, permanent, and nonnegotiable.

Our sudden musical appearance at the Cathedral of Christ the Savior with our song "Mother of God, Chase Putin Out" disturbed the integrity of this media image, created by the authorities over time, and exposed its falsehood. Without securing the patriarch's blessing, we dared in our performance to combine the visual images of Orthodox culture and the culture of protest, making intelligent people suspect that Orthodox culture may belong not only to the Russian Orthodox Church, the patriarch, and Putin: it can end up on the side of civil riot and the protest culture in Russia. It is possible that the unpleasant large-scale effect of our media intrusion into the cathedral surprised the authorities themselves. At first they tried to portray our performance as a prank by a bunch of soulless militant atheists. But they missed the mark by a lot because by this time we were already known as an anti-Putin feminist punk band that commits media attacks on the country's main political symbols. In the end, after they had appraised all the irreversible political and symbolic losses brought on by our innocent art, the authorities decided after all to protect society from us and our nonconformist way of thinking. Thus ended our complicated punk adventure at the Cathedral of Christ the Savior.

I have mixed feelings right now about this trial. On one hand, we are expecting a guilty verdict now. Compared to the judicial machine, we are nobodies and we have lost. On the other hand, we have won. The entire world can see now that the case against us is trumped up. The system cannot hide the repressive nature of this trial. Yet again the world sees Russia not as Vladimir Putin tries to present it in his daily international meetings. None of the steps he has promised to take toward a rule-of-law society have actually been taken. And his declaration that the court in our case will be objective and will announce a just decision is yet another lie told to the whole country and the world. That's all. Thank you.

The judge scheduled the sentencing for August 17, eight days later. Nadya, Maria, and Kat spent those days back in pretrial detention, going over all the signs. The prosecutor had asked for three years, but some of the victims' lawyers had asked for a suspended sentence. Plus, Putin had said the sentence should not be too harsh. All of this pointed to a suspended sentence. On the other hand, Mark Feigin, who had grown glum right after the probable-cause hearing and never really recovered, had talked about a possible sentence of a year and a half. But he had also said he would petition to have the three women kept in pretrial detention if the sentence was that short—short?—and they could work in the same jail where they were now, perhaps in the kitchen or, better yet, the library. This seemed like a good option to Kat, though Maria and Nadya were thinking they might prefer a prison colony to the cramped monotony of jail. And then again, Volkova had mentioned that hooliganism was the kind of offense that, if you were found guilty, always got you three years of real time. That could happen too. It had clearly happened to a lot of other people.

———————

THE CROWD GATHERED in front of the courthouse on August 17 looked happy. It was a sunny day, and the faces in the crowd were so good, so familiar, that it seemed nothing terrible could happen. Back when people used to come to the courthouse for arrest hearings, someone—perhaps it was Petya—had coined the term *cultural festival* to replace *protest* or *vigil*. It had been forgotten since, but now the atmosphere actually felt festive. There was music, some people held up witty signs, and an occasional balaclava could be glimpsed. Orthodox believers were there too, with their signs, but, being clearly outnumbered by Pussy Riot supporters, they looked like bad actors playing themselves and not at all scary.

The judge began reading the verdict just after three. It was "guilty," which surprised no one, but, following the tradition of Russian courts, the judge would plow through a tedious recounting of most testimony heard and evidence reviewed in the course of the trial before announcing the sentence; it could take hours. Some of the people in the crowd tuned their phones to radio stations that had reporters in the courthouse and stuck earphones in their ears; clumps of people convened around these listeners, looking at them expectantly, as though something depended on being first to hear the news.

"In sum, and in light of the danger to society caused by the offense committed, as well as the circumstances of the crime and its goals and motives," the judge said just before six in the evening, "the court believes that justice can be served and the defendants can be reformed only if they are sentenced to time behind bars and are ordered to actually serve this time."

"Two years," said the people with headphones throughout the crowd.

"Two years," the entire crowd sighed at once.

A shadow fell over hundreds of faces. The festivities were over. The mood had darkened.

It was as though something had fallen with a loud bang. A retired woman in the building across the street from the courthouse heard the sound and called the police. They discovered the sound had come from the roof, where someone had dropped a padlock. The police found a young man on the roof, and a lot of equipment: microphones, amplifiers, and four speakers large enough to blast the sound through the neighborhood, certainly large enough to make sure the windows of the courtroom across the narrow street shook. The police also found rock-climbing equipment.

It would have been a spectacular action. Three women were going to descend the wall of the building, tethered to cables hung from the roof, wearing balaclavas and singing:

> In jail the state is stronger than time.
> The more arrests there are, the happier.
> Every arrest is a gift of love to the sexist
> Who has been pumping his cheeks the way he pumps his
>   chest and his abs.
> But you can't put us in a box.

Overthrow the Chekists,* do it better and more often.

Putin lights the fire of revolution.

He is bored and frightened of silence.

An execution to him is a rotten ashberry†

*And a long prison sentence a cause for nocturnal
    emissions.*

*The country is on the march, marching in the streets with
    nerve,*

*The country is on the march, marching to say good-bye to
    the regime,*

*The country is on the march, marching in feminist
    formation.*

And Putin is on the march, marching to say good-bye.

Put the whole city in jail for May 6.‡

Seven years is not enough, give us eighteen.

Ban screaming, libel, going outside,

And take Lukashenko§ to be your wife.

---

*Chekists were members of the Cheka, the first incarnation of the Soviet secret police. The term has become generic for secret-police officers.

†This is an allusion to a line from Osip Mandelstam's Stalin epigram, which is believed to have gotten the poet arrested and ultimately killed in prison. In the Mandelstam poem, Stalin enjoyed executions like one enjoys raspberries; in the Pussy Riot version, Putin had a bad taste in his mouth.

‡A peaceful march with tens of thousands of participants on May 6, 2012, the eve of Putin's inauguration for his third term as president, turned into a riot after the marchers were attacked by police. Hundreds of people were detained that day and soon released, but by the time this song was written, more than a dozen were facing charges and likely prison time in connection with the clashes.

§Alexander Lukashenko, president of Belarus, once known as "the last dictator in Europe"—until Putin himself reached dictator status.

It had been a beautifully prepared action. The song had been mastered ahead of time, so it would blast from the speakers as the women descended the wall. The three women had trained with experienced rock climbers, practicing on abandoned buildings outside of Moscow. And they had hauled all that equipment up on the roof during the night. And Petya had told Pussy Riot's international supporters to expect a big surprise after the sentencing, and his contact people had told everyone else. Some people thought this meant Pussy Riot would be released an hour or two after the sentencing.

But then someone had dropped a padlock.

PART 3

Punishment

TEN

Kat

"THE DRIVE BACK after the sentencing was very strange. It was an open prisoner transport, the first time we had an open one." Kat made it sound like they were taken back to jail in a convertible. It was just a prisoner transport with plain windows: no dark film, no curtains. It was a rambling old bus with the three of them and several special forces officers in riot gear inside. They could see the city and breathe its dusty summer air. Nadya was agitated, and one might have thought she felt happy. Maria had an emotionless air about her. She said, "That's that," as though she had expected this all along, which she had not. Kat felt angry. She cursed Putin and the patriarch. It was like she had nothing to lose—and neither did the special forces guys, who failed to reprimand her; one of them asked to have his picture taken with the three of them. They got to the jail. Nadya hugged Kat, then Maria, then Kat again. That was that.

All talk in the "spec" was now of life in penal colonies. This struck Kat as nothing more than a coincidence: one of her cellmates had also recently been sentenced, and another one would be sentenced imminently, so the only experienced one in the cell, a woman who called herself Irina Orlova, was telling them about life in the colonies morning to night now. To be more precise, she was telling them how awful it would be. She started with the hardships of the transport; some women spent grueling weeks going from train to transit jail back to train, lugging all their crap each time, facing hazing and sleepless nights at every step. "I don't know if you'll make it," Orlova would say before moving on to the ways of the colonies. There would be hundreds of people to a barracks, she said. There would be work, unremitting, backbreaking slave labor. There would be no hot water, and the toilets would be outdoors. And the colony would likely be someplace where it was winter most of the year—with a break for a short scorching summer when the mosquitoes ate you alive and the smell spreading from the outdoor toilets knocked you over. The two less experienced inmates acted terrified. They sighed, perhaps cried a little; one of them kept repeating "I hope they don't make me go" over and over again, and then asked for more detail.

The technique of placing an older, more experienced inmate in a cell to cow and pressure younger ones into a pliable state in which they might sign confessions and testify against themselves and others—in the usually unfounded hope of securing release—went back to at least the middle of the twentieth century. Kat did not wonder why Orlova was apparently doing everything she could to frighten her cellmates. She did not wonder if it was too much of a coincidence that three of the four of them faced sentencing at roughly the same time. And, of course, she did not wonder what Orlova or whoever might have sent her could possibly want from her; after all, the trial was over and Kat was about to be shipped off to a penal colony. She just hoped it would not be that far away and the toilets would be indoors. And she really worried about surviving the transport. Whatever Orlova might or might not have been trying to do was working.

Kat escaped the harping and the whining by thinking back over the trial, reviewing it in her head day by day, hour by hour, minute by minute. It had all happened so fast. As she rewound and replayed her mental recording, she noticed new things—many new things—and they made her very angry. The defense attorneys had handled so many things so badly. There was the time Volkova ran out of the courtroom. The time Feigin snapped at the judge. The time Volkova read out the very long text of an expert opinion they had commissioned— it seemed to Kat that Volkova was simply unprepared and had nothing to say at the hearing that day. And anyway, how could she be prepared when she barely spoke to Kat? She rarely came to see her at the jail, and now, after the sentencing, with an appeal pending, she seemed to have disappeared altogether: friends were telling her they could not get hold of her.

She also suspected that the lawyers were in cahoots with Petya. They had bad-mouthed him to Kat, but this meant nothing, and anyway, they all seemed interested in the same thing: money. Petya wanted to trademark Pussy Riot, to produce a record, to have the group go on tour, and the lawyers were right there with him. They had even had Kat sign a document allowing them to register Pussy Riot the brand. This was what they discussed with her during their infrequent visits in jail—instead of talking about her defense strategy. In fact, they probably realized it was better, from the point of view of commerce, to have her and Nadya and Maria do time. It would make the story more compelling and the enterprise more profitable.

Some of the episodes Kat recalled had reasonable explanations of which she was not aware. For example, Volkova's reading expert testimony out loud was an ingenious ploy to get it into the court record after the judge had refused to allow the expert's opinion into evidence. Other incidents, such as the running out of the courtroom or the snapping at the judge, were true lapses that could only be explained by the lawyers' lack of experience and the extreme stress they were under. Still others really were expressions of profit seeking and, to an even greater extent, vanity. For example, as Kat lay on her bunk day after day mentally sifting through evidence from the trial and her friends kept dialing Volkova and the other lawyers to no avail, the lawyers were in New York, helping Petya collect the LennonOno Grant for Peace on behalf of Pussy Riot; Petya had not asked for their help.

Could the women have gotten a lighter sentence if they had had different lawyers? Kat grew convinced that they could have. After all, their lawyers had been objectively terrible: unprepared, incoherent, in addition to being rude, disrespectful of the court, and just plain ugly and stupid. Was Kat supposed to believe that if she had had, say, a smart, professional, attractive, well-spoken, hardworking, well-prepared defense attorney, she would still have been sentenced to two years behind bars? Was she supposed to believe that having a lawyer made no difference whatsoever and you could dispense with the whole pretense of the trial and just wait for Putin to name his price? That is probably what the legal trio would want her to believe—that would conveniently absolve them of all responsibility past and future—but Kat refused to believe that nothing could have made any difference. And if the choice of lawyers mattered, then the fact that she had had the worst ones on earth had to matter. It was their fault she had been in jail for six months and was about to be shipped off to an overcrowded, freezing penal colony with outdoor toilets.

Orlova and the other two kept going over the same depressing details of penal colony life; it was like their conversation was stuck in an endless loop. But inside Kat, something was changing. Despair was giving way to a new feeling, a desire to act—a desire for vengeance. It was probably too late to do something about her sentence. But it was not too late to teach the lawyers a lesson. She would disgrace them by firing them from the biggest trial of their careers.

———————

KAT KNEW SHE WAS RIGHT, but she also knew she should try to talk to Nadya and Maria about this. How, though? Ask one of the three lawyers to carry a note saying she wanted to fire them? They had offered their services before, saying they would deliver notes back and forth without looking at them, but Kat had never quite trusted their assurances—and she certainly did not now. She decided to write a note that suggested adding another lawyer to the team. Maybe that would get them thinking.

The ploy did not work. Volkova said she was searched on

the way out of the jail that day and had to dispose of the note; communication between defenders in the same criminal case is strictly forbidden, and a lawyer can be disqualified for facilitating it. Kat did not believe Volkova; she was sure lawyers never got searched. (She was wrong; lawyers do get searched, though the law forbids this.)

Kat found herself agreeing to have her fortune told by Orlova. The senior cellmate had some technique: you had to have drunk a cup of coffee yourself and dumped the grounds on a napkin that preserved whatever picture they had formed at the bottom of the cup. Orlova told fortunes incessantly—mostly her own—and Kat the computer programmer, Kat who did not have a mystical bone in her body, looked upon this disdainfully. But Orlova kept offering, and as Kat found herself growing closer and closer to Orlova—she had to admit she had been warming to her since early in the summer, the woman was so consistently kind and attentive to her—she also found herself saying, "Yeah, whatever, go ahead, I don't care."

Orlova said, "I see space all around you buzzing. I see a man running toward you." Kat thought maybe it was her new lawyer.

Two women from a human rights organization came to see Kat; they were the only people, aside from lawyers and immediate relatives, who could get visitation rights, and they had been coming occasionally. Kat had her doubts about whether she could trust them, but she decided to tell them she was firing her lawyers. They told her to be cautious, to think twice, to consider her own reputation, and Nadya's and Maria's. She told them she did not care. Once she convinced them of her resolve, one of them gave her detailed instructions about getting it done: make sure you have the motion in writing; tell the court you have a difference of opinions on your defense; and tell the court you already have a new lawyer—if you have no one to represent you, the court may deny your motion because then you will be lawyerless. Kat did not have a new lawyer. But by this time she was convinced that having no lawyer was better than having Volkova or the other two.

The next day one of the human rights women came back. "Don't do it," she told Kat. "It's not going to help. You are still going to go to the penal colony, but your reputations will be ruined." Kat objected. She said the lawyers were dishonest; she said they had been signing commercial contracts on the group's behalf; she said they and Petya were in cahoots. "What does it all matter?" the woman said, exasperated. It mattered to Kat. Also, she was certain this woman, who claimed to be a human rights advocate, was doing the lawyers' bidding. This only strengthened her resolve.

In fact, the human rights advocate had had virtually no contact with the lawyers. She was just sincerely convinced that, since Kat had no hope of changing her sentence, her firing the lawyers would be seen by the public as what it was: an act of vengeance. With so much attention still fixed on the trial, this seemed like an ill-chosen coda.

THE MORNING OF OCTOBER 1, when Pussy Riot's appeal was scheduled to be heard in Moscow City Court, Orlova gave Kat a pill. She said it was for her nerves, something mild. Kat figured they wouldn't have let her have a serious sedative in the cell. She took it, and she did not feel anything in particular.

Then they had their hair done. It was another misplaced act of goodwill; someone from the support group had paid for hair services for them, and the woman in charge of the jail's so-called salon thought it would be a good idea to give each of them a wash and blow-dry the morning of the appeal. So six weeks after they were sentenced, Kat, Nadya, and Maria met at the hair place.

Kat started by broaching the subject of money and contracts the lawyers had apparently been signing on their behalf. Maria said she knew something about this and had asked Polozov to provide the documents.

"Why should you be asking him to provide stuff?" Kat was outraged. "He should be bringing all this stuff to you without being asked."

"Why are you being so loud?" Nadya asked Kat.

"Because I'm irritated. I'm angry."

"So I guess you'll be firing them," said Nadya.

"I'm firing them," Kat confirmed.

"I'm not," said Maria.

"I'm not either," said Nadya. Then she said it was going to look bad. She said the lawyers were perceived as opposition lawyers and the firing would look like a split in the group, or even like they had broken Kat. She asked Kat to give it some more thought. Kat said she had given it all the thought it needed.

In the prisoner transport going to court, Kat threw up. It might have been that pill.

In court, things went just as the human rights activist had predicted: the judge tried to ignore Kat's attempts to make a motion, then finally asked if she had it in written form, accepted it reluctantly, and, hearing that Kat already had another lawyer lined up but that the lawyer needed time to get acquainted with the case, granted the motion and continued the hearing until October 10. Then there were a lot of cameras clicking, most of them aimed at Kat for the first time since the trial began, and a lot of microphones and Dictaphones being pushed out of the way by the court marshals, and then they were back in the prisoner transport and back at the jail. Nadya and Maria did not seem to be angry at Kat; they even said that now, thanks to her, they could pressure their lawyers into working harder and being more attentive—lest they also get fired by the two of them.

———————————

THE NEXT DAY, a prison guard told Kat to come out of her cell "lightly." That was the opposite of going "with your stuff." If you are being transferred, or even going to court, you always go with your stuff—all your stuff, including soap and books and food—because you do not know if you are coming back to your cell. If you are told to come out "lightly," you are just going for a talk, probably within the jail compound.

Kat was taken to see one of the female inspectors.

"I heard you fired your lawyers."

"Yes."

"They'll probably be going after you now, trying to come see you, pressure you."

Kat had no idea what this woman wanted.

"So just so you know, if one of the three of them comes, we are going to let you know and you can say you don't want to see them. You should put it in writing, and then we can tell them to get lost."

"Okay."

They sat in silence for a minute.

"Can I go back to my cell now?" Kat asked.

"Wait, sit here awhile," the officer said. She seemed sympathetic, and Kat felt, if not touched exactly, at least surprised by the concern she was showing. "I heard there is now a vodka called Pussy Riot," the inspector continued. "Your old lawyers seem to have had something to do with it."

Kat was surprised by her familiarity with Pussy Riot and its issues. She had never thought prison staff paid attention. But she had no desire to discuss this with her.

"Can I go back to my cell?" she asked again.

The inspector, apparently peeved, had her escorted back.

THE FOLLOWING DAY, they came for her again; again she had to come "lightly."

"Your lawyer is here."

"The old one?"

"The new one."

The new lawyer was definitely not the man Orlova had seen in the coffee grounds. She was a diminutive blonde in her midthirties. She wore her hair in a ponytail. She handed Kat a letter from her closest friends in the support group; the letter said the lawyer's name was Irina Khrunova, and she was "big guns." She did not look like big guns, but she got right down to business.

"I want to know why you fired your lawyers," she said. "I doubt you have enough information about the trial to have 'a difference of opinions' on the defense, so I'm assuming that's just a phrase you used. What's the real reason?"

Kat told her as much as she could of what she noticed as she had thought back over the trial, and the money stuff, the contracts, and even the vodka.

"I see," said Khrunova. "That's called loss of trust. I'll be your lawyer, then." And she said she had to go read the case and think about their next step.

Back in the cell, Orlova was reading Kat's coffee grounds. "I see a lot of media attention," she said. "I see the penal colony, with a tall fence around it. I don't see you behind that fence. I don't know why, but I don't see you behind that colony fence."

The new lawyer came back a few days later, two days before the next hearing. "I am pleased," she said. "I have found a lot of mistakes." She was going to tell the court what Volkova and the others had omitted: that Kat had not actually taken part in the actions for which the three of them were convicted of hooliganism.

The omission had been intentional: Volkova, Polozov, and Feigin had respected Pussy Riot's commitment to anonymity in their defense. More important, they had pointedly refused to engage the court on charges they and their defendants considered absurd. But what might have been a coherent political stand looked absurd as a legal strategy, thought Khrunova. What she was doing was going back to the venerable tradition of defense attorneys who had represented Soviet dissidents: they had often had a clear division of roles with their clients. While the defendant objected to the charges as such and sometimes even claimed not to understand them, the lawyer would look for ways to lessen his client's punishment within the existent legal framework. Khrunova would now do the same: while Kat as a person might choose not to be differentiated from her comrades who committed the sacrilege of lip-synching, Kat as her client should get the benefit of having bungled her way out of performing.

"What are my chances?" asked Kat.

"I don't know," said Khrunova. "You know how unpredictable it all is. All I can tell you is I see a legal mistake here and I am doing everything I can to correct it. But I can't promise you anything."

Kat felt she should talk to Nadya and Maria, so she decided to do something she had not dared to do in her six months in the jail: she would try to talk to Maria through one of the forbidden routes. She knew Maria was in the cell right above hers. Normally, that would open the way for passing notes and even simply talking through the open windows, but the first and second floors were separated by an additional horizontal barrier that extended out from the building's outside wall; it made passing notes extremely difficult and it even got in the way of shouting.

So Kat decided to knock on the ceiling using a bucket. Orlova gave her blessing. If an inmate was caught communicating with other inmates, the entire cell was penalized, but Orlova said, "We see that you have to get in touch with her, so go ahead. We'll cover for you."

While one of her cellmates stood watch by the door to make sure no one was looking in from the hallway, Kat knocked. And knocked again. And again. Finally, she got a response: a single knock. What in the world could a single knock mean? For that matter, what could a series of knocks mean?

"Either you are really stupid and can't figure out how to communicate, or something else is going on," said Orlova. In fact, something else was going on: an inspection in Maria's cell just as the knocking began—at the worst possible moment. Maria had simply stomped on the floor to try to get Kat to stop.

Orlova, meanwhile, let fly a series of curses and instructed Kat to try shouting out the window. Since sound would not carry over the horizontal barrier, Kat needed to ask a cell kitty-corner from hers but on the second floor to relay a message. Orlova had taught her she could not just stick her head out and ask for a favor; she had to make small talk first.

"Hey, two-oh-eight," Kat shouted to the cell on the floor above. "How is it going? Any chance you can call out to two-ten?"

"All right, let's see. Their windows are closed. Another time, then."

But Kat hardly had any time. So a few hours later she knocked on the ceiling first and then opened the window and started screaming. She felt she was so loud the entire jail could hear her. "Two-ten!" she screamed until she was hoarse. "Two-ten!"

She finally heard Maria's high-pitched voice.

"What's up with the lawyers?" Kat screamed.

"Same old," screamed Maria.

Kat tried screaming something else, or hearing something else, until she finally heard Maria shout: "Wait! I'll write!"

Kat waited all night and then all morning. She stopped waiting only when an inspection started in her cell. In this weekly ritual, jail staff went through literally all their belongings, first laying them out as though on display, then examining them, sometimes confiscating them or disposing of them. Maria's rope with the weighted sock at the end, with a letter inside the sock, made its appearance in the window at the worst possible moment: just as the inspectors appeared in the doorway. Orlova panicked and hissed at Kat—"Idiots"—but the inspectors, miraculously, noticed nothing. As soon as the door closed behind the inspectors, Kat ran for the window.

The sock dangled about four feet away; the horizontal barrier had pushed the rope out that far. Orlova grumbled but quickly fashioned the tool Kat should have made by now: a broomstick, or something like it, with a hook at the end, made of twisted pages torn from glossy magazines—someone had sent Kat a copy of the Russian edition of *National Geographic*, which she hated ripping up, but which made the best possible hook. She used the hook to pull the rope into the window and remove the sock. Soon she placed her response back in the same sock, tied it to the rope, gently guided it out the window with the help of the hook, and tugged on it to signal the upstairs cell to pull it up. Kat was terrible at working the hook, so Orlova did it for her.

Still, the fourth letter in the exchange—Kat's response to Maria's second note—broke off from the rope and tumbled down to the ground in its sock. For all their effort, they had barely managed to have a conversation. Maria wrote Kat a note about fund-raising efforts in the United States, but it assumed too much knowledge and Kat did not understand anything.

Kat wrote back outlining her new defense and urging Maria to try to get a lawyer who would represent all three of them so they could at least communicate with one another. Maria wrote, "I'm sorry the lawyers have been saying horrible things about you. But don't worry about that right now. I am worried about you. I don't like the state you are in." This hurt Kat's feelings, but her response never made it upstairs. She had written, "If they'd been like that to you, I would have fired them."

And there was no chance of communicating with Nadya at all; she was all the way up on the third floor. Anyway, Kat did not think there was a point to talking to her. Nadya always knew exactly what was going on.

———

THE MOOD IN THE PRISONER transport was all wrong. Kat did not know what to say, and so kept quiet. At one point Maria and Nadya started speaking to each other. But in the cage, when they saw Khrunova, they addressed Kat together, laughing: "So you got yourself a younger, better-looking lawyer!" Khrunova always wore tailored dresses to hearings, with a cardigan sobering up the outfit. She looked as different as a woman could look from the obese Volkova.

Kat was the first to make a statement. She said the action had been political. "We didn't want to offend anyone. And if we did, we said we are sorry. But a punk prayer is not a crime." She then switched from first-person plural to first-person singular and quickly muttered that she had not actually done anything at the cathedral.

Maria had prepared a long speech, in which she intended to reiterate what she had said during the trial. She had said in the prisoner transport that she would keep repeating her message as long as it took to get through to people. "We are serving time for our political beliefs, and even if we are sent to a prison colony, we are not going to keep quiet, no matter that you want us to," she said, apparently addressing the court.

"Stick to the topic at hand," said the judge.

"I'd like to address Putin's statement regarding 'slapping us with a two-ie.'"

The judge raised her voice. "Topic at hand!"

"I'm still going to say it. Unlike Putin, I can say the name of our group out loud. It's called Pussy Riot. And that sounds and is a lot better than his calls for 'snuffing the enemy out in the outhouse,'" she said, referring to a speech that first made Putin popular in Russia back in 1999. After this, the judge started shouting and people both inside and outside the courtroom started applauding, and no one could hear anything anymore.

Most of Nadya's speech was drowned out by the screaming and the applause. She said the case had proven the repressive nature of the Russian state. "I demand a reversal of the verdict, and I want to warn you that Putin's continued rule will drive the country to civil war." She had raised her voice.

"This is not an election campaign!" screamed the judge, even louder.

The three old lawyers' speeches turned into a shouting match between them and the judge, so ultimately only the words *president*, *church*, and *demand* could be distinguished.

But Khrunova addressed a hushed courtroom.

She said she did not think Nadya, Maria, and Kat had committed a crime. But, she added, Kat had not even taken part in the actions the court had deemed criminal: "She did not jump, pray, or sing."

She spoke for no more than seven minutes, and then, almost immediately, she realized something was wrong. One after another, the so-called victims' lawyers rose and said something good about her, her speech, and her position, even though they said they disagreed with it. They said she had made a great speech. They said it was a relief to hear legal arguments after a trial dominated by political speechifying. They said they respected her. Khrunova felt like she had stepped into a trap, though she could not figure out who had set it or for what purpose. Her best-case guess would be that everyone, including the other side, was so genuinely tired of the farce they had been witnessing instead of a trial that a plain, clear, decidedly legal speech seemed so refreshing that they were moved to praise her—in unison. Her worst-case guess would be that this was a setup in which Kat was either a willing participant or an unwitting pawn whose role it was to break ranks—and be rewarded for it.

THE JUDGE TOOK forty minutes to make a decision. Kat waited in a tiny room with a stranger, a defendant in a different case who could not stop talking. Kat was trying to think, though she was not sure what she was trying to think about; the woman kept interrupting her efforts, and Kat could not figure out what the woman wanted, though for some reason it appeared to be pity.

The judge read her decision: she left Nadya's and Maria's sentences unchanged but changed Kat's to a suspended two-year sentence. "The defendant is to be released in the courtroom."

Maria jumped up and started hugging Kat, squeezing her hard, trying to put into this hug all the joy that had washed over her. Nadya looked stricken and momentarily lost, and then she too stepped over to hug Kat. She seemed to be in a bad mood, but she had seemed to be in a bad mood on the way over to the court as well, and Kat thought this was perfectly understandable on the eve of her being shipped off to a penal colony.

The marshals opened the cage door. Nadya and Maria were led out in handcuffs, as usual. A marshal uncuffed Kat and told her to come with him. He took to her to a room downstairs and told her to wait for her papers and left her—left her alone in a room with no handcuffs, a window with no grates—and she paced the room like a free woman for half an hour as she waited for her papers. Out in the hallway, Stanislav Samutsevich teared up as he gave interviews and teared up again as he looked at Maria's mother.

Kat finally got her papers and stepped out on the porch. There were many cameras—she had a sense that Orlova had mentioned seeing something like this in her coffee grounds—and many microphones, and Kat just stood on the porch for a few minutes, until two young men came up very close to her. She knew one of them—he had helped with some actions—and he said, "You can trust him" about the other, and they led her away from the courthouse. At one point one of them said, "Let's run," and they ran.

ELEVEN

Maria

Hi, Olya,

*Today is October 30. I am in a pretrial detention center
in Perm. I am to be shipped from here to a penal colony
sometime very soon. I don't know which colony it's going to
be, but it's definitely in the Perm region, and here there are
only two of them: one is within city boundaries, the other
about 150 km away. All of this probably sounds silly; with
access to the Internet, you probably have more knowledge
about my whereabouts than I do. It's been almost a week
and a half since I left the pretrial detention facility in
Moscow. I feel an acute lack of information. I spent four days
in Kirov and no one came—I mean none of the lawyers did.**

---

*No one else came either, but the defense attorneys would have been virtually
the only ones in a position to demand a meeting with Maria. It is not, however, standard practice for defense attorneys to visit their clients while they are in transit.

Two weeks without communicating makes me extremely anxious. I feel awkward admitting that. I have six envelopes left, and this is the only thing that gives me a bit of hope: I send out letters without the slightest idea whether they are going to be received. I had the wherewithal to take about 30 kilos of stuff with me when I left Moscow, so I still have some reserves of food, but these will not last me more than 2 weeks (and that only if I am very frugal). Meanwhile, the absurd system for transferring funds from pretrial detention to the penal colony means they will not get there for an entire month after I finally arrive. And there is still no sign of the lawyers. I mentally curse them up and down. The helplessness makes me want to stomp my feet or go on a hunger strike.

You can't imagine how much I want to know something, anything, about what's going on in Moscow. I suspect interest has dropped and will only continue to drop from now on. Of course this matters to me, but it's not paramount. I still believe in the power of the gesture, the power of taking a stand—and there will always be people who will see it and understand, I am sure of this.

None of the scary stuff they told me about the transport was true. The transfer process is hugely engaging, albeit physically exhausting. I have put together a list of things that need to be done to make the system at least remotely resemble a humane one. Now I'm wondering who I should give this list to. I'm writing in a journal a bit, reading

Mamardashvili* a bit, and hoping not to lose my mind—or,
if I lose it, to do it publicly. Don't forget me!

Dear Olya,

I don't know how to begin this letter. December. You may
place any punctuation mark after that word and still it will
barely begin to describe what I feel. It is already December,
it is only December, it really is December—or is it?
Something tells me you'll get this letter when everyone is
frantically getting ready for the New Year while I continue
to sit in this "safe place." I'd wanted to write right away
after you came to see me here, but then I couldn't and now
it's December 2.

MARIA ARRIVED at Penal Colony Number 28 in early November. By the time she was out of "quarantine"—solitary confinement that launches the term of incarceration in the colony—snow had covered the grounds and blizzards were a daily occurrence. This was the colony about one hundred and twenty miles from Perm, in the town of Berezniki. One of Russia's oldest industrial towns, with four large chemical plants dominating its economy and its difficult air, Berezniki had been completely rebuilt in the 1960s. It looked like scores of identical gray-brick five-story buildings had been airlifted and

---

*Merab Mamardashvili (1930–1990) was a Soviet Georgian philosopher.

dropped in perfectly indistinguishable parallel and perpendicular rows.

Penal Colony 28, one of two colonies in the city, sat at the outskirts of Berezniki; a solid concrete fence topped with barbed wire surrounded a grouping of two-story buildings, sloppily assembled of the same gray brick. Each block housed two units, one per floor. The space available would accommodate around seventy people if inmates were housed in accordance with official instructions, but the administration managed to squeeze twice that number into the metal beds that formed a tight grid in the vast, unpartitioned bedroom space. Small wooden cubbies separated the beds, one for every two inmates. Any personal belongings that could not be concealed in this tiny space had to be packed into an enormous black bag stuffed, along with scores of other enormous black bags, into a storage space.

A unit's quarters included, in addition to the giant bedroom, a kitchen with two tables, a refrigerator, a microwave oven, and a teakettle, for the minority whose relatives sent them food to store and reheat what could replace the inedible cafeteria fare; a "leisure room" equipped with a television set and a DVD player and benches and chairs for people who never materialized because inmates here were always either working or sleeping, dead tired from the monotonous, endless work; and a bathroom with three toilets and no partitions. Bathing was to be done one day a week, when inmates were marched to the colony bathhouse. At other times the women had to clean themselves using the toilets and the pair of sinks in plain view of the toilets; the process was so humiliating that none of the former inmates whom I interviewed would agree to describe it. Some, but not all, of the units had hot water in those bathrooms.

Before Maria was transferred from quarantine, Unit 11 underwent renovations. Some of the inmates were transferred out and distributed among other units, so the population of Unit 11 went down to the roughly seventy people its physical quarters could legally accommodate. Some of the walls got a paint job and hot water was piped into the bathroom. Later, when a high-profile human rights activist interviewed Maria in the colony, partitions went up between the toilets.

Maria had been readying herself for the transfer as well. She continued reading the Criminal Procedure Code and the Criminal Executive Code, which she had begun studying in pretrial detention. At first she felt her humanities-steeped brain might shatter under the weight of the dense language, but in court hearings she began to see that she knew more about what was going on from a legal standpoint than her co-defendants, her lawyers, and, she suspected, the judge. Now, after a month in transit and two weeks of quarantine, Maria was more than conversant with the penal code: she felt it was her job to ensure that law as she had learned it was observed.

Maria talked to everyone, or tried to, as she always did. Most women were here on drug-related charges. Some were honest-to-goodness dealers, most were users who had unsuccessfully ventured into dealing, and some had just been in the wrong place at the wrong time. They had sentences averaging seven years, the vast majority were under thirty, and few of them had contact with their families. The killers were different, older and with strong family ties, though most were serving roughly the same sentences as the drug offenders. A few women were in for fraud. Russian prosecutors often charged people with fraud—it was a wastebasket crime, and the best charge for extorting money or settling scores between business partners (one of whom would often pay off the prosecutor). Fraudsters were considered the intellectual and economic elite of the Russian prison population, and most of them were men; many managed to secure accommodations in city jails, so one did not encounter many inmates serving time for fraud in the penal colonies.

Lena Tkachenko was an exception. As a staff member at a real estate agency in Perm, she would rent an apartment for two days and then flip it ten times in twenty-four hours, conducting ten showings, signing ten contracts, handing out ten sets of keys, and collecting ten first month's, last month's, and security deposits. The new renters would then show up when the unsuspecting apartment owner returned, and it would be up to him to deal with the rage and the police. Lena had rules: she never fake-rented to people who looked to her like they could not stand to lose the equivalent of a few months' rent or who looked like they needed the money more than she did. On the other hand, she needed the money a lot. Lena and her colleagues at the real estate agency got away with this scam for a year, until she got caught. At twenty, she was sentenced to seven years, and five of them had passed.

Lena liked to talk about music, and she was impressed when she heard that Maria had been in a band. She had heard of Pussy Riot and the trial, and though television news portrayed them as witches—or, rather, because of this—she figured they deserved her sympathy. Lena also liked to talk about a particular guard, a woman in her forties whom she had been courting for months, bringing her a flower every day in the summer and some other token of her affection in winter. The guard accepted the gifts, but, Lena complained, treated her like a child. For her part, she saw Maria as a bit of a child, a child who needed to be protected because she was too smart and too stubborn to be liked by others. Lena made sure she told Maria in detail how the place worked—she was good at systematizing, she was going to be a lawyer when she got out of here—and soon she was fielding questions she thought no one would ever ask.

Was it not against the rules, Maria was asking, to make inmates work twelve-hour shifts? The colony's sewing factory worked around the clock, with half the inmates working the 6 a.m. to 6 p.m. shift and sleeping from nine thirty to five thirty while the other half worked evening to morning and were awakened at two in the afternoon. Yes, it was illegal to make them work twelve-hour shifts. Plus, local work such as lugging bricks for perennial construction projects was often added between the end of the work shift and lights-out. What was worse, said Lena, was that the penal colony secured huge sewing orders by undercutting regular manufacturers' prices for everything from bedsheets to uniforms and then pocketed half or more of the supposed labor costs, so that inmates received only a few kopecks for every ruble to which they were entitled. This was slave labor—there was no other name for it—and Lena had been documenting violations for years, though she'd had no one to show this documentation to. But human rights activists and officials, inspectors, journalists—everyone—would be coming to see Maria at the colony, Lena thought, and this would allow her finally to expose these violations to the world.

THREE DAYS AFTER Maria was transferred to Unit 11, seven inmates showed up in the late afternoon, just as Lena was leaving to work the night shift. Lena had an idea of who these seven were: they were all known to do the administration's dirty work. Now they were all in Unit 11, supposedly moving in, except all they had with them were their rolled-up mattresses. It was like they were here for a special-assignment sleepover. Maria had not yet been assigned a shift, so she would be here, in the unit, while Lena was at work. "Don't talk to them," Lena said quickly. "We'll talk in the morning." But even as she was leaving, she saw the seven women surround Maria. She heard them saying, "It's your fault."

When Lena came back from her shift, Maria was gone. Someone had seen her crying and signing some papers and the duty officer taking her away. She had asked to be moved to solitary for her own protection.

> I think it was the day after we saw each other that they
> brought me a package from Mama, and in it was
> everything I had asked for. There was a watch, and I put it
> on. I think they had already brought the books.* It was
> evening. It is almost always quiet in this cell—not at all like
> the barracks where the unit is—and so I put on the watch,

---

*Books are brought separately from the rest of the package because they must be seen by the censor. The censor disallows any books in a foreign language or books with any handwritten marks in the pages, as well as anything deemed subversive or likely to aid in organizing an escape.

*and it was ticking on my hand, and I started reading a
book. I think it was Gandelsman*—(I keep writing "I think,"
it's like a parasitic word, but this is because I cannot
remember anything with certainty—the days blend into one
another)—I just wanted to say that it was a very poignant
moment. I am not a very good person, and here I was,
surrounded with such wonderful poetry and things sent by
people who love me. It's hard to explain, but all of this
becomes incredibly important when you are in prison.
Don't worry about my blabbing on about silly things
when you were here. I just can't let myself feel things here
like I can there. Here it cannot be. And at the trial it could
not be.*

*It's December 3. I am attending trade school, have been
for two days. I am sewing mittens. They are big and warm.
They have cotton stuffing on the inside. I get there, take off
my coat, put a kerchief on my head, and dive straight into
socialist realism. Then again, I am submerged in it all the
time. I have on a white kerchief with sharp ends that stick
out, and the machine is burring and is made up of parts
with frightful names. I see fat iron constructions covered
with thick paint and black cables that take the electrical
current away, into the ground next to the barracks. If earth
conducted electricity, the current coming out of all the
barracks and the factory and everywhere would make
worms jump, and bugs too, creating tiny hills on the
surface. Being humane, of course, we would find a way to
breed the kind of worms who feel no pain from this. As for*

---

*Vladimir Gandelsman is a contemporary Russian poet.

*humans, to whom we are not generally humane, they will
wear boots with a special isolating sole. The state will
supply this place with these special boots, but corruption
will do its thing and the supply will be sporadic and the
Chinese-made soles will be unreliable, while human rights
defenders will say all is well (this part requires no
imagination). In time, inmates will figure out how to
make their own soles, but the process of making them
will be considered a violation, so we have to be careful.
I mean, we will have to be careful. But that's in the
future—for now everything is good. I spend my time
in the company of remarkable interesting people:
Hemingway, Shakespeare, Grass—well, you know them
all. I seem to have lost the ability to write. Or is it just that
sort of evening?*

As a convicted felon, Maria was entitled to one four-hour
visit with up to two adults and one child every two months
and one conjugal or family visit of three days every three
months. Natalya Alyokhina and Olya Vinogradova visited in
November. Nikita came in December. They talked mostly
about Philip, who had looked so scared when Nikita brought
him for a visit at the pretrial detention center. He had turned
red and sat very straight, and Nikita had grown anxious and
tried hurrying both him and Maria, who was tongue-tied:
"Dudes, we don't have much time, don't just sit there." Two
subsequent visits went better—Nikita actually thought the
third one was great, it was like talking to his mother behind a

glass partition was natural for Philip now—and then Maria was transferred to the penal colony.

Nikita had told Philip what happened right away: "They've put Mama in jail." It was hard to explain why, of course—not because Philip was a child, but because how could you explain it to anyone. Nikita said that Maria had gone into the Cathedral of Christ the Savior, and Philip had heard it as "the savior's castle," which seemed perfect to Nikita. So he said, yes, she had gone into the savior's castle and sung a loud song, which you are not allowed to do there.

Maria filed an application to have her sentence deferred until Philip turned fourteen. There was precedent: a woman in Irkutsk had recently been convicted of vehicular homicide for running over three young women on a sidewalk and had had her sentence deferred. But that woman was a prosecutor's daughter, and Maria realized that the court would not be so charitable to someone who had sung a loud song in the savior's castle. Still, there was value in fighting for the sake of fighting. And there was value in getting out of her cell and into a courtroom where she would see familiar faces. And there was just a little bit of hope too.

The Civilian Collegium in Berezniki got a paint job in anticipation of all the media who would come for the hearing January 16. Petya had mounted a successful campaign to draw media attention—and to force the authorities to move the hearing from colony grounds to the town. A glass case was constructed in the courtroom, which had not, apparently, previously been equipped to host dangerous felons. The courtroom was filled with journalists and supporters—a ragtag

group that had assembled around Petya over the last months—
and an overflow of several dozen people were watching the
proceedings in the lobby, on a monitor the court had installed
for the occasion.

Maria and Nadya had both fired the lawyers who had represented them. In Moscow, they had been embarrassing, but
once the women were transferred to colonies, the lawyers
were simply absent. This time Maria was represented by a local attorney experienced in working with inmates, along with
a former Soviet political prisoner from Moscow. The prosecutor and a representative of the penal colony, a copper-haired
woman in a sky-blue uniform, argued that Maria did not de-
serve to have her sentence reduced because she had been
racking up infractions in the colony. Twice she had failed to
rise when awakened by a staff member at five thirty. Once she
had been caught carrying notes to a meeting with her lawyer,
and these were deemed to be correspondence that she was
trying to smuggle out past the censors. And once she had refused to testify in a disciplinary hearing against herself—this
too was an infraction.

The local lawyer badgered the penal colony's representative with requests for documentation and a printed copy of the
colony rules. The former dissident pointed out that all of these
supposed violations were of the nuisance variety, the sort of
thing a colony would normally ignore unless it was out to get
an inmate. Maria said, "This is where one would mention Gogol, Kafka, and Orwell, but that seems redundant."

Olya, I am having trouble with my emotions. I cannot
manage them, and I despise myself for this. Some little

thing, an underhanded little thing, begins to look like a whole big act of injustice. I know they are not going to release me, so what difference does it make whether they pin one more or one less infraction on me? I am indifferent to the whole idea of release. What is it, then? I know what it is, and I despise myself—no, I do not despise myself, I pity myself and this humiliates me. It is their triumph, their petty power—and it is, their power is itty-bitty, but they use it to the fullest. This is so low . . . They serve the state. Think about what kind of state it is, Olya: I see it every day now, and it terrifies me. It terrifies me to see the monster they re-create with every one of their actions. This is what we mean when we say "the system," but this is not a system at all, it is incapable of creating anything or even destroying anything, it is nothing but a bloated desert. And I will leave, but this thing will stay here and continue to reproduce itself . . . There is only one thing I want: to preserve this memory. And if I don't have the gift or the strength to show what I have seen here, then maybe someone else will. Otherwise, why am I seeing this and feeling it so acutely? Possibly because I am neurotic.

After about six hours, the judge, an older woman with a kindly school principal's way about her, retired to her chambers to write the decision. The support group sent a runner out for fast food. Journalists recharged their equipment and recorded stand-ups outside the courtroom. An hour and a half later, the journalists and assorted others were herded into a closed corridor off the lobby so Maria could be marched back into the courtroom without seeing any of us.

"It has been demonstrated that the child is harmed by his mother's absence," the judge read out. "However, said absence is the result of the mother's committing a felony. Having a child did not keep Alyokhina from committing a felony. Furthermore, it is the court's opinion that Alyokhina will not be reformed if she lives at home and concentrates on raising her child."

Hi, Olya! We finally talked today. February 25. You said, Get out already. You said, Get out of prison. But I can't even get out of solitary and into the barracks.

"It's all for your own safety." Television news is full of tanks and guns—VVP's* favorite toys. Expensive toys. The message is similar: ALL OF THIS (a pile of metal scrap no one needs) "for your own safety." Rising defense capability, rising interest meaning investment, rising, rising, rising—it's a Freudian nightmare: how far can it rise, and what for? We keep raising it and it keeps falling—falling: rockets fall, salaries fall, interest falls. But they keep up the pomp, the noise, and the moments of silence. Parliament members held a moment of silence when a child adopted from Russia died in the U.S. If they held a moment of silence for every child who dies in Russian adoptive families, for every inmate who dies in jail, for everyone who loses her mind in a hospital, then their work would turn into mourning 8 hours a day, 7 days a week. And I want—I demand—to see real mourning, not the ritual laying of a wreath at the eternal flame but the kind of mourning that makes them sweat.

---

*Vladimir Vladimirovich Putin.

26 February

You are very lucky in the way you get your news. I've been getting it from television for the last year and now I hate journalism. And don't tell me that what I'm watching has nothing to do with journalism. People like me—the ones who watch TV—are in the majority, and what's worse, only the very few view any of it at all critically . . .

Our wonderful penitentiary system has a special place for so-called malevolent violators. The "malevolents" go in a special "prophylactic registry," which mandates close monitoring of the inmate's behavior and "prophylactic activity." You can be deemed a "malevolent" for committing a dangerous violation, planning to commit, or "having a tendency" to commit one (this is my favorite part). Dangerous violations are: smuggling drugs into prison; attempting to escape; stealing; petty hooliganism, belonging to a criminal group—Article 115 contains a full list, and this list also contains male homosexuality and lesbianism . . . I wonder what sorts of "prophylactic activities" these people are subjected to. Most likely, they just repeat, robotlike, that this is wrong, this is an infraction, read the rules out loud to you—but what else? What do they tell the person? They probably say it's a sickness—I'm willing to bet that's exactly what they say. Getting back to the point that you can be put in the registry for "having a tendency." I love Oscar Wilde, ancient Greeks, and Marina Tsvetaeva's poetry. If I declaim their poetry, would that be seen as proof of a "tendency"? I'm sure it could. And if you are in the registry, they make a special mark in your

personal file, and once that's done, there can be no parole.
That's all, I have to go to trade school.

I've come back for lunch. I have good news: I have received
written responses to my queries and proposals.
I now have a piece of paper that says I have the right to
wash my hair every day! That it's not a violation! This is a
victory. Another small victory is this: I am no longer
subjected to the gynecological chair before and after
meeting with my lawyer. This went on for a month, and
now I have finally managed to get this canceled. It was
painful and disgusting, and anyway, no one can stand
being subjected to this 4 times a week.

These were not Maria's only victories. She kept writing
official complaints. She appealed all the infractions with which
she had been charged. The court in Berezniki convened again
on the last day of January to review the infractions, and a hearing that should have taken fifteen minutes went on for a week.
This time the prison authority did not let her go to the courthouse in Berezniki. The journalists were there—not as many
as two weeks earlier, but still at least a dozen people—and the
support group was there, though her mother did not come this
time, but Maria herself was only an image on a small flat-
screen to the right of the double-headed eagle that is the symbol of Russia, and a voice in the loudspeakers.

"Maria Vladimirovna, can you see us?" asked the judge
when the trial began.

"I can barely see you," she answered, squinting on screen.

"To me you are just a dark silhouette. And I can neither see nor hear the prosecution at all."

"You can hear us," stated the judge.

The hearing went on in fits and starts. Maria insisted on her rights—the right to be represented by counsel with whom she could consult in confidence, which would mean being in physical proximity—and the judge allowed the defense attorney to go to the penal colony and sit next to Maria on the screen. Maria also insisted on reviewing procedures and demanded paperwork from the colony. As the days dragged on, what began as a humiliating bureaucratic procedure turned into something resembling a court hearing. At the end, the judge did something perhaps no other Russian judge had ever done in such a situation: she struck down two of Maria's supposed infractions and she ordered the penal colony to put its house in order.

In her final statement at that hearing, Maria said, "A philosopher named Heidegger once said that language is the house of being. And I have to tell you that being within the language of these secure objects and special-purpose objects and decrees and amendments and administrative orders and mandated procedures and transport is a nightmare. And I feel it during this hearing, I am dying here. I need to realize my potential, I need to work on what I believe I was born to do. And I would very much like to do it. I would like to get out as soon as possible and do my work. I believe that this all-out, all-around victimization of inmates will stop. And I assume that the decision in my case has already been made and it's probably not in my favor, but this hearing this week has perhaps made the administration of the penal colony understand something. More than anything else I want them to understand that we are human beings and that their uniform and badge does not change that. We are human beings."

After that hearing Maria stopped dying inside the language of legalese and started living in it. The administration, apparently realizing it could not get rid of her and could not keep her in solitary indefinitely without facing more complaints and legal sanctions, released her into the barracks. Lena Tkachenko was transferred to a different unit, but she and Maria found ways to meet and organize: Lena would pass Maria notes instructing her to go to the infirmary at a particular time and they would meet there as if by accident. Maria accumulated documentation of violations; everywhere she went, she carried a bulging folder. Many of the inmates at Penal Colony 28 started working eight hours a day instead of twelve.

Hi, Olya!

It looks like it's been a month since I last sent you a letter. The last one went out February 26. What in the world have I been doing? Today is March 27. Spring is here. We were smoking on the trade school porch today when snow fell off the roof—so much snow that several people were pinned under it. Could the coming of spring have been announced any more clearly? A whole mountain of wet snow—I wish you had seen it. All the smokers jumped away from the porch and wouldn't return even though there was no snow left on the roof. They still kept their distance, smoking in a flock.

What should I write about? About the fact that I live behind bars and I sew? Those are silly words. I live behind

a multitude of doors and a multitude of bars, and I have
been sewing for 4 months. I'll tell you in detail. I'm not sure
my story will have literary value, but I'll try to make it
interesting.

Look at your bedsheets. See how their edges are folded
in? Now I too know how to do this. First you fold 0.7 mm
over, then 1 cm, then you lay down a stitch 0.2 mm from the
edge. 0.2 mm is important, and it also turns out to be
possible. Actually, I would even say more: it's a simple
operation. The word operation used to put me in mind of
hospitals or the police, but now I think of sewing machines
as well. The entire clothing manufacturing process is
subdivided into operations (division of labor). There are
simple operations and complex ones, and the complex ones
are to be performed by seamstresses who have a higher
ranking. What's considered complex? Stitch a collar into
the orifice (what a creepy word, don't you think?)—I can
do that. I can also set up piping, which is also not simple
but has a great sound to it.* But a motorized sewing
machine is a regular object—many people own something
similar, as do you (or do you?), but you definitely don't have
a machine that sews on buttons and makes buttonholes.
I can do this too.

Buttonholes get stitched very fast. That zigzagging
thread you will see if you look at a buttonhole—that is put
on by a machine in the space of about 10 seconds, and then
a knife lands in the middle. Then you shift the cloth over

*The Russian word for piping is kant, as in the philosopher, which may be why Ma-
ria thought it sounded great.

*and the process repeats: shift, stitch, knife. Shift. Stitch,
knife. Next item. I put buttonholes onto housecoats.*

*There are machines that use 3 or 5 spools of thread
simultaneously. They overstitch the edges. First you slip the
cloth underneath the tab, then you press the pedal, and a
tiny knife starts trimming the cloth very very quickly while
a needle (or two needles) cover the edge with a pattern
using a mechanism I don't understand. If you needed to
undo regular stitching, it would take you a while, but you
can undo the edge stitch in a second simply by pulling on
the right thread.*

*I like the sound of the overstitching machines; they are
like little animals willing to eat all the cloth you can feed
them. I like the smell of oil that you feel when you clean a
machine; you flip it and lay it on the back part of the table
and you can see the oil trickle into the tray from the
different internal mechanisms. I like cutting buttonholes;
they look like mouths. I like the view from the workshop
window: a small grove with factory stacks visible beyond it,
and there is always smoke coming out of them. If you spend
a long time sewing fast, the same thing over and over
again, and then you stand up and look out the window, you
feel like you spent much longer than a minute staring. It is
a wondrous thing, to look out the window. Just to look out
the window and nothing else. It is like all the noise in the
world recedes and there is so much silence that it fills up
my entire head.*

TWELVE

Nadya

Nadya looked like she was going to cry. "Gera is acting like I'm a stranger! Gera is being shy around me! But just you wait, I'll get out."

"That's odd," said Petya. "Gera is usually perfectly relaxed around strangers." This did not help.

Gera had not seen her mother since the last family visit, two months ago. In the interim she had gone to the Montenegrin seaside and become very tan and a little grown-up and shy.

"You are not tan," Petya said to Nadya. "Do you not get to be outside?"

"Oh, I get to be outside all right," said Nadya. "Take yesterday, for example. We were lugging rocks. The rocks were in bags. Gera, I work on the factory floor. You know what a barn looks like?" There was no reason for her daughter to know what a barn looked like any more than she knew what a factory floor looked like. "It's like a barn with very very many sewing machines in it. And very very many women. And on the factory floor, they are changing the floor. It used to be wooden and they are going to put down tile. And we are carrying rocks so they can put them down first and then cover them with tile. All right, I am going to read to you."

Gera was still standing stiffly next to her mother. This four-hour visit was taking place in a tiny rectangular room that was cut up with tall desks. Nadya sat at the desk farthest from the door, with her back to the window. Petya and I sat about two yards from her, behind another desk, with our backs to the door. A penal colony officer sat in the space between us. After some consideration she had allowed Gera to cross over to Nadya's side of the room.

"Have you learned to read yet? So I guess I'm going to have to come out of prison and teach you to read. Do you at least play the hedgehog game?" Nadya leaned into Gera's neck and made sniffling sounds. Gera giggled uncomfortably. "You don't play the hedgehog game? What do you do all day? Who is Andrei Usachev?" This was the name on the book of children's poems Gera had with her. "Why aren't you reading the classics? Do you read Kharms?"

Daniil Kharms was an absurdist poet who was killed in the Stalinist purges of the 1930s. Petya had diligently memorized a Kharms poem with Gera, and he had even sent it to Nadya in a separate e-mail so they would all know the same poem, but this was months ago and Gera had forgotten most of it while she was in Montenegro. They all tried to recall it together now, but they started by putting the words in the first line in the wrong, too-obvious order, and this got them into trouble; it got them to where the bulldog's bone had a wrinkly forehead. Gera finally laughed like a kid.

"Can you wrinkle your forehead? Since I've been in prison, I have gotten wrinkles on my forehead." Nadya was now trying to draw a bulldog. She was too far away for us to see what she was doing, and the desks had odd little barriers that obscured whatever was there, but apparently she did not think the drawing was very good. "I know a woman here who can draw anything at all because she is a professional artist."

Time was, Nadya had thought of herself as a professional artist. Petya called her on it now, and she laughed bitterly. At most, she said, she could convince people here that she was "creative," which was just a fancy word for weird.

Petya tried to change the subject to something positive: "Did you make that smoothie yet?" Nadya had been dreaming of making one and had asked for bananas and cinnamon, which she planned to mix with milk, available from the colony concession.

"I haven't had the time. There is no time here."

"What about your two hours before lights-out?"

"It doesn't exist. They keep giving us extra maintenance work."

The colony was laying pipes underground: at the moment the gas, water, and sewage pipes were elevated. Endless ditches were now being dug and the dirt had to be removed. The inmates lugged it off using those all-purpose giant square bags.

"Don't you have wheelbarrows?" I asked.

Nadya laughed an angry laugh.

"And we don't have planes and trains either."

"Someone told me recently that I walk like the Terminator," she said.

"You do have an unusual gait," said Petya.

"What's unusual about it? Verbalize. Oh my God, I can use that word!"

Petya thought for a long minute.

"If a person's gait can express emotions, yours expresses anticipation. You hop."

"That's what they told me. That I hop and that I walk very confidently and that I hold my arms like so." Nadya placed her hands on her hips and spread out her elbows. "And that I walk around as though I owned the world. So I've been trying to walk a bit more modestly, but I don't seem to be very good at that yet."

At the age of twenty-four, Nadya was confronting the idea that it is not always good to be noticed. She had been that very unusual kind of girl and young woman who always thought that standing out, being more beautiful, smarter, and louder than everyone else was a good thing. Even in prison it had seemed a good thing at first—or it just took her a long time to realize that it was not. Nadya's relationships with other inmates seemed smooth at the beginning; she was too unusual to form the kinds of intense bonds that got Maria into instant trouble, and this same otherworldliness seemed to make her attitude of anthropological curiosity acceptable to others. She did not rack up violations like Maria—in fact, she was ambushed by her first violation for walking to the infirmary unescorted on March 2, the last day of her first year of incarceration, which happened to be the last day she could be slapped with a violation that would serve as an excuse to deny her parole. Soon waves of hostility started rolling through the penal colony: one day Nadya would approach an inmate in the factory with a work-related question and the inmate would hiss back, "Don't talk to me." Nadya would be ostracized for about a week and then things would normalize, only to flare up again a week or two or three later, for no apparent reason.

For the first time in her life, Nadya found herself in a setting where she did not know and could not intuit the rules. She would be reprimanded for not taking part in social activities such as the Miss Charm beauty contest or the singing contest, and she would sign up to sing and go to the clubhouse to rehearse only to be told that she was in violation for being in the clubhouse without an official permission slip. Though this requirement did not seem to apply to other inmates, Nadya needed an escort to walk from her barracks to the clubhouse. But while she waited for the escort, her permission slip expired. She never made it to the clubhouse and never took part in the contest.

Petya had a pile of legal paperwork with him. He had developed as great a passion for jailhouse lawyering as Maria had. Attorney Irina Khrunova, who was now representing both of the Pussy Riot inmates, called him the best lawyer's assistant she had ever met. Now seemed like a good time to give Nadya some papers to sign; these were some legal motions Maria was testing, and Nadya could follow. She waved him off.

"I am not interested at all. I don't believe in the courts." Petya tried to convince her that Maria had succeeded in changing her own and other inmates' lives for the better through legal means. Nadya did not have an argument to counter this and grew even more irritated. "Petya, we have a conjugal visit in two weeks, right? Can't you bring it up then? You have nothing to talk to me about right now? What are you, going to burst?"

Petya showed no sign of being hurt. It was now an hour and forty minutes into the visit and Gera was finally comfortable in her mother's lap.

"Gera, what is your favorite food now?"

Gera could not think of an answer.

"I am giving Petya an assignment, to find out what your favorite food is and send it to me here so I can taste it too."

"You know, Maria doesn't understand how it's possible not to be fascinated with the intricacies of the law; she has immersed herself completely."

"She is lucky. My excuse is that everyone has her own language. I am growing increasingly convinced that I am not interested in politics as such."

"But this is the system's bloodline. It allows you to see how the state really works."

"You don't think I have a good sense of how this state works? I have intimate knowledge now, and I really understand how bureaucrats work. And the more I learn, the less hope I have. It's all based on a set of blind beliefs that are impossible to shake even using an individual approach. Their very concept of state power—they see it as a static structure that is unchangeable by its very nature. The same goes for the way the penal colony is constituted. And art. No one wants to listen; they tell me to go get lost. They are afraid of new information: 'Tolokonnikova, stop it right now.' Even though all I'm doing is trying to talk to them about art. Which I try to do all the time, because I'm an expert in that area. As opposed to sewing, for example."

There was another reason she did not want to file any more complaints: she wanted time in the colony to go faster. "That's all anyone here wants. And court hearings or anything else that breaks up the monotony doesn't help because it slows time down."

Petya was surprised. He would have thought that time in the colony dragged on, and interruptions would help speed it up. He clearly did not know the first thing about monotony.

On Sundays the inmates watched movies. "Last week they screened an hour-long American film about dental hygiene. It was dubbed. But the funniest one they showed us was about the need for leisure time. I was sitting next to women who work until one in the morning every day. And here they were telling us that when a person does not get any rest, he becomes a destructive member of society because of the elevated risk of accidents. The women were laughing so hard they fell off their chairs."

WHAT NADYA REALLY wanted to see was *Laurence Anyways*, a film by Xavier Dolan. I had not heard of the film or the filmmaker. "He is a Canadian director," she explained, "who's made a movie about a man and a woman and the man decided to become a woman. The other thing that I'm interested in is that the director is twenty-four years old and he's already made four movies and each one of them has been shown at Cannes. He was born the same year I was. It always touches me when someone my age does something. And it really hurts that I have to spend this time behind bars."

Being behind bars was not only a waste of time; it was also an experience that had changed Nadya in ways from which she already feared she would not recover. "I know that when I get out of here I will be able to find people capable of understanding me and acting with me. But I realize that we will only ever be understood by a small circle of people. This is a crisis of sorts. I am not interested in classical art forms, but it is they that can be used to explain things to people. So I am facing the task of using the mechanics of pop to create something that's mine. This is a complex technical challenge, so I am feeling a little stymied."

"But that is a replay of the Soviet attitude, when you were only considered an accomplished poet if your books had press runs of three million," said Petya, somewhat unfairly to Soviet-era poets.

"Say, *War and Peace* leaves me completely cold," said Nadya, trying a different tack either to make herself understood or to understand what she was trying to formulate herself. "Whereas Tolstoy's ridiculous attempts to educate and organize the masses inspire me."

"Interesting that it was when Tolstoy tried to address the masses that he was noticed as problematic by the Church." Petya was trying hard to hold up his end of the conversation, even if he had a difficult time grasping what Nadya meant.

"'Being noticed'—I used to think that was a good thing," said Nadya. She was not hearing Petya either.

I thought I might as well bring up something Nadya and I had been corresponding about: language. Pussy Riot had subverted Soviet-speak, which had perverted language. But how does one pull off that trick in a more traditional art form?

"I really feel the problems with the language in here," said Nadya. "Yes, words being used to mean their opposites, and this is handed from the top down. And at every step, as they pass the word down, people feel that they are doing it but they still do it in order to keep the status they acquired through this use of upside-down language."

"And this use of upside-down language is what you were referring to when you talked about sincerity in your closing statement in court?"

"I had a fit of absolutism then," Nadya said, sounding a bit embarrassed. "I got overheated. I started talking about 'the truth.' Because this endless flow of lies—" Of course, talking about "the truth" in earnest would embarrass a twenty-four-year-old student of Theory.

"I always thought this was strange," Petya chimed in. Apparently, they had not discussed Nadya's closing statement, which had been translated into most of the world's languages. "The truth is not a political concept at all."

"So what that it's not a political concept? I just wanted to be understood. I could have used constructions from contemporary philosophy that are better suited to describing this precisely, but I wanted to be understood."

Petya persisted in his criticism, and he and I fell into an

argument about whether Nadya had fallen into a modernist trap. Nadya and Gera tried singing a song about polar bears, but they could not remember the words.

"You look beautiful," said Petya.

"It's just the green color of the uniform," Nadya responded. "When I danced in a green dress, that suited me too. Especially when a yellow mask used to cover my face."

EPILOGUE

Activist Ambition sat on the second floor of a café near Chistye Prudy metro. She had no way of knowing it was the same table at which Violetta Volkova and Nikolai Polozov had met almost exactly a year earlier. She chose the table because it had a good view out the window. She was drinking wine. Activist Ambition—she did not remember exactly, but the nickname must have been coined by Petya when he recruited her for Voina near the end of that group's active life—was in her late teens, which in Russia meant she was of drinking age. This did not change the fact that she was small and not a very experienced drinker: she felt the effects of the alcohol by the time she got to the bottom of her first glass, and on her second, she grew maudlin and sentimental. She started thinking of Pussy Riot.

No one had made her leave: she had decided herself, for all the right reasons. It was the time Pussy Riot was detained in the Metro for singing on the platform. Activist Ambition had been very clear with Kat and Nadya from the outset: she told them she only had three hours before her lecture, and unlike them she arrived not in Pussy Riot dress but in her school clothes—Kat had had to shield her while she changed. A few minutes later she was up at the top of the platform looking down. The song was over and police had surrounded the platform. She started throwing confetti at the police, and this did not make a difference. A train came: all she had to do now was climb down and jump on board the train before the police could grab her. She did—but the train did not move. Women in gray tried to force her back out through the open doors. Several men in black ran in and quickly grabbed her—and Kat and Nadya and Morzh, who she discovered were next to her—and twisted their arms behind their backs.

At the police station, while Nadya haggled with the cops and Tasya kept filming and Kat fretted that they had called her father, Activist Ambition realized something important: not only did none of them care that she had missed her lecture, but they would not have cared even if one of them had missed a lecture. They lived for the actions. She had been trying to be like them for several months. After the Feed the Road action, which had been her first, her father had stopped giving her pocket money, and she had been reduced to finding ways to ride public transit for free and to shoplifting, which she learned from Nadya and Petya and Kat. Now, at the police station, she realized that she had landed there not by accident but by design: the life they led had to include incarceration. And she was the only one in the group who cared.

They kept inviting her to actions after that, and she did

help in filming one, but by the time the Cathedral of Christ the Savior happened, she learned about it from the media. While Maria, Nadya, and Kat were in hiding, they gathered several women in a safe space—it was some sort of cellar, which seemed fitting—and Activist Ambition went, of course. They talked about future actions. The feeling of being part of the group was elusive, it kept teasing her and dissipating, leaving a painful longing in its place.

Then the three women got arrested, and regret replaced the longing. She tried to help by joining in press events organized by Petya: several women would sit down in balaclavas and be interviewed on camera. The balaclavas were not foolproof: Activist Ambition's boss recognized her and she was fired—for giving an interview to the television channel where she was interning. The worst part was, the interviews did nothing to help with the regret. She felt like an actress who had retired from the stage—she had enough irony to think of herself that way, but this did not help either. There is that moment in every action, when you have handed over your personal belongings to whoever is helping and you know exactly why you are there and you know what you are about to do and you feel that you can do anything at all and at the same time it is as though you could see yourself, so lithe, so young, so bright in every way, climbing up onto that platform—it was this moment she remembered when she brooded alone at a table on the second floor of a café overlooking a desolate autumn park.

She saw Kat. She knew Kat had been released from prison a few weeks earlier. She had been hoping to hear from her. Activist Ambition could have called Kat herself, but she wouldn't have known what to say: she wanted Kat to need her, to call her to action. She slapped a few bills on the table and ran out of the café after the woman she thought might be Kat.

It was Kat. She was friendly in a flat way, as she always was—Activist Ambition thought Kat generally kept all her feelings and most of her thoughts inside—but she seemed happy enough to spend time talking. She talked about the lawyers. She said they had betrayed her and Nadya and Maria. She said the only way to get justice for everyone was to confront them, fight them, and expose them for the traitors they were. Activist Ambition agreed—how could she not agree—and tried to change the subject. She asked what new actions Kat was thinking about. Kat talked about the lawyers. And when Activist Ambition asked straight out—even though it seemed a little tactless and possibly illegal—what Pussy Riot was going to do, Kat talked about the lawyers.

Activist Ambition decided she was going to wait for Nadya to get out of prison. She knew that once she did, Nadya would start something—and Activist Ambition would feel that feeling again. She read all she could about Nadya to try to get a glimpse of what she might do next. Sometimes she even thought she could tell what it would be.

Kat was living back at the apartment with her father. For the first few weeks, maybe two months, she was a celebrity. She went to parties thrown by foreign journalists; she was recognized on public transport; people asked to have their pictures taken with her. She obliged—Kat usually did what people asked, if she could—but she was not sure she liked it. And they all wanted to know what she was going to do—what Pussy Riot was going to do. As though they did not realize that a suspended sentence meant she was on parole, and her sentence could be un-suspended at any moment.

Lest she forget, once a month she had to report to an office on the first floor of one of the yellow apartment towers not far from her home. It smelled of stale sweat, a faint reminder of the stench of the pretrial detention facility. She waited in a narrow corridor with her fellow paroled felons, then entered a small office where a squat policewoman shoved a piece of paper across a desk without looking and told her to sign it, using the condescending, familiar form of the imperative. The piece of paper certified that the officer had conducted an educational talk with Kat. She signed and got another piece of paper, instructing her to report back in another month.

Once, the police summoned her for questioning in the case of the cutting down of an Orthodox cross at a chapel outside of Moscow. It had been said that Pussy Riot might be responsible. Kat was questioned, said she had nothing to do with it, and was released.

If she could not be Pussy Riot in any visible, familiar way, Kat could at least get justice for Pussy Riot. If she could only prove that they had been denied proper legal representation, then the sentence could be overturned. To do that, she would have to expose the defense attorneys as the traitors they were. Irina Khrunova, the lawyer who had secured her release, slowly backed away from Kat's case. "I can't really claim that a thirty-year-old woman with a master's degree did not understand the proceedings," she told Kat, whose claim by that point more or less amounted to this. They agreed they would tell the larger world that Khrunova was too busy to handle Kat's complaints. Kat found a lawyer on the Internet. She was doing most of the work herself by now, helped by a self-styled and self-taught legal expert, but she needed someone with a defense attorney's license to sign her complaints. The new lawyer would meet her outside his apartment building in a suburb clear on the other end of Moscow and sign the papers she brought, using the trunk of a parked car as his desk. Then Kat would deliver the papers to the court—the guards at Khamovnichesky recognized her from when she'd been on trial there, and were nice to her—or to the Defense Attorneys Collegium, the rough equivalent of a bar association, where she also filed complaints. The collegium reviewed her long list and found only one clear violation of legal procedure among the many she had attempted to document: Violetta Volkova had failed to enter into a proper remunerative contract with her client, an offense under Russian regulations, which banned pro bono representation.

Kat still thought of herself as Pussy Riot, as did three other women who spent time with her. They were the two participants in the cathedral action who had not gone into hiding and had not gotten caught, and Natasha, Kat's Rodchenko classmate and collaborator, who had participated in Voina but had not been living in Moscow during Pussy Riot's brief period of activity before the arrests. They were quick to condemn as fake a tightly produced video that appeared in the summer of 2013, in which women in brightly colored dresses and tights and balaclavas belted lyrics—at least partly written by Nadya—that took aim at the unholy alliance between Putin and the oil industry. Among other things,

Kat's group felt that it did not correspond to Pussy Riot's idea of serial performance: it consisted of several performances, but these, Kat's group believed, had been staged solely for the purpose of producing the video rather than as independent actions. It was a subtle distinction, and a difficult argument to make given the group's brief but varied history, but for Kat's Pussy Riot, it was serious.

Arguably, serial performance—a months-long joint serial performance, unrehearsed and largely unscripted—was exactly what Nadya and Maria were engaged in. Their venues were the courtrooms of Berezniki and Perm in the Urals, Zubova Polyana and Saransk in Mordovia, and Nizhny Novgorod, where Maria was eventually transferred. Although, as convicted felons and coconspirators, they were banned from communicating with each other, they located their roles, as they always had, through a series of public performative experiments. They found ways of doing exactly what they had, in effect, promised to do in their closing statements in the Moscow court in August 2012.

Nadya had then said that it was the regime that was on trial and had pledged to continue to "act and live politically" to fight Russia's overarching problems: "the use of force and coercion to regulate social processes" and the "forced civic passivity of the majority of the population as well as the total domination of the executive branch over the legislative and judicial ones." That and the "scandalously low level of political culture . . . intentionally maintained by the state system and its helpers." And the "scandalous weakness of horizontal links in society" and the "manipulation of public opinion, carried out with ease because the state controls the vast majority of media outlets."

Maria had chosen the opposite approach in her closing argument, moving from the general to the specific. Like Nadya, she had addressed the sham nature of the trial, but it was the particulars that engaged her. She had talked about the psychiatric facility for children—in part because her visits there, of all her experiences before jail, had prepared her best for life behind bars, but also because the similarities between its specific horror and the insanity of the court proceedings served to highlight the absolute absurdity of the trial. Nadya, on the other hand, pointed to the trial as a small example of the larger travesty—of justice, decency, and reason—that Pussy Riot had been screaming about.

And Kat had spoken only of the results of the trial and conclusions from it.

Almost as soon as Nadya and Maria arrived in their penal colonies and arranged for new legal representation, both began filing all the appeals, complaints, and motions they and their lawyers—but mostly Maria with her legal books—found grounds to file. Petya shuttled back and forth between the colonies, the inmates, and the lawyers, collecting paperwork and delivering messages. Most important, he coordinated the ragtag support group, fashioning it into a working entity that distributed information, served as bodies—tweeting, texting, and videotaping bodies—at every hearing, and ultimately helped ensure that all hearings were open to the public and covered by the media. In late January, less than three months after leaving pretrial detention in Moscow, the Pussy Riot inmates commenced a regular schedule of court hearings, which also guaranteed them regular appearances in Russian and international media.

If Pussy Riot ever edited their court performances into a clip, its refrain would be "It seems that the court is denying my right to a defense." (Indeed, the same might be claimed by any defendant in any court in Russia.) After a few hearings, Maria worked out her MO. She confronted the court to the point where the violations, and their routine nature, were exposed, obvious even to the clerks and court marshals, who had long ago stopped paying attention. At this point, the judge usually lost composure, along with the seemingly inherent sense of his or her own superiority. Judges snapped at Maria, screamed at her, and sometimes became belligerent. As soon as that happened—and it happened every time—Maria, whose own voice, by this point in the proceedings, had begun to crack traitorously, instantly regained her calm. And then she said, "It seems that the court is denying my right to a defense."

After the very first hearing in Berezniki, the one where Maria had quoted Heidegger and Martin Luther and had merely mentioned Orwell and Kafka because quoting them would have been redundant, courts and prison authorities kept her out of the courtroom: she participated by a video uplink from the penal colony or another local facility. In late July 2013, the regional court in Perm took up her appeal of a denial of parole.

It started, as it usually did, looking like an actual court proceeding. The recently built regional courthouse, an eight-story structure of glass and concrete and modest but evident architectural ambition, would not have looked out of place in a medium-size U.S. city. The lobby was decorated with large glass panels engraved with Latin sayings of the *Dura lex, sed lex* variety, and the court's press secretary was exceedingly polite and made sure everyone had a seat. The marshals manning the metal detectors did not do quite as well: one barked at Khrunova, "Lady, place your shopping bag in the metal detector!" Khrunova shot back, "I am not a lady, I'm a lawyer, and these are not shopping bags, this is the legal case."

The large and well-ventilated wood-and-glass defendants' box in the courtroom was empty: Maria was visible on two large flat-screen monitors in the courtroom. She had been delivered to a pretrial detention center in Perm, and there she sat in a metal cage. The camera was positioned outside the cage, so the court had a view of Maria through the grates.

The Perm judge lost his composure soon after lunch, when Maria requested, for the fourth or fifth time that day, a break in the proceedings to allow her to consult with counsel. Every time she did this, the video link had to be broken and rerouted to a separate office in the courthouse, where Khrunova could go to talk with Maria in confidence. Maria had mentioned, a time or two or ten, that this kind of conferring would have been carried out easily and without disrupting the proceedings if only she had been allowed to be physically present in court. In any event, now that the court was moving to the substantive part of her complaint, the moment had come when she needed to discuss with Khrunova their strategy for the remainder of the hearing.

"And what were you and your lawyer discussing before?"

screamed the judge. He was tall and thin and he looked elegant in his long black robe. His fine-featured face, framed by salt-and-pepper hair, was handsome in a way that put one in mind of a mythic, refined, aristocratic Russia. Now this face was contorted in annoyance. "I mean if it's not a secret, of course. You did not discuss your strategy for the remainder of the hearing?" Of course, it was a secret, by law.

"It seems that the court is denying my right to a defense," said Maria, and it looked like she might be smiling a little up there on her screen in her cage.

After a short conference with Khrunova, Maria announced that she had decided not to take part in court proceedings where her right to a defense was being violated. She had done this once before, in May, when the Berezniki court heard her original motion for parole. Back then she had not only pulled out of the proceedings herself but forbade her defense team to participate. The judge had had something resembling a breakdown and ended up appointing an attorney to represent Maria, who had refused to be represented—or to meet with this court-appointed lawyer. Now the Perm judge was terrified he would find himself in a similar position.

Maria was kinder to him. She said she would allow Khrunova to continue to participate in the hearing on her behalf. And then she turned her back to the court. Literally—she was seated on a swiveling office chair in her cage, and she swiveled it around until all the court could see on its screens was the mane of slightly frizzy red hair that covered most of Maria's back.

It took the judge a few minutes to realize he should order the video link cut.

If Pussy Riot put together a video clip of their court performances, it might cut from Maria's back, turned to the court, to an April 2013 hearing in Zubova Polyana—the first time Nadya went to court after she left Moscow. The largest courtroom in Zubova Polyana was too small to fit all the journalists, cameras, and assorted supporters. The courtroom was sweltering, and the smell of human bodies hung heavier as the afternoon wore on. The judge, a prim middle-aged woman with a blond perm, tried to conduct an exemplary hearing in these trying circumstances. "I felt like I was in television court," Khrunova told me later. "I've never seen a Russian judge act like that—asking the marshals to carry papers from the defense table to the bench, for example. Except on TV, of course."

But in the late afternoon, something snapped: either the judge's resources had run dry, or someone had called to tell her to wrap up the hearing, which was being broadcast live by every independent media outlet in Russia, and a couple of foreign ones too. And so the judge asked for the prosecution's opinion, called a break in order to draft a verdict, and hurried out of the courtroom. Nadya stared out of her cage, her mouth slightly open. She had drafted a four-page speech to deliver at the end of the hearing. Khrunova looked like she was having a breakdown. Standing behind the defense desk, all five feet of her, she screamed hoarsely as the judge left: "In my fifteen years as a defense attorney, nothing like this has ever happened to me!"

Nadya made sure nothing like that ever happened to her

again. Before every court hearing, she drafted several speeches of various lengths. She ranked them according to importance and started saying them, in turn, whenever and as soon as she had the opportunity to say anything in court.

Two days after Maria's hearing in Perm, at Nadya's own hearing on the appeal of her denial of parole, before the Supreme Court of Mordovia, she said her longest and most important speech at the first opening.

"I would like to discuss the very concept of correction," she began, standing up in the steel cage in the court. "I have once again observed that the only true education possible in Russia is self-education. If you don't teach yourself, no one will teach you. Or they'll teach you who knows what." She had been thinking about this at least since she wrote that turgid article titled "What's the World Coming To" at the age of fourteen. Her life since then had been a series of confrontations and adaptations to educational institutions, of which IK-14 was the latest.

"I acknowledge that I have a great many stylistic disagreements with this regime, this aesthetic, and this ideology." She was quoting Andrei Sinyavsky, a writer and literary critic, one of the Soviet Union's first dissident political prisoners and one of the earliest political emigres of the post-Stalin era. He had said that his disagreements with the Soviet regime were "purely stylistic in nature." Not that the judge or any other member of the court would recognize the quote, of course, but Nadya was not addressing the court: she was speaking to the public outside the courtroom and outside Mordovia, and to some of the public outside of Russia as well.

"So it stands to reason that a state institution that represents the dominant aesthetics would not see me as having been re-formed," she conceded.

"What can a state institution teach us? In what way can I be reformed by a penal colony and you by, say, Russian TV Channel 1? In his Nobel lecture, Joseph Brodsky said, 'The more substantial an individual's aesthetic experience is, the sounder his taste, the sharper his moral focus, the freer—though not necessarily the happier—he is.' We in Russia once again find ourselves in a situation where resistance, especially aesthetic resistance, becomes the only viable moral choice as well as a civic duty."

Nadya then lectured briefly on the origins of contemporary Russian aesthetics, which she called a combination of imperial Czarist aesthetics and "a faulty understanding of the aesthetics of socialist realism." This, she said, was on display at IK-14. At the parole hearing in April, penal colony representatives had reproached her for not taking part in reformative activities such as the singing contest or the Miss Charm contest. "I assert that it is the principles in accordance with which I conduct my life—feminist, antipatriarchal, and aesthetically nonconformist principles—that are the basis for boycotting the Miss Charm contest. These principles—and mine alone, for they are certainly not shared by the guards who run the camp—lead me to study books and magazines, for which I have to wrestle time away from the colony's stupefying daily schedule."

When Nadya began detailing some of the infractions with which she had been charged—such as concealing her notes on life in the colony; failing to greet a member of the administration; being present at the clubhouse without a permission slip—and the system of aesthetic values that would view these as violations, the prosecutor interrupted her and asked to address "the substance of the case and not the Putin regime."

The judge nodded kindly. "I will allow you to continue," he said, "but please try to stick to the topic at hand. The question before the court is a little narrower."

"But I am calling on you to take a wider view," Nadya responded frankly, and continued reciting her prepared speech. "I know that as long as Russia is subjugated by Putin, I will not see early release. But I came here, to this courtroom, so that I could shed a light, once again, on the absurdity of oil-and-gas justice that condemns people to spend senseless years in jail based on the fact that they wrote a note or failed to cover their head."

After a few procedural remarks by the prosecutor, the judge, and Khrunova, Nadya saw an opportunity to read her second prepared speech, a slightly shorter one.

"I am proud of everyone who is willing to make sacrifices for the sake of standing up for their principles. That is the only way to achieve large-scale change in politics, values, or aesthetics. I am proud of those who sacrificed their quotidian comfort on a summer evening and went out into the streets on July 18 to affirm their rights and defend their human dignity." She was referring to the largest unsanctioned protest in contemporary Russian history. A week before, about ten thousand people had come out into the streets of Moscow after opposition leader Alexei Navalny was sentenced to five years in prison, and Navalny had been released the following day— all of which Petya had told Nadya the day before the hearing, when he visited her. "I know that our symbolic power, which grows out of conviction and courage, will eventually be converted to something greater. And that is when Putin and his cronies will lose state power."

Not too much later, she found the opening for her third speech.

"I'll be happy if I am released when my term runs out rather than slapped with an additional term, like Khodorkovsky was . . . The word 'correction' is one of those upside-down words characteristic of a totalitarian state that calls slavery 'liberty.'"

Here the imaginary Pussy Riot clip might have come back to Maria turning her back to the court and saying, "It seems that the court is denying my right to a defense."

Nadya's, Maria's, and Kat's arrests had heralded a new Russian crackdown. In the months following, dozens of people were arrested on charges stemming from various kinds of peaceful protest. Twenty-eight people were facing trial in connection with police-instigated violence that broke out during a march to protest Putin's inauguration in May 2012. Thirty more were facing piracy charges for being on a Greenpeace ship protesting oil and gas drilling in the Arctic. The courts had become Russia's sole venue for political conversation, the only place where the individual and the state confronted each other. Not that most political defendants in Russia had a clear idea of how to use such a venue, or a language for speaking in it. But Maria and Nadya knew a stage when they saw one. In the old dissident drama, Maria was choosing the role of the person who fights the court on legal grounds and Nadya was refusing to recognize the court as such and choosing to use it only for the pulpit it offered.

They were doing what Pussy Riot had always done: illuminating the issues and proposing a conceptual framework for discussing them. As is often the case with great art, most people did not understand what they were doing. But eventually, Nadya and Maria knew, they would.

Maria had always been moved to activism by the events or circumstances of her own life—as when she became a defender of the Utrish national park after camping there with infant Philip. Now her home was a penal colony and other inmates were her family. She felt obligated to give voice to their experience and to use her place in the public eye to draw attention to the injustice they all faced. Nadya, on the other hand, had always been driven by theory rather than experience, and now she naturally separated her public, performing persona from the daily existence of an IK-14 inmate. She endeavored to either accept or ignore the circumstances of her daily life: as she told Petya during that June visit, she just wanted her time in captivity to pass quickly and uneventfully. That was also part of the reason she deflected attempts to elicit more details of colony life that day. That, and the fact that too detailed a description would have been both shameful and dangerous.

Some things were never talked about. Even Maria's friend Lena Tkachenko, who described the violations in IK-28 with precision, driven by a natural aptitude for detail multiplied by five years of observation and by the will to tell as much as she could to help those she had left behind—even she would not talk to me about the particulars of what they called "personal hygiene," or what might better be called a desperate quest to maintain dignity in the face of circumstances she was too ashamed to describe. Other things not only could be described but had to be publicized and fought. Maria did that by filing complaints on her own behalf, but more often on behalf of other inmates, against the systematic violations of inmates' rights: the long work hours, the close quarters, the lack of hot water. The administration of IK-28 retaliated by restricting inmates' freedom of movement further and stopping the movement of packages to inmates—closing off the prisoners' lifeline. Maria responded by declaring a hunger strike. A war of nerves ensued. On Day Ten of her hunger strike in May 2013, Maria had to be hospitalized; she could no longer walk. On Day Eleven, the administration admitted defeat: locks that had been added to barracks apparently to teach Maria a lesson were removed and packages once again started being delivered. Petya was convinced that someone from Moscow had directed the administration to avoid at any cost having Maria die on them.

Khrunova was devastated: "They'll never forgive her for this," she told me. "They've caved in and they've now made it clear to the entire inmate population that it's Maria Alyokhina who sets policy there. And they also know this will persist even after she leaves—inmates will know they can make the administration cave." She was right: within weeks, IK-28 engineered Maria's transfer to a colony in a different region. After the initial shock and a bit of outrage, everyone involved had to admit that everybody had won: IK-28 was now rid of Maria, Maria was in a colony with much better living and working conditions, and the inmates of her new colony now had the benefit of sharing their lives with Maria Alyokhina, who immediately commenced her jailhouse lawyering there.

A few months into Nadya and Maria's sentences, the legal team had established a pattern of testing motions with Maria and following up with Nadya. After securing a judgment against IK-28 in a Berezniki court in the winter, in May they filed complaints against IK-14 in Mordovia. It backfired disastrously. Nadya woke up to discover she had become a pariah in the colony. Inmates would not speak to her. Brief moments of fun and camaraderie—like the times the inmates, finding themselves alone in the factory, would crank up a radio, climb right up on their sewing machines, and dance, moments worth living for—disappeared. For Nadya, they were replaced with humiliating experiences she was loath to describe to anyone. She concluded the complaints had been a mistake. She should not have picked this battle: the war for better conditions for Russian prison inmates was not her war. She reached for monotony, but monotony was now elusive. Things kept getting worse.

Petya pinged me in the middle of the night of September 23. "Nadya is declaring a hunger strike tomorrow morning," he wrote. He sent me an open letter Nadya had written over the preceding few days, as her decision had gelled. Some paragraphs were smuggled out on scraps of paper; others she had dictated to Petya. Together, these paragraphs made up the most affecting piece Nadya had ever written. It had none of the stilted quality of her letters from prison or the forced bravado of her letters from jail. It held nothing back—not even the embarrassing parts.

On Monday, September 23, I am declaring a hunger strike.
This is an extreme method, but I am absolutely convinced it
is my only recourse in the current situation.

The prison wardens refuse to hear me. But I will not back down from my demands. I will not remain silent, watching in resignation as my fellow prisoners collapse under slave-like conditions. I demand that human rights be observed at the prison. I demand that the law be obeyed in this Mordovian camp. I demand we be treated like human beings, not slaves.

It has been a year since I arrived at Penal Colony No. 14 [henceforth, IK-14—Trans.] in the Mordovian village of Partsa. As the women convicts say, "Those who haven't done time in Mordovia haven't done time at all." I had heard about the Mordovian prison camps while I was still being held at Pre-Trial Detention Center No. 6 in Moscow. They have the harshest conditions, the longest workdays, and the most flagrant lawlessness. Prisoners see their fellows off to Mordovia as if they were headed to the scaffold. Until the last, they keep hoping: "Maybe they won't send you to Mordovia after all? Maybe the danger will pass you by?" It didn't pass me by, and in the autumn of 2012, I arrived in the prison country on the banks of the Partsa River.

My first impression of Mordovia was the words uttered by the prison's deputy warden, Lieutenant Colonel Kupriyanov, who actually runs IK-14. "You should know that when it comes to politics, I am a Stalinist." Colonel Kulagin, the other warden (the prison is administered in tandem*) called me in for a chat my first day here in order to force me to confess my guilt. "A misfortune has befallen you. Isn't that right? You've

---

*A reference to the way Russia was said to be governed during the four years Dmitry Medvedev held the office of president: believing the president was ineffectual and directed by Prime Minister Putin, political analysts referred to the regime as "the tandem."

been sentenced to two years in prison. People usually change
their views when bad things happen to them. If you want to be
paroled as soon as possible, you have to confess your guilt. If
you don't, you won't get parole." I told him right away I would
work only the eight hours a day stipulated by the Labor Code.
"The code is the code. What really matters is making your
quota. If you don't, you work overtime. And we've broken
stronger wills than yours here!" Colonel Kulagin replied.

My whole shift works sixteen to seventeen hours a day
in the sewing workshop, from seven-thirty in the morning
to twelve-thirty at night. At best, we get four hours of sleep
a night. We have a day off once every month and a half. We
work almost every Sunday. Prisoners "voluntarily" apply to
work on weekends. In fact, there is nothing "voluntary"
about it. These applications are written involuntarily on the
orders of the wardens and under pressure from the inmates
who help enforce their will.

No one dares disobey (that is, not apply to go to the
manufacturing zone on Sunday, meaning going to work
until one in the morning). Once, a fifty-year-old woman
asked to go back to the dorm zone at eight p.m. instead of
twelve-thirty p.m. so she could go to bed at ten p.m. and get
eight hours of sleep just once that week. She was not feeling
well; she had high blood pressure. In response, a dorm unit
meeting was called, where the woman was scolded,
humiliated, insulted, and branded a parasite.

"What, do you think you're the only one who wants
more sleep? You need to work harder, you're strong as a
horse!" When someone from the shift doesn't come to work
on doctor's orders, they're bullied as well. "I sewed when I

had a fever of forty centigrade, and it was fine. Who did you think was going to pick up the slack for you?"

I was welcomed to my dorm unit by a convict finishing up a nine-year sentence. "The pigs are scared to put the squeeze on you themselves. They want to have the inmates do it." Conditions at the prison really are organized in such a way that the inmates in charge of the work shifts and dorm units are the ones tasked by the wardens with crushing the will of inmates, terrorizing them, and turning them into speechless slaves.

There is a widely implemented system of unofficial punishments for maintaining discipline and obedience. Prisoners are forced to "stay in the local* until lights-out," meaning they are forbidden to go into the barracks, whether it is fall or winter. In the second unit, where the disabled and elderly live, there was a woman who ended up getting such bad frostbite after a day in the local that her fingers and one of her feet had to be amputated. The wardens can also "shut down sanitation" (forbid prisoners to wash up or go to the toilet) and "shut down the commissary and the tearoom" (forbid prisoners to eat their own food and drink beverages). It's both funny and frightening when a forty-year-old woman tells you, "So we're being punished today! I wonder whether we'll be punished tomorrow too." She can't leave the sewing workshop to pee or take a piece of candy from her purse. It's forbidden.

---

*The "local" is a fenced-off passageway between two areas in the camp.

Dreaming only of sleep and a sip of tea, the exhausted, harassed, and dirty convict becomes obedient putty in the hands of the administration, which sees us solely as a free work force. So, in June 2013, my monthly wages came to twenty-nine rubles [just less than one dollar]—twenty-nine rubles! Our shift sews one hundred and fifty police uniforms per day. Where does the money made from them go?

The prison has been allocated funding to buy completely new equipment a number of times. However, the administration has only had the sewing machines repainted, with the convicts doing the work. We sew on obsolete and worn-out machines. According to the Labor Code, when equipment does not comply with current industry standards, production quotas must be lowered vis-à-vis standard industry norms. But the quotas only increase, abruptly and suddenly. "If you let them see you can deliver one hundred uniforms, they'll raise the minimum to one hundred and twenty!" say veteran machine operators. And you cannot fail to deliver, either, or else the whole unit will be punished, the entire shift. Punished, for instance, by everyone being forced to stand on the parade ground for hours. Without the right to go to the toilet. Without the right to take a sip of water.

Two weeks ago, the production quotas for all prison work shifts were arbitrarily increased by fifty units. If previously the minimum was one hundred uniforms a day, now it is one hundred and fifty. According to the Labor Code, workers must be notified of a change in the production quota no less than two months before it is goes

into effect. At IK-14, we just woke up one day to find we had
a new quota because the idea happened to have popped into
the heads of the wardens of our "sweatshop" (that's what
the prisoners call the penal colony). The number of people
in the work shift decreases (they are released or
transferred), but the quota grows. As a result, those who
remain have to work harder and harder. The mechanics say
they don't have the parts to repair the machinery and will
not be getting them. "There are no spare parts! When will
they come? What, you don't live in Russia? How can you
ask such questions?" During my first few months in the
manufacturing zone, I nearly mastered the profession of
mechanic, out of necessity and on my own. I would attack
my machine, screwdriver in hand, desperate to fix it. Your
hands are scratched and poked by needles, your blood is all
over the table, but you keep on sewing. You are part of an
assembly line, and you have to do your job alongside the
experienced seamstresses. Meanwhile, the damned machine
keeps breaking down. Because you're the newcomer and
there is a lack of good equipment in the prison, you end up
with the worst equipment, the most worthless machine on
the line. And now it's broken down again, and once again
you run off looking for the mechanic, who is impossible to
find. You are yelled at and berated for slowing down
production. There are no sewing classes at the prison,
either. Newcomers are immediately plunked down in front
of their machines and given their assignments.

"If you weren't Tolokonnikova, you would have had the
shit kicked out of you a long time ago," say fellow prisoners
with close ties to the wardens. It's true: other prisoners are

beaten up. For not being able to keep up. They hit them in the kidneys, in the face. Convicts themselves deliver these beatings and not a single one of them happens without the approval and knowledge of the wardens. A year ago, before I came here, a gypsy woman was beaten to death in the third unit. (The third unit is the "pressure cooker": prisoners whom the wardens want subjected to daily beatings are sent there.) She died in the infirmary at IK-14. The administration was able to cover up the fact she had been beaten to death: a stroke was listed as the official cause of death. In another block, new seamstresses who couldn't keep up were undressed and forced to sew naked. No one dares complain to the wardens, because all they will do is smile and send the prisoner back to the dorm unit, where the "snitch" will be beaten on the orders of those same wardens. For the prison warden, managed hazing is a convenient method for forcing convicts to totally obey their lawless regime.

A threatening, anxious atmosphere pervades the manufacturing zone. Eternally sleep-deprived, overwhelmed by the endless race to fulfill inhumanly large quotas, the convicts are always on the verge of breaking down, screaming at each other, fighting over the smallest things. Just recently, a young woman got stabbed in the head with a pair of scissors because she didn't turn in a pair of pants on time. Another tried to cut her own stomach open with a hacksaw. She was stopped from finishing the job.

Those who found themselves at IK-14 in 2010, the year of smoke and wildfires said that when the fire would*

---

*Throughout Russia, because of anomolously high temperatures.

approach the prison walls, convicts continued to go to the manufacturing zone and fulfill their quotas. Because of the smoke you couldn't see a person standing two meters in front of you, but, covering their faces in wet kerchiefs, they all went to work anyway. Because of the emergency conditions, prisoners weren't taken to the cafeteria for meals. Several women told me they were so horribly hungry they started keep diaries to document the horror of what was happening to them. When the fires were finally put out, prison security diligently rooted out these diaries during searches so that nothing would be leaked to the outside world.

Sanitary conditions at the prison are calculated to make the prisoner feel like a disempowered, filthy animal. Although there are hygiene rooms in the dorm units, a "common hygiene room" has been set up for corrective and punitive purposes. This room can accommodate five people, but all eight hundred prisoners are sent there to wash up. We must not wash ourselves in the hygiene rooms in our barracks: that would be too easy. There is always a stampede in the "common hygiene room" as women with little tubs try to wash their "breadwinners" (as they are called in Mordovia) as fast as they can, clambering on top of each other. We are allowed to wash our hair once a week. However, even this bathing day gets cancelled. A pump will break or the plumbing will be stopped up. At times, my dorm unit has been unable to bathe for two or three weeks.

When the pipes are clogged, urine gushes out of the hygiene rooms and clumps of feces go flying. We've learned to unclog the pipes ourselves, but it doesn't last long: they soon get stopped up again. The prison does not have a plumber's snake for cleaning out the pipes. We get to do laundry once a week. The laundry is a small room with three faucets from which a thin trickle of cold water flows.

Convicts are always given stale bread, generously watered-down milk, exceptionally rancid millet, and only rotten potatoes for the same corrective ends, apparently. This summer, sacks of slimy black potato bulbs were brought to the prison in bulk. And they were fed to us.

One could endlessly discuss workplace and living conditions violations at IK-14. However, my main grievance has to do with something else. It is that the prison administration prevents in the harshest possible way all complaints and petitions regarding conditions at IK-14 from leaving the prison. The wardens force people to remain silent, stooping to the lowest and cruelest methods to this end. All the other problems stem from this one: the increased work quotas, the sixteen-hour workday, and so on. The wardens feel they have impunity, and they boldly crack down on prisoners more and more. I couldn't understand why everyone kept silent until I found myself facing the mountain of obstacles that crashes down on the convict who decides to speak out. Complaints simply do not leave the prison. The only chance is to complain through a lawyer or relatives. The administration, petty and vengeful, will meanwhile use all the means at its disposal for pressuring the convict so she will see that her complaints will not make anything better for anyone, but will only make things worse. Collective punishment is employed: you complain about the lack of hot water, and they turn it off altogether.

In May 2013, my lawyer Dmitry Dinze filed a complaint about the conditions at IK-14 with the prosecutor's office. The prison's deputy warden, Lieutenant Colonel Kupriyanov, instantly made conditions at the camp unbearable. There was search after search, a flood of disciplinary reports on all my acquaintances, the seizure of warm clothes, and threats of seizure of warm footwear. At work, they get revenge with complicated sewing assignments, increased quotas, and fabricated defects. The forewoman of the neighboring unit, Lieutenant Colonel Kupriyanov's right hand, openly incited prisoners to sabotage the items I was responsible for in the manufacturing zone so there would be an excuse to send me to solitary confinement for damaging "public property." She also ordered the convicts in her unit to provoke a fight with me.

It is possible to tolerate anything as long as it affects you alone. But the method of collective correction at the prison is something else. It means that your unit, or even the entire prison, has to endure your punishment along with you. The most vile thing of all is that this includes people you've come to care about. One of my friends was denied parole, which she had been working toward for seven years by diligently overfulfilling quotas in the manufacturing zone. She was reprimanded for drinking tea with me. Lieutenant Colonel Kupriyanov transferred her to another unit the same day. Another close acquaintance of mine, a very cultured woman, was thrown into the pressure-cooker unit for daily beatings because she had read and discussed with me a Justice Ministry document entitled "Internal Regulations at Correctional Facilities." Disciplinary reports were filed on everyone who talked to me. It hurt me that people I cared about were forced to suffer. Laughing, Lieutenant Colonel Kupriyanov said to me then, "You probably don't have any friends left!" He explained it was all happening because of Dinze's complaints.

Now I see I should have gone on a hunger strike back in May, when I first found myself in this situation. However, seeing the tremendous pressure put on other convicts, I stopped the process of filing complaints against the prison.

Three weeks ago, on August 30, I asked Lieutenant Colonel Kupriyanov to grant the inmates in my work shift eight hours of sleep. The idea was to decrease the workday from sixteen to twelve hours. "Fine, starting Monday, the shift can even work eight hours," he replied. I knew this was another trap because it is physically impossible to make our increased quota in eight hours. So the work shift would lag behind and face punishment. "If they find out you were the one behind this," the lieutenant colonel continued, "you definitely will never have it bad again, because there is no such thing as bad in the afterlife." Kupriyanov paused. "And finally, never make requests for everyone. Make requests only for yourself. I've been working in the prison camps for many years, and whenever someone has come to me to request something for other people, they have always gone straight from my office to solitary confinement. You're the first person this won't happen to."

Over the following weeks, life in my dorm unit and work shift was made intolerable. Convicts close to the wardens incited the unit to violence. "You've been punished by having tea and food, bathroom breaks, and smoking

banned for a week. And now you're always going to be
punished unless you start treating the newcomers,
especially Tolokonnikova, differently. Treat them like the
old-timers used to treat you back in the day. Did they beat
you up? Of course they did. Did they rip your mouths?
They did. Fuck them up. You won't be punished for it."

I was repeatedly provoked to get involved in conflicts
and fights, but what is the point of fighting with people who
have no will of their own, who are only acting at the behest
of the wardens?

The Mordovian convicts are afraid of their own
shadows. They are completely intimidated. It was only the
other day that they were well disposed toward me and
begging me to do something about the sixteen-hour
workday, and now they are afraid even to speak to me after
the administration has come down hard on me.

I made the wardens a proposal for resolving the conflict.
I asked that they release me from the pressure artificially
manufactured by them and enacted by the prisoners they
control, and that they abolish slave labor at the prison
by reducing the length of the workday and decreasing the
quotas to bring them into compliance with the law. But in
response the pressure has only intensified. Therefore, as of
September 23, I declare a hunger strike and refuse to be
involved in the slave labor at the prison until the
administration complies with the law and treats women
convicts not like cattle banished from the legal realm for
the needs of the garment industry, but like human beings.

---

*Translated by Bela Shayevich and Thomas Campbell.

By the time she declared her hunger strike, Nadya had been depleted by a summer of abuse, sleep deprivation, and undereating. Once she stopped eating, she quickly became very ill. Then she disappeared. IK-14 officials would not let anyone call her, and even the defense lawyers, when they showed up, were turned away. Nadya, they were told, had been hospitalized in serious condition. After two weeks she resurfaced at a prison hospital. Her hunger strike was over and she was awaiting transfer to a different penal colony. On October 18, she was, instead, sent back to IK-14. She declared a hunger strike again. Then she disappeared again. Prison authorities said she had been sent to a penal colony in a different region but they would not say which or where until she had arrived there. Every two days or so, rumors placed her at a new colony somewhere in the Urals or in Siberia or in Chuvashia—but no one really knew where she was.

I kept thinking of the first book I sent to Nadya in prison: *My Testimony* by Anatoly Marchenko, which she had requested. Marchenko had been an odd bird among Soviet dissidents, a manual laborer whom self-education had turned into a "political." He spent about fifteen of his forty-eight years in camps, including in Mordovia, and jails and political prisons. It was at a special prison for "politicals" in Tatarstan that Marchenko declared a hunger strike in August 1986, demanding that Mikhail Gorbachev make good on his talk of reform by releasing all political prisoners. Many dissidents thought then he was rash and irrational: it would take years for the Soviet Union to rid itself of political prisoners, they believed, if it ever happened at all. Marchenko was hospitalized, force-fed, started his hunger strike again, and finally stopped after more than three months. Less than two weeks later he fell ill. He died in prison in December 1986. A few days later, Gorbachev launched the process of releasing all Soviet political prisoners. I am sure that in perestroika-era USSR no one had really wanted Marchenko to die: he was an almost accidental victim, a side effect of a system created to exert maximum pressure on anyone who resisted it. The system had changed little since the 1980s, and now it was crushing a woman, not yet twenty-four years old, who had not even wanted to fight it.

It had been two years since Pussy Riot started recording its first song, "Free the Cobblestones."

Moscow, October 2013

Postscript, December 2013

Twenty-six days passed before there was any news of Nadya. Petya and the support group roamed Russia, first camping out in Mordovia, then following one in a long series of leads to Siberia. It was in Siberia that Nadya finally surfaced, in a prison authority-run TB hospital in Krasnoyarsk. She had apparently been greatly weakened by the hunger strike and the nearly four-week transport, but she was alive. She was told she would be allowed to serve out the last three months of her sentence in the relatively comfortable conditions of the prison hospital and would be given a job there if she regained her physical strength.

AUTHOR'S NOTE

Writing about people whom I cannot, for one reason or another, interview has become something of a specialty for me. It has taught me to cast a wide reporting net. Nadezhda Tolokonnikova, Maria Alyokhina, and Yekaterina Samutsevich all knew I was working on the book from the moment this project began, and each helped me collect information. Yekaterina sat for many hours of recorded interviews, allowed me to trail along with her some days as she went about living the life of a convicted felon on parole, and also provided me with documentation of all her legal battles. Nadezhda and Maria corresponded with me, answering my questions to the extent that time, their physical condition, and prison censors allowed. I was also fortunate to be able to meet with Nadezhda in the penal colony for nearly four hours in June 2013. Maria and her friends and family gave me access to letters she had written to them; excerpts from these letters are reproduced in this book with her permission. I attended most of the court hearings described or mentioned in the book; where I could not be physically present, I used audio and video recordings prepared by journalists or lawyers. Defense attorneys Mark Feigin, Nikolai Polozov, and Violetta Volkova not only sat for interviews but also gave me access to case documents, correspondence, and audio recordings. Defense attorney Irina Khrunova made herself available for interviews and accessible for running commentary before, after, and even during many legal proceedings. Friends and family of the three Pussy Riot convicts talked to me at length: all of their quotes in this book come from original interviews. Tasya Krugovykh shared film footage documenting the group's history. Finally, I interviewed seven Pussy Riot participants other than the three whose names are known to the public; some but not all of them are quoted in this book. The one unfortunate omission are the two participants in the Cathedral of Christ the Savior action who were not arrested. I was forced to forgo interviewing them because one of them asked that I pay for the interview; I do not know whether she was asking for herself or for both of them, because the other one never responded to me directly. In the many months of intensive reporting for this book, this was the only interaction that contradicted the spirit of openness, accessibility, and free flow of information that had always marked Pussy Riot. The rest of the time, I was not only grateful for but often awed by the ability of Pussy Riot and their family and friends to maintain this spirit under the most trying of circumstances.

Keep in touch with
Granta Books:

Visit grantabooks.com to discover more.

GRANTA